ACCLAIM FOR

William Langewiesche's

Sahara Unveiled

"Whether dealing with the geography and history of the region, observing its psychological impact on the natives and outsiders, describing the beauty of its swirling sand patterns or discoursing on the characteristics of the scorpion . . . Langewiesche writes with style and flair. . . . This is travel writing with a human face."   —*Parade* magazine

"Langewiesche . . . exploits the harshness, forlornness, and political hopelessness of the vast desert to fashion an entertaining and edifying tale."   —*The New York Times*

"A reader's dream. . . . With spare lyrical cadences and cool sensuality, Langewiesche summons up the landscape itself. . . . *Sahara Unveiled* has a masterful dry chill to it, a power that stays coiled and ready to spring and a prose that fits its subject as cleanly as skin to the bone."   —*Seattle Times*

"Like Charles Doughty, Freya Stark, T. E. Lawrence, Antoine de Saint-Exupéry, Wilfred Thesiger, and many others . . . Langewiesche finds places of his own amid the vast mysteries of the desert. . . . His travels are filled with intense characters and scenes so vivid you can feel the grit between your teeth."

—*The Advocate Literary Supplement*

BOOKS BY

William Langewiesche

Cutting for Sign
Sahara Unveiled

William Langewiesche

Sahara Unveiled

William Langewiesche is the author of *Cutting for Sign* and a correspondent for *The Atlantic Monthly*. For many years a commercial pilot, he now lives in Davis, California.

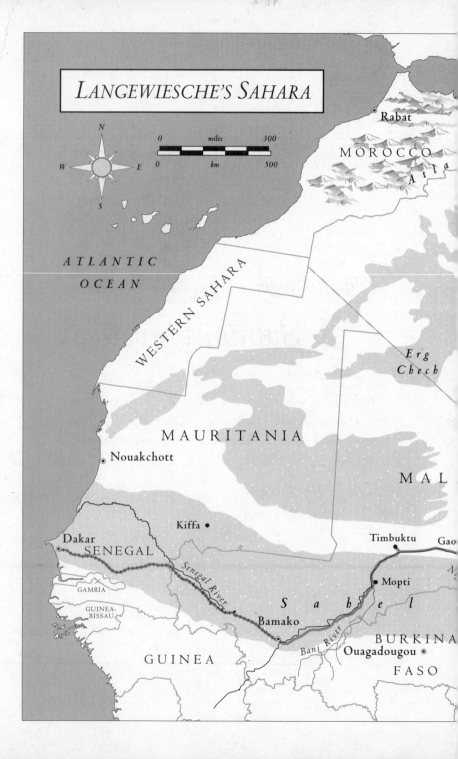

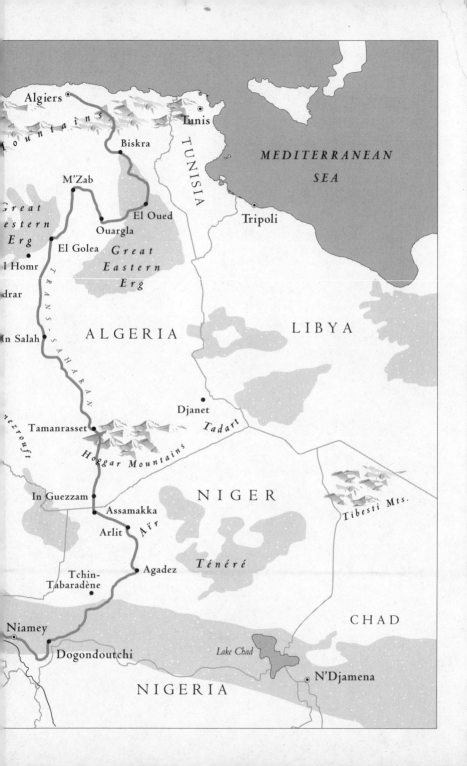

SAHARA
UNVEILED

William Langewiesche

SAHARA
UNVEILED

A

JOURNEY

ACROSS

THE

DESERT

VINTAGE DEPARTURES

Vintage Books   *A Division of Random House, Inc.*   *New York*

FIRST VINTAGE DEPARTURES EDITION, JULY 1997

Copyright © 1996 by William Langewiesche

All rights reserved under International and Pan-American Copyright
Conventions. Published in the United States by Vintage Books, a division of
Random House, Inc., New York, and simultaneously in Canada by Random House
of Canada Limited, Toronto. Originally published in the United States in hardcover
by Pantheon Books, a division of Random House, Inc.,
New York, in 1996.

Portions of *Sahara Unveiled* have appeared in *The Atlantic Monthly*.

Grateful acknowledgment is made to the following for permission
to reprint previously published material:

Chapman & Hall: Excerpts from *The Physics of Blown Sand & Desert Dunes*
by R. A. Bagnold (New York: William Morrow & Company, 1942).
Reprinted by permission of Chapman & Hall.

Editions Jean-Claude Lattes: Excerpts translated by William Langewiesche
from *Touareg, La Tragedie* by Mano Dayak. Copyright © 1992 by Editions
Jean-Claude Lattes. Reprinted by permission of Editions Jean-Claude Lattes.

Illustration credits: Photographs on pp. 49 and 50,
copyright © E. D. McKee/ U.S. Geological Survey; photograph on p. 178,
copyright © Eric Lessing/ Art Resource, N.Y.
Map © 1995 by Vikki Leib.

The Library of Congress has cataloged the Pantheon edition as follows:
Langewiesche, William.
Sahara unveiled : a journey across the desert / William Langewiesche.
p.   cm.
ISBN 0-679-42982-4
1. Sahara—Description of travel.
2. Langewiesche, William—Journeys—Sahara. I. Title.
DT333.L26   1996
916.604'329—dc20
95-48864
CIP
Vintage ISBN: 0-679-75006-1

Author photograph courtesy of William Langewiesche
Book design by Jo Metsch

Random House Web address: http://www.randomhouse.com/

Printed in the United States of America
10   9   8   7   6   5   4   3   2   1

To Minouche

CONTENTS

Contents

ACKNOWLEDGMENTS

Thanks to Dan Frank, Cullen Murphy, Chuck Verrill, and Bill Whitworth for their years of support. Thanks also to Gail Boyer Hayes for her enduring faith and her intelligence. Finally thanks to the Saharans themselves, among whom I count close friends. I have judged them frankly. I know they will understand.

THE NORTH
IS A DESERT

1

BEFORE

THE

DESERT

Do NOT REGRET the passing of the camel and the caravan. The Sahara has changed, but it remains a desert without compromise, the world in its extreme. There is no place as dry and hot and hostile. There are few places as huge and as wild. You will not diminish it by admitting that its inhabitants can drive, and that they are neither wiser nor purer nor stronger than you. It is fairer to judge them squarely as modern people and your equals. They were born by chance in a hard land, at a hard time in its history. You will do them no justice by pretending otherwise. Do not worry that their world, or yours, has grown too small. Despite its roads, its trucks, its televisions, the Sahara remains unsubdued.

In its scale and complexity, it is a difficult place to know. Consider just the external dimensions—a desert the size of the United States, filling the northern third of Africa, extending south nearly to the edge of the tropical forests. Only a fifth of

3

this vastness is the sand of popular imagination, formed into the great dune seas called *ergs* in Arabic; the rest is rock and gravel plain, and high rugged mountain. On that much we can agree. But beyond such crude description, geographers begin to quarrel over the most basic measures. For instance, if "desert" is defined by dryness, should the threshold be six inches of yearly rain, or twice that? Should "desert" be defined by variability of rainfall? By rates of evaporation? By hours of sunshine? Or should we choose a biological standard and define the Sahara as a place where only certain plants and animals can survive? If the questions seem endless, it is because the desert defies such delimitations. You cannot even assume you will know it when you see it. My own impression is that the Sahara is indeed advancing south into Africa, despite the evidence from satellite surveys that perhaps it is not. The satellites measure temperature, soil, and vegetation. But my measure is mostly human. It starts far to the north, in Algiers, a port city on North Africa's green coastal plain, which at first glance is not the Sahara at all.

Algiers was once the loveliest city of the French colonial empire. As the capital of an independent Algeria now, it still sparkles across hills above a blue Mediterranean bay. It has a whitewashed center with boulevards lined by stuccoed French-style apartment buildings, and a gentle climate nurtured by maritime breezes. The Sahara proper lies a day south by bus, across a farmed coastal plain, and out beyond the snowy Atlas Mountains. Visitors mention the desert's pull, the fabled attraction of that imagined horizon. They say the Sahara has the presence of an unseen ocean. That is true. But you can also find the desert closer, in the poverty and crowding of Algiers.

Algeria won its independence bitterly in 1962, after war, and then as a new nation found itself pressed against the Mediterranean by its vast hinterland. Ninety percent of the country lay out there beyond the mountains. Cynics who claim that the fight for independence came down to a fight for the desert's oil are misreading history. The Algerians fought a classic guerrilla war for their families and towns and cultural ideals. Perhaps a million people died. Afterward the army ran the country, and spent the income from oil and natural gas on a long and troubled experiment with socialism that in the end left the people with little of the desert but the desert itself. It was as if the Sahara had refused to be reduced to oil. If the desert appeared on the map as a national treasure, it existed in reality as a forbidding land that denied Algeria's fast-growing population the room to expand. Algiers became a city of two million in a colonial shell built for a fifth as many—one of a string of such towns in which nearly all Algerians now crowd the coast.

By the early 1990s, the economy had collapsed and the crowds had begun to quarrel violently. A long-awaited Islamic revolution that broke out in the north was sparked by bread riots. The military dictatorship answered in the only way it knew, by fighting back. The fight continues today. Deep in the Sahara, the oases remain relatively calm; they are conservative and religious places where the local Islamic radicals have little real opposition. But in the crowded north, with its close ties to Europe, the cities are infested not only with revolutionaries but with soldiers, spies, and other agents of the established order. People are dying by the tens of thousands. You cannot blame the Sahara alone for the troubles. But you should also not see the desert simply as some faraway place of little rain. There are many forms of thirst.

I STAYED NEAR the center of Algiers, beside the National Assembly building, in a hotel I knew from earlier visits, and had come to appreciate for its high colonial ceilings and the glowering of its guests. They were government men and party hacks, heavy smokers who stayed up late in the lobby and talked in low voices, acting worried and conspiratorial. They draped sports jackets over their shoulders, leaving the sleeves to dangle. They cast ominous looks in my direction. I found them strangely reassuring—proof that the old Algeria still endured, teetering as always on the edge of the political abyss.

Thunderstorms battered the city. My hotel room, which overlooked the street from the third floor, had a dripping ceiling, a door that would not lock, and French windows that kept blowing open, letting in the wind. A nightly curfew had been imposed. I kept the light off and watched in darkness as an army patrol moved cautiously up the street through torrential rain. Lightning flashed. An armored vehicle stood in an intersection near the casbah. The casbah is the oldest part of the town. It climbs a hillside above the harbor in a maze of streets too narrow to drive. During the colonial years it was the Algerian ghetto. Now all Algiers is the Algerian ghetto. Gunshots puncture the nights. The city teaches you to sleep away from the windows.

I lay on the bed and listened to the storm with satisfaction, expecting within days to cross the mountains to the place where rain so rarely falls. I had been to the Sahara before, but for short stays, and by air. There I had found a land unknown, as masked by the dreams built upon it as by drought and distance—and yet a land where the interplay between Europe and its former colonies lay exposed in the crisp sunlight. That interplay came as a surprise. It seemed to act through a set of mirrors by which

Europe unwittingly found itself in its images of the desert, while the desert people in turn defined themselves not as they actually were, but as they were reflected in Europe. I saw in this another reflection, larger even than Africa, a metaphor for desert all over the world.

This time I would linger, and travel by ground. The Sahara is the earth stripped of its gentleness, a place that consumes the careless and the unlucky. But all you need to navigate it is a suitcase, a bit of cash, an occasional bus ticket, the intention to move on. Such simplicity appeals to me. Wars and borders allowing, I expected now to cross the Sahara in an arc from the Mediterranean south to the African savanna, and west to the Atlantic. The route would take me through the desert's hyperarid core—a place with plateaus nearly sterilized by drought, where bacteria cannot survive, and where cadavers, partially mummified, decompose slowly like sun-dried dates. The Sahara has horizons so bare that drivers mistake stones for diesel trucks, and so lonely that migrating birds land beside people just for the company. The certainty of such sparseness can be a lesson. I lay in Algiers in a hotel in a storm, thinking there is no better sound than the splash of rain. The desert teaches by taking away.

ALGIERS LOOKED CLEAN in the morning. The sun reflected brilliantly through the canyons of whitewashed buildings. Laundry hung from all the windows, turning the city's insides out, betraying its density and the youth of its population. Most Algerians are children, and they wear children's clothes. Families of ten now crowd into apartments built for two.

In the morning, when the curfew ended, the young men spill into the streets, then stand around all day. Factories have closed, offices have closed, and the men cannot find work. Economists could count them in the streets, and find that unemployment has overwhelmed the city. Whether the unemployment runs at 40 or 50 or 60 percent hardly matters. A paralysis has set in. Islamic radicals want to make a big change. Some are truly religious, and some only pretend to be. Some think of Islam as an expedient jobs program that moves the female half of the population out of the way.

When the killing began, the radicals shaved off their beards and discarded their traditional robes. Now they look like the modern city boys they have always been. I walked sidewalks thick with them. They were slim and well groomed, and could afford to drink espressos at the stand-up coffee counters. This is the face of the new revolution, dressed in counterfeit clothes, with proud labels—but largely unemployed. The only money to be made is on the black market, which is the key to this revolution. A young Algerian can, for instance, smuggle Peugeot carburetors into the country from France, sell them illegally at a fivefold markup, and buy a gun. With just a few such transactions he can also support his family. In fact, it is the efficiency of the black market that allows unhappy men the time to drift through the streets and think of change. There are so many of them in Algiers that beneath the sound of traffic you can hear their footsteps.

Algiers lives under this siege. As I walked by the main post office, a car backfired, and a policeman stumbled in panic, fumbling a pistol from his white leather holster.

The car may simply have needed a new carburetor. There were men in the street who could have provided one. But you could hardly blame the policeman for overreacting. A bomb had recently exploded nearby. And other policemen kept getting assassinated—along with journalists, professors, and military men. Anyone representing the state or the intellectual establishment was at risk. Soldiers stood guard on the corners, watching the crowds intently, cradling submachine guns, fingers on the triggers.

Foreigners, too, were at risk. Some had been attacked and had their throats cut. I was not worried, since I did not intend to stay long, and I have learned to walk purposefully on hostile streets, to keep moving, and never to ask directions. Moreover today, for once, I knew the way.

By afternoon I had walked to Hussein-Dey, a run-down residential district where Malika Belouard now lived in a two-bedroom house with her four children, her older sister, her sister's husband, and her ancient Berber mother.

I had met Malika in the Sahara. At thirty-four, she was a gentle woman, with a soft build, brown skin, full lips, and wiry black hair which she tied back from her face. Her husband, Ameur, had been my friend, too. He had taught me the first rule of the oases, that only fools and foreigners stand in line. But then he had hit his head in a driving accident, and had lost his mind forever. His mother had taken him home.

With no means of support, Malika had left the Sahara and crowded with her children into this tiny house up an alley in Hussein-Dey. She needed to find a job, but there were no jobs. Then the Islamic revolution broke out, and the house in Hussein-Dey became her fortress. It faced the alley with a heavy metal gate and a concrete wall topped by barbed wire. The family lived like prisoners. I arrived on time, but they had been waiting for me for hours.

Malika looked rested. Her sister, who was twenty years older and childless, required me to admire Malika's beauty, which I naturally did anyway. Malika knew. There was little pretending between us. I asked about Malika's husband, Ameur, and she said there would be no point in visiting him.

In French she said, "He can speak, but if you tell him the sky is red, he will answer, 'Yes, the sky is red.' " She was both sad and angry. "He did this to himself, you remember."

She had her own concerns now—the ferocious worries of a single mother bringing up four children in a dangerous neighborhood. Her oldest boy, Ali, had turned fourteen. She put her hand on his head, and as Ali looked at me, she said, "He is a bad student, interested only in basketball. He is getting too familiar with the streets. But what should I do? I can't keep him inside forever."

That opposition between the street and household was on their minds. Malika's older sister, whose name was Zora, had witnessed rapes and killings in the last Algerian war, and she could not bear the thought that such savagery could occur twice in a lifetime. "We keep to ourselves," Zora said firmly, as if by insistence she might protect the family.

Their cherished living room was small and heavily furnished. It had two overstuffed chairs, a sofa, and velvet drapes. A brother who had died for Algeria's independence gazed steadily from a photograph hung in black on the wall. Beside him stood the television, whose screen was red and green and alive.

The favorite program was a Mexican soap opera, dubbed in Arabic, about a rich family living on a distant Pacific coast. Malika said, "I like it because it carries me so far away." I wasn't sure how to read this. As a woman living in an Islamic world, she had a habit of talking in code.

When the evening episode started, all conversation stopped. After the episode, Zora smiled wryly and said, "So you see how we pass our time. It's not a real life when the television gives you your only escape."

I asked Malika if she thought of returning to the Sahara. She answered, "The Sahara is no place for a woman."

Zora said, "Here at least we have each other."

She meant, "Here at least Malika has me to protect her."

And she was right. Zora was smarter than Malika, and more sentimental, and always strong. She was the head of the household. Her husband was a gendarme, a member of the national police force, but a meek man by comparison. Once in my presence he suggested wistfully that she should retire from her job managing a neighborhood medical clinic. He thought she might play the more traditional Muslim wife. Zora snorted, and said to me, "You see? The religious crazies are getting to him!"

Later she said, "He asked me to wear the veil. I told him I would leave Algeria first!" She would serve his dinners, and do his cleaning, but his opinion mattered to her only when it wasn't irrelevant. Her job was important, and the family needed the money.

Without intending to, they had taken sides in the struggle. The gendarme was a civil servant with no fight in him, and he was tired of the barracks life. He would gladly have retired, and lingered at the café by the neighborhood mosque; he would gladly have the new rulers. But Zora could never have stood for it. At work she was known as a disciplinarian; in the neighborhood she was known for her fierce rejection of the revolutionaries. She was a religious woman, and had twice made the pilgrimage to Mecca, but she could no longer stand to attend the local mosque, and now said her prayers at home. This was noticed. Zora's idea that the family could keep to itself was an impractical fantasy. The civil war would not be so easy to escape.

I don't know how much she said in public. In private, she detested especially the coming of the veil. Blaming the synthetic fabrics, she talked about the pimpled faces of the women she saw at the medical clinic. She talked about hypocrisy, about women who strip off the veil away from home, and about the sinning that goes on under the holiest of clothes.

"But people do change," I said.

Zora scoffed. "Before, these women were alive and full of talk and laughter. And now, it's as if they are dying, or already dead. Suddenly they're silent. They hide behind their veils and make a show of disapproving."

Night came, and with it came the rain again. Before the curfew the sisters loaded me into Zora's old Fiat for the trip across town to the hotel. Malika sat in the back with her three youngest children. She spoke little in the presence of her sister. Zora drove awkwardly, with uncharacteristic caution. We nosed out of the alley by the house, then down a street where Islamic slogans had been scrawled on the buildings, then out around the mosque.

Zora gestured angrily at the men standing in the doorways. "They can put on their holy airs, but they forget we have known them since they were babies! We remember! Are they going to tell *me* about Islam? A few years ago they were nothing but hoodlums and drinkers!"

We came to a stop sign, by men talking in the downpour. "Look at them," Zora snapped. "They will make a show out of staying on the street until the last minute before the curfew. They don't even have the sense to get in out of the rain."

I was in a quiet mood. I wanted to be alone with Malika. Zora was too angry, and could not appreciate the rain. Earlier she had hustled the children into the car as if the drops might hurt them. Malika had lingered and turned her face toward the sky. Malika believed the Sahara is no place for a woman—but she had been taught by it nonetheless.

The revolutionaries had been taught by it as well. At the start of the troubles, the army swept thousands of young men from these city streets, and shipped them to camps deep in the Sahara for punishment and persuasion. But the camps did not dampen the revolution. The Sahara teaches by taking away. The revolutionaries learned to do without. When they returned to Algiers they had grown beyond city life. The men standing by the stop sign in the storm did not look idle. Their conversation engaged them. I thought they had learned to love the rain. I saw the desert on them.

2

ABOUT

PARADISE

THE FRENCH CONQUERED the Sahara early in the twentieth century, then set about trying to understand it. Ethnologists spread through the desert recording its folkways, which they published in small books, which burrowed into the libraries where they sit today. I have read, for instance, that the prophet Mohammed had a donkey, and that one day he set out to ride him to a nearby oasis. Halfway there the donkey looked at the Prophet and, seeing a stick in his hand, asked, "Why do you carry the stick?"

"It is to use when you refuse to walk," answered the Prophet. "It is for beating hardheaded beasts like you."

"Throw away the stick," said the donkey. "If I am not obedient, you can do with me what you like."

The Prophet pretended to throw away the stick, but hid it under his coat. Soon afterward the donkey refused to go on. The Prophet said, "But you promised to keep walking!"

"Yes, I promised," said the donkey. "But I've changed my mind. Do what you like. You have bare hands, and I have hooves."

Hearing this, the Prophet took the stick from his coat and struck the donkey a hundred blows until the donkey's tongue hung out. Then he cursed the donkey, condemning him to another hundred blows every day of his life. And if some future master spared the donkey, because he obeyed and worked hard, he would receive those blows from the angels.

These are the stories that Saharans may have told their children to explain the miserable lot of desert donkeys. More important, they are the stories that the French repeated.

One ethnologist heard that God once took pity on the donkey, and that He pronounced, "Enough of this unhappiness! I have decided to allow the donkey into Paradise."

The donkey was delighted, and exclaimed, "At last, I'll be able to rest!"

When he came to the threshold of Paradise, the great gates opened for him. He stuck his head inside, and found there a green oasis of flowers and fruit trees, where the rivers flowed with milk, wine, and honey, and the women were amorous. But he also spotted groups of children playing in the streets.

The donkey hastily backed out and said, "Can this be Paradise? The children who torture donkeys on earth are allowed here as well? Then I will not stay. Better to return to the suffering of life!"

He left Paradise, but not before its brilliant light had bleached his muzzle. Ever since, donkeys have had white muzzles.

The French taught that when a donkey is found without a white muzzle, a Saharan might say to a child, "Poor beast, he has not seen Paradise!"

The French were sympathetic administrators. Their ethnologists helped to explain why Saharan children pelted donkeys with stones, as if French children did not.

3

ACROSS

THE

ATLAS

I TOOK THE early bus for Biskra, an Algerian oasis on the eastern border with Tunisia. The bus was called *Express* because it required merely a day to cross the mountains. The passengers who boarded at the station in Algiers filled the seats and crowded the aisle, and waited with closed expressions for the bus to start, as if only through silence could they endure the trip. The bus pulled out of the station at dawn, listing and groaning, stinking of sick engine, hot oil, and dirt. I worried because Biskra lay 300 miles ahead, and I wanted to put the distance behind. The desert teaches patience, but patience is a hard quality to learn.

We moved through Algiers in a drizzle. The outer city stretched for miles along the Mediterranean in clusters of bleak concrete apartment towers that surrendered gradually to cultivated fields. Occasionally, ruins of French farmhouses stood at the end of palm-lined drives. The soil looked fertile but unloved.

The morning passed. Traffic on the road dwindled. We came to muddy towns of oversized brick and unfinished construction, where rubbish littered the gullies and factories stood idle. Passengers climbed on and climbed down, and slowly the bus grew less crowded. We passed army checkpoints, and a convoy of unhappy soldiers stalled beside the road like bait for the revolution.

In the deepest farmland, two university students flagged down the bus and sat beside me discussing a political text. They spoke in French because the text was in French, and loudly because they wanted me to overhear. The subject was the absorption of Muslim immigrants into Parisian schools. The students had adopted the book's viewpoint, which was European and fearful, and they agreed now that head scarves on Muslim girls were unacceptable. They never acknowledged my presence, perhaps because it was enough to know that I was listening. They seemed to want to see themselves in my eyes, to distinguish themselves from the less thoughtful Algerians on the bus. It is probably not surprising that thirty years after national independence, some in the middle class still harbor those hopes. Even their opponents, the Islamic revolutionaries, require an audience of outsiders to define themselves.

The students climbed down near a failing state farm. They fell silent, and waited glumly on the road's muddy shoulder while the bus drove off, headed away from Paris.

Ahead the Atlas Mountains formed a dark wall that rose into the mist and cloud. The road narrowed, wandered, then found a steep-walled valley, and climbed it. The bus could barely make the grades, and had to creep uphill bellowing in the lowest gear. The earth near the road was raw, eroded, and slick with rain. We passed through forests of stunted evergreens, and basins where alfalfa and vegetables grew. Men on donkeys watched as we labored by. In the afternoon the view widened and we rolled out across the high grassy plateaus that occupy the core of the Atlas, 3,000 feet above sea level. The landscape was punctuated by higher peaks and outcroppings, and by tabletop mountains like those of the American Southwest.

Beyond the town of Bou Saâda, in continuing drizzle, the country grew slowly drier. We came to rows of planted pines, the heralded Green Barrier that stretches east to west across Algeria, and by which the Algerian army once tried to hold off the Sahara. The idea was to stop the sand, as if sand were contagious or a cancer, the cause of the land's decline, and not its symptom. The Sahara frightens those within its reach. When windstorms lift its surface into the stratosphere, and the desert dust falls as far away as Europe and the Caribbean, people there feel dread. Algerians are no different. They worried they might be pushed into the sea—and many were indeed forced to emigrate. But it was overpopulation and incompetent farming, not advancing sands, that consumed their land. The army marched out to confront a myth, and ignored the real enemy at home.

The Green Barrier has served a purpose nonetheless. The trees are like caged canaries in a mine. Their survival confirms that the coast is for the moment safe. The reason is that the Sahara is simply not advancing toward the north. If it were, it would swallow the trees effortlessly. The essence of any desert is its overwhelming power, and the Sahara is the most powerful of them all. It exists beyond the scale of human engineering. In simple words, it is created by global weather patterns that cause the atmosphere over all of North Africa to press toward the surface and to dry out. To stop such a desert from advancing you would need a barrier stronger than anything an army could build—say, a mountain range called the Atlas. And even that might not work. The Sahara swallows mountain ranges whole.

The Atlas Mountains do act to change the weather, but in the reverse direction, by squeezing the maritime moisture from the Mediterranean winds. The last of that moisture fell now, as the bus climbed a thousand feet above the plateau and the rain turned to snow and mixed with clouds to sweep the barren hills.

We stopped for Berber nomads herding goats across the road. The nomads looked cold. Their low-slung tents, pitched in the distance, offered scant shelter from the weather. The snow fell harder.

Berbers are the ancient inhabitants of North Africa, and though few still live as nomads, they constitute its base population. They are copper-skinned, dark-haired, good-looking people, neither Arab nor Negro, whose origins remain largely unknown. Malika is one of them. Nineteenth-century French imperialists claimed the Berbers had descended from Celts, and now deserved to come home. Romantics claimed they had descended from the lost people of Atlantis. Berbers had their own myths. Current theories are more tentative: they propose that the Berbers descend from Eurasian horsemen who invaded Africa 4,000 years ago, or that they descend from still-earlier inhabitants. Anthropologists are certain only that North Africa has been inhabited for at least 200,000 years, and by successive populations. When the Romans built colonies on the North African coast, the land was occupied by the same people who occupy it today. The Romans dismissed them as "Berbers," from *barbarus,* which in turn derived from the Greek for "foreign and uncivilized," which indeed they were.

In that sense the word "Berber" still expresses a common European attitude toward North Africans, though "Arab" is more commonly used. But the Arabs are if anything overcivilized. Inspired by Mohammed's teachings, their armies came to North Africa from the Middle East in the seventh century A.D. and didn't stay long. When the soldiers left, their followers remained behind as merchants and missionaries. They began to trade south into the Sahara. They interbred with the Berbers, and taught them a new philosophy and religion, and the language to understand it. Over the following centuries this potent combination spread into every corner of the wilderness, replacing the original Berber tradition. North Africa did not surrender to the Arabs, but was persuaded by them, and underwent a collective change of mind. The most determined holdouts were these tough mountain herders of the north and the even tougher Tuaregs of the central Sahara, a Berber people also originally from the north, who to this day have retained their Berber customs and language. But they, too, converted to Islam.

The bus stopped in a village of cold stone. Women came from their houses to greet their returning husbands and sons. They trilled high-pitched ululations, the warbling cry that so spooked the French patrols during the war for independence. The men wore burnooses, brown woolen gowns with pointed hoods like the garments of medieval monks. Children scampered through the mud, excited by strangers and the scent of travel.

The bus driver was a Berber too, but generations removed from the mountains. He was a sharp-faced man with styled hair. At one stop he caught my eye in the overhead mirror and grimaced, as if he wanted me to know that he had no patience for these peasants. I noticed that he spoke to them as little as possible. He wore black slacks, a silky white shirt, and thin-soled shoes more suitable for dancing than for driving. The farther we got from Algiers, the less he cared to look beyond the road. The bus was his oasis. Only once did he get off, to grab a coffee at a stone-shack café. Armed with cassettes of bad European rock, he seemed to dream of a faster life somewhere else. He must have hated the way the land on the southern edge of the Atlas had emptied.

WE CAME TO the Sahara late in the afternoon, during the descent from the mountains, as if we had passed through a transparent wall. The rain suddenly stopped, the air warmed, and a strong sun dissolved the clouds. We crested a rise, and the Sahara appeared below—a brilliant and treeless plain stretching south in naked folds to the horizon. A trace of smoke marked some unseen oasis. The view was so wide you could imagine the curvature of the earth.

The road led down into it, and the uniform plain became a rolling desert of yellow sand and ochre dirt, strewn with stone, and cut sharply by gullies. Spiny bushes had rooted along the gullies, and in the shelter of rocks. A camel grazed on thin and fragile grasses. The bus grew hot. I opened a window to let in the wind. The air smelled of baked soil, and tasted of sand. In the distance a cluster of date palms survived untended. The sky was close, fierce, relentless. It pushed away even the memory of rain.

BISKRA WAS A town of well-kept cement and adobe houses, French colonial arcades, and 20,000 people. It stood along a dry riverbed that snaked from the mountains before spreading into the desert and disappearing. Dry riverbeds are the most important feature of any desert, and they have many names. Within the United States alone, depending on the region, they are called washes, gulches, gullies, creeks, coulees, and arroyos. To see a desert clearly it helps to apply the local term. In the Sahara the term is *oued,* which is Arabic for "river." *Wadi* is used farther east. Everywhere, it is understood that the rivers are dry.

Nonetheless some *oueds,* like Biskra's, store large amounts of water close below their surfaces. The underground water was how Biskra lived. In that sense Biskra was a typical Saharan oasis—not the waterhole of public imagination, but a settlement built around plentiful wells. What Biskrans themselves called the oasis was not the town proper, but the grove across the *oued,* a garden three miles wide where vegetables, fruit trees, and 150,000 date palms grew. The number of date palms was widely known because date palms in the Sahara count for a lot. The number of people was less important. Biskra was a regional capital not because of its population, but because it commanded a string of oases where altogether 1,500,000 palms grew. It also had several large date-processing factories.

One of those factories exploded on the afternoon of my arrival. The explosion killed twenty workers, and burned, and made the national television news because it was an old-fashioned industrial disaster, and not an act of revolution. That evening around the central square, men lingered in small sidewalk cafés. Women did not linger, but walked close to walls, wearing veils and bulky robes. A few wore jeans, but even they hurried by in tight groups. The men watched them with an uneasy combination of lust and disdain. Biskra was a cosmopolitan place. When the sun went down, street lamps bathed the square in pools of orange light. I drank a slow bitter coffee, and to the surprise of the men beside me took it without sugar. They asked me about cowboys. I said that cowboys drink weaker coffee, which surprised and pleased them.

The hotel was a state-run place whose only guests were the foreign technicians residing there. They formed a small group— British, French, and one American—sent by their respective governments, and paid hardship salaries to brave the revolution and bring their ideas to the desert. Out of necessity they stuck together. I met them in the hotel restaurant, which played Michael Jackson tunes and had a menu made up entirely of unavailable choices.

After dinner we retired to the bar, which for religious reasons no longer served alcohol. The British especially seemed angry about the deprivation. They were experts in irrigation pumps and mixed drinks—cynical men who, having indulged in the remnant privilege of the white man, could no longer stand the natives, nor stand to return home. The sole American was different because he seemed in his heart never even to have left home. He came from Tuscumbia, Alabama, on the Tennessee River, and called himself Chuck. Chuck was sixty-five. He had a lean, lined, battered face, a glass eye, and a visored cap emblazoned with an American football. The cap read: *Show Pride— Alabama—Roll with the Tide.* I was the first American he had seen in nearly a year. He said, "I'm loving this," and plied me with soft drinks.

The British wanted to talk about the missing alcohol. They described something they called iced tea, a mix of white liquors that would have knocked them senseless.

I changed the subject to Algeria.

They groaned. One said, "What takes forty-eight hours in Morocco and Tunisia takes eighteen months in Algeria."

I answered, "Or maybe things just look better across the fence."

Chuck said, "What does it matter? It's all a desert out here anyway."

He meant the world away from home, including Britain.

He wanted news of American football. The University of Alabama was his special interest. He was disappointed that I had not kept track.

He invited me to his room, where he lived with Guy Lombardo cassettes, Robert Ludlum novels, a water purifier, and a hot plate. He showed me his cartons of candy bars, instant mashed potatoes, beans and franks, and macaroni. The room smelled of canned deodorizer, which he sprayed daily to mask the stench of the toilet. He told me he felt like a prisoner. He meant that he lived in isolation and felt lonely.

Chuck was a chicken man. He had come to Biskra on behalf of the United States to build a demonstration farm intended to teach Saharans how to raise production-line chickens. But Chuck himself was not convinced. "This is our tax dollars," he complained. "Yours and mine. It's a goddamned giveaway."

He was angry because he was partly to blame. We sat in his room in two chairs by an open window, and talked late into the night. He asked about my work in the Sahara, and I said something empty about events there, as if there were any. He saw through this, and asked where I had been over the years, and why I traveled. I said I traveled out of curiosity about the horizons. Chuck was not that kind of man. He said he hated the damned horizon. He traveled too, and had most of his adult life, but only because he was known in some corner of the Department of Agriculture for his willingness to endure. He wanted to tell me about it.

"They're sitting in some damned office over there, and some damned somebody says 'Chickens,' and somebody says, 'Send Chuck—he'll take the job.' "

And Chuck would.

He said, "I didn't think much about it at first. Korea, Vietnam in the early days, Pakistan. After a while I didn't know what else I'd do. The money was good, for chickens. Vietnam again, Egypt, a bunch of others. Algeria? I wish I'd told somebody even just once to go to hell."

Here in Biskra he kept threatening to quit, which is not the same.

"It wouldn't be so bad if these people wanted chickens, but they don't. They never do."

To show for his life he had some money in the bank.

He peered at me with his good eye, unaware that his glass eye had slewed. "You a married man?"

I said, "Yes," but I don't think he heard me.

He said, "I've been single twenty years. I swear my next wife's gonna be deaf and dumb and own a bar." It was a stock joke, a verbal twitch, and he did not smile. The years had reduced his family to a widowed sister on an Alabama farm. He placated himself with thoughts of retirement. "Florida for the bad months, Alabama for the fishing."

In the morning I accompanied him to the post office, where he checked his box, which was empty. He complained that it took over a month to get a letter from his sister. I sympathized.

He gave me Algerian postal *Par Avion* labels to paste on my own letters.

He didn't want to let me go.

We exchanged addresses, and I left him standing at the center of town, a little man in plaid pants, flip-down sunglasses, and sneakers.

CITY

IN

THE

DUNES

BEYOND BISKRA, THE Sahara starts in earnest. This is the Great North, the desert as people imagine it—a scorching flatland of pale soil, a palm grove like a shimmering green line floating in the distance, an ocean of dunes. You can close your eyes to see it.

But the north is also a desert of surprises. The first is the oil that required the new nation beyond to pay attention. The second is the ample subterranean water that allowed small towns to become large ones. The third, which grew from the wealth and water, is the web of paved roads that makes driving the north almost easy. The roads are narrow, and sometimes interrupted by drifting sand, but they are maintained and easy to follow.

Away from the roads this is still a big desert: flat, scorching, and difficult to navigate. Distances between neighboring oases are a hundred miles or more. Drivers who set off cross-country and miscalculate their directions by a few degrees may miss their destinations by miles, then drive in frightened circles until they can drive no more. Satellite navigation would be useful, but drivers can barely afford to keep recapped tires on their cars. So it is better to stick to the pavement, where help is usually near. The roads are frequented by refrigerated trucks, army convoys, private cars, and swarms of yellow taxis. Those taxis are the desert's fourth surprise. When you close your eyes and think of the Sahara, you don't naturally picture a fleet of smoky Peugeot station wagons in need of repairs. They operate under license, shuttling between neighboring oases, and, unlike the bush taxis of sub-Saharan Africa, they rarely carry more than the legal maximum of seven people, plus luggage. But they also rarely depart without a full load. So you go to the station, find the right Peugeot, check its tires, negotiate a price, and wait. You don't ask about the departure time because the driver has no idea, but will always answer "soon."

The wait may last an hour or several days. Open-ended waiting is good training for the deeper Sahara, a place with no roads or taxis, where even at its best, the transportation is uncertain. But waiting anywhere is unpleasant work. In the north, you try to find shade within sight of the taxi. There are no reservations. A taxi that is one person short may suddenly be three people too full, and if you don't fight for your place, you lose it. Then you start again. I have been stranded for days in some oases, unlucky, and unable to grab a cab. But in Biskra I escaped that fate.

The driver I found was an aging man with a tasseled ski cap and gold-rimmed teeth. He did not speak much, but asked to fasten our seatbelts as we approached the roadblock on the edge of town. We were as usual six passengers. The police checked our belts, then had us undo them and step out of the taxi for an identity check. Two veiled women were allowed to remain in the car. The driver handed over his permits wordlessly. The police found no subversives, and let us go.

A mile later, we discovered that Biskra's only gas station had run dry. We would have to wait until a tank truck arrived to replenish it. No one asked how long this would take. Out of modesty, the women again stayed in the taxi, looking straight ahead. The men climbed out and crouched in the dirt beside the road.

A clean-shaven young man told me his name was Leuilli. The women were his mother and sister. It was Friday, the Islamic Sabbath, and he was escorting them south to visit his uncle. I asked him if the women weren't suffering from the heat inside the car. He looked surprised and said no. But the temperature outside had climbed to 100 degrees.

Leuilli spoke difficult French and a little English. Dates had rotted his teeth. He told me he was a student: twice he had failed the *baccalaureate,* but he would try again as soon as he found time to study. He wanted to talk about the United States.

Eventually the tank truck came, and replenished the station, and the taxi gassed up, and we set off for El Oued, a city in the dunes, 150 miles across the desert. Leuilli insisted on sitting beside me. I insisted on a place by an open window.

The Sahara undulated under pale blue sky. The ground was made of dirt and gravel, and was tan and barren, but not bare. It supported patches of grass and small bushes. We passed a ruined mosque alone in a stand of palms, and a camel wandering untethered. An *oued* filled with refracted sunlight shimmered like a lake. The road followed it, descending, and stretched across the Chott Melrhir, a salt flat below the level of the sea. Seeking relief from the heat, I leaned into the hot breeze pouring through the open window.

The human animal is the most adaptable of all species, and the most successful in the desert, but it cannot stand to be over-heated. The body requires about ten days to get used to the ex-tremes of the desert climate, makes small adjustments, which allow it to dissipate heat more easily, but it never learns to con-serve water. Of course some people can just naturally stand the heat better than others. Because human cooling works by sweat, it works best on people with a lot of skin in proportion to their weight—people who are short and skinny. But there is no such physical type as a desert rat. Saharans are born small, but also tall and fat. Visitors are as comfortable after ten days as after ten gen-erations. During the summer when the afternoon air sears your lungs, Saharans feel the pain as well, and complain frequently about the weather.

Beliefs make their suffering worse. Women in the Sahara would feel cooler in light, full clothing, but they dress in heavy robes to hide even the hint of their sexuality. The most pious of them willingly wear bunched ski socks around their ankles, and heavy woolen gloves to hide the shape of their hands. The desert is full of such self-imposed tortures. I have been told in the Sahara to avoid drinking water to avoid sweating. I have been told that hot liquids cool better than warm ones, and that warm ones cool better than cold ones, and that cold ones will overheat you. Now, in this taxi without air-conditioning, I was asked by the other passengers to roll up my window because I was letting in the hot wind. Leuilli agreed. Afterward we all suf-fered together.

Our driver put on a tape of the Koran, a lovely, melodic read-ing of the holy book. "If you're bad, you'll go to Hell," Leuilli said. He meant a place of drought and fire. "But if you're good, you'll go to Paradise." He meant a place where only donkeys suffer.

We stopped at a lone adobe house, the color of the earth. A boy emerged and offered sweet tea in shot glasses. I bought a round for everyone. Leuilli was pleased, and took tea to his mother and sister. They drank behind their veils, still looking ahead. The men walked into the desert and washed ritually with dust before kneeling toward the east to say their afternoon prayers.

Later we came to the sand. It started in sheets and streaks and pockets on the gravel, floated and swirled across the road, and built into yellow dunes on the horizon. Desert sand is made of eroded and weathered rock, mostly quartz particles, pushed and rounded by the wind. It crept into the taxi and settled on the floorboards. The driver switched off the cassette player, and wrapped a strip of cotton around his mouth and nose. No one spoke. The dunes marked the shore of the Eastern Erg, a sand sea covering 120,000 square miles, an area slightly larger than the state of Arizona. The erg is 70 percent sand. It contains hidden salt flats, and here and there, the gravely surface of the desert floor. At its core lies an area of 90 percent sand that itself is the size of New York state, and has a population of zero. Other sand seas are larger.

The Eastern Erg is an erg because the basin in which it lies has been trapping sand for over a million years. The sand comes from ancient river and lake beds, and more recently from the weathering of rock at the foot of the Atlas Mountains near Biskra, where over the past 2,000 years the winds have excavated the desert floor by as much as thirteen feet. The wind gathers the grains from the desert floor, then soars, skids, and bounces them across flat land until they come to a basin. Inside the basin the winds slow and swerve, tangle with the dunes, and drop their load.

M. Mainguet, a French geographer, writes that the Eastern Erg still has a "positive sand budget." He means that the erg has a wealth of grains, and keeps getting richer. The sand continues to accumulate by six million tons every year. If all the grains in the Eastern Erg were evenly leveled, they would lie eighty-five feet thick. But they do not. As the sand begets sand, it forms into dunes, which grow nearly 400 feet above the basin floor, repeat every mile, and shift about. Most sand seas are uninhabitable. El Oued, our destination, is one of the few places where people have chosen to make a stand. It was settled about six billion sand tons, or a thousand years ago, and named for the water that still seeps close below the surface. It is justifiably famous for its survival.

Sand spilled onto the road, and the pavement grew worse. Leuilli thought we were driving too fast; he worried that we would blow a tire. The driver carried no spare, because no one does. Tires are scarce and expensive, about six hundred dollars apiece at the official exchange rate. Leuilli asked me about the situation in the United States. When I admitted that tires are plentiful and less expensive, he asked me the price of jeans. I answered, relatively low. Leuilli sighed. "You know, I dream about America."

When the old Peugeot began to stutter, the driver acted as if he hadn't noticed. The passengers exchanged glances and said nothing. Then the car lost power entirely, and coasted to a stop. The driver went forward to fiddle under the hood. This time, optimistically, we stayed inside.

Leuilli asked again about the United States. "Is the living cheap there?"

"No cheaper than in Algeria."

"Is there unemployment."

"Not like here. But many people are poor."

Leuilli refused to believe it. He smiled. "In America life is easy."

Another passenger interrupted crossly, "You speak nonsense." He was an older man in a suit and fez, holding a briefcase on his lap. He said, "You must not compare Algeria with America or Europe. They are rich and powerful countries. Our histories are different."

Leuilli looked rebuked.

The gentleman formally introduced himself. His name was Mr. Miloudi, and he was traveling to El Oued on business. He asked me if I had been to Ouargla, the oasis where he lived. I said I had. Ouargla had been the home of Malika and Ameur Belouard in the years before the accident. It is an unattractive oil and government town of 100,000 people. But Mr. Miloudi didn't see it that way. He spoke proudly about Ouargla's wide boulevards and modern buildings. "All that was built since we threw the French out."

Mr. Miloudi had fought in the war of independence. He was the rare Saharan who seemed truly not to care about the West. Now he wandered off to urinate in the desert. Leulli was unrepentant, and took the chance to talk about American military power: the Persian Gulf War, the earlier bombing of Tripoli—these attacks on his brethren had only strengthened his belief in the unfailing magic of the United States. You could no more dissuade him of it than you could dissuade a conspiracist, and knowing this, I did not try. The driver got the engine started. We limped on.

The dunes loomed larger, bore down on the pavement, and pushed their sandy tongues across the road. Road signs warned of SABLE!, French for Sand!, as if otherwise a driver might not notice. The sand streamed in jets from the crests of the dunes like snow streaming from alpine peaks. It eddied downslope and out over the road at knee level. It swirled and slipped across the pavement. It wore the paint off the warning signs.

We came to a yellow bulldozer belching diesel smoke, a machine engaged in endless battle. The operator was a man about my age, with a black beard. He paused placidly while we stopped to consider a way across a patch of sand, and he and I exchanged curious glances. His features were hawklike. His eyes were deep and calm. I admired his resignation and his ability to labor on, just as from a distance I sometimes regret my own ambitions. Still, I won't pretend that I envied him his life. I would tear myself inside with frustration. So much of who we are is where we have been.

Closer to El Oued we came to a group of farmers with shovels, flinging sand. Farmers in an erg fling sand in order to survive. They plant clusters of date palms in the depressions between dunes, then spend their lives defending them. Only from the depressions can the palms tap into the underground water; but the palms then interrupt the wind and bury themselves in sand. Untended, the depressions would not stay depressed for long.

But the farmers are more clever than they seem. They fight back by ambush, ringing their gardens with thatched fences, which do not stop the sand directly, but intercept the winds. Sand builds against the fences, grain by grain, and engulfs them.

Artificial dunes are born. They rise as the farmers build new fences on the graves of the old. After years, the dunes tower in tight circles above the palms, providing shelter to the trees. To the casual observer, the effect is of holes dug by hand, but the real work is done by the wind. Farmers from El Oued have learned how to grow the sand.

Within the city, still greater accommodations have been reached. The residents sweep and shovel the sand, but rather than shunning it, they invite it into their houses. They soften their sleep with sand, spreading it thickly across the floors, then overlaying it with handwoven rugs, the most beautiful in the Sahara. Inviting in the sand keeps people from regretting the obvious, that the sand gets into everything anyway. They say you can complain about the grittiness of the bread, but might better just chew it. Chewing sandy bread is a good discipline, because it teaches forbearance. The people of El Oued pray in the sand, and wash ritually in it. Once a year, they shovel out the old grains, then turn around and shovel in the new. They embrace their fate.

THERE WAS A time when the socialist regime built large hotels in the northern oases, and tried to promote the Algerian Sahara as a vacation spot for Europeans. For a few years in the late 1980s, it looked as if this might work. But even then there were problems: having thrown the Europeans out once, few Algerians wanted to serve them again, while within the puritanical Sahara people equated the hotels with sex and drink, and shunned them. Waiters and clerks had to be imported from Kabylie, a rugged area in the northern mountains, where Islam's grip was less strong. Isolated from the communities around them, the hotels festered like sores in the desert. I knew Saharans who would not enter a lobby or restaurant even for a cup of coffee. Inevitably, hotel guests were made to feel unwelcome.

The less adventurous tourists in particular complained about the treatment. I remember a typically empty hotel in the western oasis of Timimoun, during the high heat of summer. Two French families had been stuck there for days because the town had run out of gasoline. We sat together after dinner, and talked about decay.

One of the men was a teacher in Paris. He had nervous eyebrows, and a thin face. He said, "There is the man in the office, and there is the assistant to hand him his pen, and there is another assistant to hand him his paper, and *none* of them works!"

I thought that in some ways such honest reaction though full of racial scorn was less corrosive than the excuse-making of more tolerant visitors. He had seen the desert squarely, though for the wrong reasons. I said, "You're not enjoying your holiday."

He got carried away. "Frankly, everyone hopes for military intervention."

The other man at the table, a reporter for a newspaper in Normandy, said, "There are already so many of them in France. It will explode here, and then what? Of *course* we are worried. Aren't you?"

I told him I was more interested than worried. But he was right, too—Algeria did explode, and then even France could not escape the parcel bombs, the identity checks, the police roundups.

Now the hotel in El Oued was falling into ruin. It was a dismal place with a dome and a watchtower, badly in need of fresh sand. It had neither power nor plumbing. To warm their hands one winter night, the clerks had made a little campfire of the tourist brochures. The fire had blackened the lobby's tile floor and soiled the ceiling. I doubt whether the clerks felt guilty about this. They seemed surprised by the few guests still drifting through.

On the night I arrived there were two others. They were a Parisian couple, traveling by car. The woman had a boy's haircut and intellectual mannerisms. She introduced herself as Brigitte, and addressed me in the familiar *tu* form. The man's name was Alain. He looked tired, and older, and had a fleshy face beneath a gray beard.

Alain was a *pied-noir,* one of the colonials who after generations in North Africa had to flee to the motherland in 1963. *Pied-noir* means "black foot," and refers to the black boots of the early French soldiers, and, later, to the bare and blackened soles of their impoverished descendants. The *pieds-noirs* were haughty in the way of colonial masters, but few ever found their fortune. Maybe because they were poor they lacked the political courage to invite Algerian independence. Finally Charles de Gaulle had the courage for them. When he pulled the French army out of Algeria he was understood by the *pieds-noirs* to have stolen their lives. They felt betrayed. Algerians understood the events better: after more than a century of unnatural advantage, the *pieds-noirs* were simply fated to lose.

The anger on both sides was so deep that in the end the *pieds-noirs* had to leave. It's not surprising that even today so many remain full of hate. They lost their balance. When they return to Algeria on vacation, they do not judge the country squarely, but dwell on what it could have been, and dream bitterly of an Algeria without Algerians.

This may explain why, in El Oued, Alain and Brigitte looked glad to find me at the hotel. They insisted that I join them for dinner, where they shared a bottle of Beaujolais they had brought from Paris. Alain started by saying, "You'd never know that Algeria once produced some of the finest wines in the entire world." Then he said, "It's shocking how low a place can sink. I was here in El Oued before, and the streets were alive and well kept. Now look at them."

I had, and I had found nothing unusual about them. They were poor, hot, and closed-off in the manner of many desert streets. They were more sandy than most, but probably always had been. But I don't think Alain cared about El Oued anyway. After two weeks in the country, he just wanted to talk. What kept emerging was a memory of his youth.

"For three generations my family had a farm in the north, a small place, but very beautiful. There was a stream that flowed along one edge. My brother and I had a few cows to look after, milk cows you know, but otherwise we were free. We spent our summers wading and fishing. Sometimes we rode the tractor out into the fields with our father. He was a careful farmer, and a gentle man. He hired men from the village, and tried to treat them well. When the trouble started, the workers came and said they were our friends, and told us we had nothing to fear. But later when the trouble spread, the same men came to tell us we were no longer safe. Oh, they said they were loyal, but afterward there were attacks nearby—who knows by whom? And we were sent an anonymous threat. My mother was terrified. My brother and I could no longer go out alone on the farm. Father began to carry a rifle on the tractor."

"How did it end?"

"We had to abandon the farm altogether and move in with our cousins in Algiers. Father found work as a butcher's assistant. Finally of course we had to leave for France. I was fourteen, and it was the end of my childhood. After three generations our family had nothing to our name. And the farm?" He snorted. "Our loyal workers moved onto it, cut it up, wrecked it within a few years. They were greedy and stupid. By now you might expect their feelings to soften, but I know that still today the Algerians blame us."

Brigitte spoke of El Oued. She said, "We went to the market this afternoon, and all we got were hostile stares."

I was struck by the extent to which Brigitte had contracted Alain's anger. She was a Parisian, and too young to remember an old Algerian war. But she had picked up the colonial habit of talking loudly about the Algerians as if they were not present or did not understand French. Similarly, she wore a short skirt and a sleeveless shirt, and through the thin fabric displayed her nipples in disregard of local sentiment. And now she sat drinking French wine. These were not acts of indifference, but of aggression. And Algerians understood the difference.

Alain said their trip had gone badly from the start. The couple had entered the country from Morocco. Seeing an Algerian birthplace on Alain's passport, and recognizing him as a *pied-noir,* the Algerian border-control officer had snarled, "Why don't you take your vacation in Israel?" It was for him like telling them to go to hell.

By some standards, Alain and Brigitte did just that. The lushness of the north brought forth too many angry memories. They fled south across the Atlas Mountains, and drove into the harshness and solitude of the Sahara, where they consoled themselves by collecting scorpions. Scorpions are little dragons—mindless, venomous, unlovable creatures, dreaded throughout history and by all peoples. Alain and Brigitte had not planned to wander the desert at night, tipping over rocks. But having fled the north, collecting scorpions had given them something to do.

Now at the hotel after dinner, our conversation flagged. Alain placed a shoe box on the table, and Brigitte lifted the lid to let me peer inside. Two scorpions sat motionless at opposite ends, each on its eight legs, with its claws extended, and its stinging tail curled over its back. They were pale, baleful specimens, the color of sand, about five inches long. Brigitte had placed a rock in the box to make them feel at home. She gazed at them worriedly, then turned to me for answers. Were they thirsty? Did they have enough to eat? Had the car been too hot for them? Would Paris be too cold? I told her not to worry because honestly I did not care.

Respect is due, nonetheless. Scorpions are among the oldest creatures on earth, living fossils, largely unchanged from species that lived 350 million years ago. About then they emerged from the sea, developed legs and lungs, and eventually crept across every major landmass except Antarctica, into habitats from the equatorial forests to the savannas and the snow-covered mountains of the high latitudes. They thrive in the harshest habitat of all, the Sahara. This is because, beyond being adaptable, they are just plain tough. Scorpions don't require plants. They eat spiders, worms, and insects, as well as the occasional snake, lizard, or rodent. When they emerge from their burrows their usual purpose is to hunt for food or a mate—and the females are prone to confuse the two. Most scorpions hunt by ambush. They have up to twelve eyes, and multiple motion-sensors.

They wait by their burrows, and when prey passes by they move fast, and can snatch a fly out of midair with their claws. When they find bigger prey, they do not hesitate to strike with their tails. But they prefer to kill simply, by crushing with their claws. They are extraordinarily diligent about their eating: certain species can gain up to 30 percent of their body weight in a single meal. Scientists describe such feedings with some awe as "the conversion of prey biomass into scorpion biomass." Afterward the scorpions look swollen.

They can survive a year between feedings. They conserve their bodily fluids so assiduously that some never drink, but absorb sufficient water from the flesh of their prey. It helps that their outer shells are impermeable, that their feces are dry, and that they release a crystalline form of urine. And scorpions don't sweat. They regulate their body temperatures by stilting, by burrowing into the ground, and by hunting only at night. If for some reason they get caught out on a hot day, they can withstand baking, up to a point. Nonetheless, evolution has hardly prepared them for captivity in a shoe box. Alain jiggled the box to make them move, and they refused. He introduced a fork, and they backed into their corners and raised their tails defensively. Saharans say that a scorpion surrounded by a ring of fire will sting itself to death. But scorpions are immune to their own venom. And as a British zoologist has pointed out, suicide requires imagination, which scorpions lack.

I was relieved when Alain put down his fork. There are over fifteen hundred species of scorpions worldwide, of which only twenty-five are man-killers—but of those twenty-five, four are native to the Sahara, where they live in abundance. I thought it prudent not to provoke these two. Scorpion venoms are complex neurotoxins, among the most potent in nature. As measured by molecular weight, some are 100,000 times more toxic than cyanide. A bad sting can lead within hours to convulsions, followed by cardiac arrest or respiratory failure. Despite the availability of antivenoms, scorpions across the globe still kill more people than any other predator except snakes—over five thousand a year. Certain Algerian oases are infested with them. During the high summer season, you do not reach into the dark corners of your rooms, or dress without shaking out your clothes, or however long you live there ever feel quite at home.

This may explain why Alain and Brigitte had collected the scorpions—an instinctive affinity for the creatures who still terrified the natives. But there is also a more charitable explanation. Forget the past—as modern Parisians they may with distance simply have romanticized the desert. Think of the Germans who visit the American West by the thousands, yearning for a fabled frontier. The Sahara is visited by French people on equally wistful quests. Even those who are not *pieds-noirs* retain a sense of possession, however dated, and say things like "You are never alone in the desert," which is wrong but sounds right. For the same people, scorpions may seem like souvenirs.

THE
PHYSICS
OF BLOWN
SAND

I STAYED ON in El Oued, and in the early hours walked south along a crumbling paved road under assault from the sand sea. The morning was bright and hot, and the dunes carved crisp lines against the sky. I passed a turbaned man on a donkey carrying empty gas cans into town. There was no other traffic. The minarets of El Oued disappeared behind me. The road led eventually to a village, or what was left of it. It was a village that had been mostly buried in drifting sand. The corners and roofs of stone structures still showed, but only three houses remained inhabitable, and from the evidence of digging around them, they, too, were threatened.

I drank at a well with a rope and bucket. There was no farming here. The only sign of industry was a freestanding stone oven, a baker's oven, against which palm wood had been stacked. The wind blew sand, but otherwise nothing stirred. Two men sat in the shadow of a wall by a fire on which they had placed a blackened pot. They motioned me over and offered me tea in a dirty glass. The men were older than I, bearded and thin, and had no work. We spent a few hours together. They pointed to where the school lay buried, and to where most of the village stood beneath the sands. I asked them the details of its burial.

They said the sands are fickle. Dunes may drift for decades in one direction, or not drift at all, then suddenly turn and consume you. Consumption by the sand is like other forms of terminal illness: it starts so gently that at first you don't worry. One day the grains begin to accumulate against your walls. You've seen the grains before, and naturally assume that a change in the wind will carry them away. But this time the wind does not change, and the illness persists. Over weeks or longer, the sand grows. You fight back with a shovel, and manage to keep your walls clear. Fighting back feels good and gives you something to do. But the grains never let up, and one morning while shoveling you realize that the dunes have moved closer. You enlist your sons and brothers. But eventually the land around your house swells with sand, and you begin standing on sand to shovel sand. Finally no amount of digging will clear your walls. The dunes tower above you, and send sand sheets cascading down their advancing slip faces. You have to gather your belongings and flee.

But your house is your heritage, and you would like somehow to preserve it. As the dunes bear down on it they will collapse the walls. The defense is again the Saharan acceptance of destiny: having lost the fight against the sand, you must now invite it in. Sleeping on the sand, covering your floors with it for all these years, helped prepare you mentally. But shoveling in the sand is not enough. Your last act is to break out the windows, take off the doors, and knock holes in the roof. You allow the wind to work for you. If it succeeds, and fills your house, the walls will stand. Then in a hundred years, when the wind requires it, the dunes will drift on and uncover the village. Your descendants will bless God and his Prophet. They will not care that you were thin and poor and had no work. They will remember you as a man at peace with his world. The desert takes away but also delivers.

I LEFT THE men to their contemplation, and climbed out over the dune that had engulfed their village. From its crest I discovered a valley two hundred feet below, where the desert floor was exposed and a stretch of blacktop emerged from the sand. The road was not on the map. It lay beyond the village and ran south toward the empty center of the Eastern Erg. I thought it might lead to an old settlement, perhaps one that had been uncovered by the wind, and I set off to follow it.

I should have been more careful. I was traveling too lightly, with neither a hat nor water nor any enduring sense of direction. The road kept turning, diving into sand, reemerging. Eventually it ran under a mountainous dune and disappeared entirely. I climbed that dune, and a string of the highest ones beyond it, and knew even as I proceeded that I had gone too far. The dunes were like giant starfish, covered by ripples, linking curved tentacles to form lines. In all directions, the erg stretched to the horizons in a confusion of sand.

This was the landscape that inspired the British officer Ralph A. Bagnold, history's closest observer of Saharan sands. Bagnold was an English gentleman of the old school. He fought in the trenches of Flanders during World War I, then earned an honors degree in engineering from Cambridge, and later reenlisted in the British Army for overseas assignment. While stationed in Egypt and India between 1929 and 1934, he led expeditions in modified Fords to explore the sand seas of Libya. These were big places in need of understanding. One *erg* alone was the size of all France.

Bagnold had a strong and inquiring mind. He marveled at the desert's patterns, saw magic in the dunes, and wanted it all explained. To his surprise, he found that scientific knowledge was as yet merely descriptive: dune shapes had been catalogued, but little was understood about the processes involved in their formation. Bagnold set out to understand for himself. In 1935 he went back to England, retired from the army, hammered together a personal wind tunnel, and began a series of meticulous experiments with blown sand. He considered himself to be a dabbler, a tinkerer, an amateur scientist. But his research resulted in the publication, in 1941, of a small masterpiece of scientific exploration: *The Physics of Blown Sand and Desert Dunes.* It was a treatment so rigorous, and so pleasantly written, that it remains the standard today. Throughout it, Bagnold never lost his wonder. He wrote:

Here, instead of finding chaos and disorder, the observer never fails to be amazed at a simplicity of form, an exactitude of repetition and a geometric order unknown in nature on a scale larger than that of crystalline structure. In places vast accumulations of sand weighing millions of tons move inexorably, in regular formation, over the surface of the country, growing, retaining their shape, even breeding, in a manner which, by its grotesque imitation of life, is vaguely disturbing to the imaginative mind.

Bagnold's genius was his ability to think grain by grain. He defined sand as a rock particle small enough to be moved by the wind, yet not so small that, like dust, it can float indefinitely in suspension—and he proceeded from there, exploring the movement of each grain. He did his best work on that level, in a laboratory far from the desert. But he was never a tedious man. He understood the power of multiplication. And when he returned to the Sahara, and stood as I did on the crests of the great ergs, he found in these accumulations his truest companions. Just before his death, in May 1990, he wrote a short memoir—an unintentionally sad remembrance of a strong life. He wrote about two world wars, about great men he had known, and about his beloved family. But again he wrote best about the sand. Bagnold's health was declining. It is a measure of the man that when he described the dunes' ability to heal themselves, his writing remained free of longing.

I GAVE UP on finding the road. For all I knew it ended where I stood, in a lost village hundreds of feet below. My tracks led back toward El Oued in the thinnest trace, softening already in the wind. The sand was a brilliant shade of tan that reflected the sun and filled the air with its heat. Bare rock can produce the same effect. As a result, the Sahara is one of the most reflective places on earth: in heat and light, it fends off 90 percent of the solar energy that assaults its surface. For burrowing creatures like scorpions, this has an essential side effect—it means that just inches underground life feels cool. For creatures above the surface, however, all that redirected energy poses problems. This is something that Bagnold hardly bothered to mention: by early afternoon, when you walk across the sands, the sun burns you from below.

Though I happened to carry a small thermometer, I did not measure the temperature on the Eastern Erg. It was autumn, a gentle season, and I had already been through the greater heat of Saharan summers. Still my hands trembled, and I suffered from the dryness of mouth and tightening of the throat that marks the onset of deep thirst. Retracing my path across the sandy swells, I thought wishfully about more genuine seas.

Imagining water is a normal human reaction to the Sahara. For that reason, and because of the superficial resemblance of the ergs to stormy seas, comparisons to the ocean are inevitable. Still, they have been overdone. Camels are not ships, and nomads do not sail across the sand. *Erg* is Arabic not literally for a sea but for a vein or belt. Dunes do undulate, but they never form genuine waves. Bagnold wrote:

> The resemblance [to a wave] is in appearance only. For the essence of a true wave is the propagation of energy, either through the body of a material as in the case of sound, or along its surface as with a surface water wave. In a sand ripple or wave there is no such propagation of energy. A sand ripple is merely a crumpling or heaping up of the surface, brought about by wind action, and cannot be regarded as a true wave in a strict dynamical sense. The similarity lies only in the regular repetition of surface form.

On the subject of sand, Bagnold was disciplined. He distinguished sternly between drifts, which form below windbreaks, and "true dunes," which achieve their greatest perfection on flat, featureless ground. True dunes breed incestuously, and live in immense look-alike families, sometimes extending across hundreds of miles. Their features depend on the wealth of the sand supply, and on the force and direction of the prevailing winds. In detail they seem infinitely variable. However, it is possible to distinguish between a few basic types.

The barchan is the elemental one—a migratory, crescent-shaped formation with a gentle windward slope up which grains slowly creep, and a steep leeward slip face down which those same grains eventually cascade. Barchans advance by avalanche, sending shallow horns ahead on each side. They are solitary by nature, and careful conservationists: born of unidirectional winds and limited resources, they retain their shape and bulk by constantly turning over their supply of sand.

Where sand supplies are abundant, the barchans multiply in ever-denser colonies, until eventually they link horns to form scalloped chains perpendicular to the wind.

As the sand thickens, the chains become high ridges across which smaller secondary barchans may begin to migrate. Such compound crescent-shaped dunes are common to the northeast corner of the Eastern Erg, and to other parts of the Sahara where the wind blows from a single direction.

Where the wind is fickle, the sand assumes an entirely different form. Bidirectional winds herd the grains by pushing them first from one angle, then shifting and pushing them from a slightly different angle, finally organizing them into elongated formations that stream downwind in parallel ranks.

Bagnold described these dunes with the word *sief,* which is Arabic for "sword." But they are more like serpents in the way they hump and crawl across the desert floor.

Where the winds blow energetically from around the compass, typically in a pattern of regular seasonal shifts, the sand crawls around less, but builds upward into high-peaked imitations of starfish.

Star dunes embrace El Oued with their tentacles. When one of them stretches, whole villages may disappear.

The forms that dunes take in real sand seas are rarely as simple as their idealized models. Even the concept of sorting—by which the dune types are meant to keep mostly to themselves—is more useful as a theoretical tool than as a practical guide to the field. Bagnold's first achievement, without an airplane and in a time before satellite mapping, was to visualize the geometry. Star dunes sprout on the crests of crescents, which bleed into barchan-crossing barchans. Bagnold's "simplicity of form," his "exactitude of repetition," and his "geometric order," tangle together with the symmetry of a maze.

I blundered into that maze now. Having left my earlier tracks to skirt the highest peaks, I climbed a ridge to reconnoiter, and instead of spotting the old road where I had expected it, found only sand. I could have doubled back to my earlier tracks, but I felt sure the road lay nearby—over the next ridge, or the one beyond. My thirst urged me ahead. I had a few hours still, because the season was not summer, so I was not immediately afraid. But I knew enough about the Sahara to want to keep moving. I ignored the romance of the erg and the mechanics of its dunes. I remembered the stories.

IN A NORTHERN oasis I once met an old drunk named Lag Lag, who as a young man had made his living driving cargo trucks across the roadless Sahara. We met one night by a campfire, to which our mutual friends had lured him with an offer of cheap wine. He was a wiry, good-humored old man with unkempt hair and ragged clothes. His friends told me he had been a pious Moslem in his younger years, but they warned me that his drinking had made a mockery of his faith. They thought his story needed to be told anyway, and they wanted me to write it down. Lag Lag was a famous man, not because twice he had been lost in the Eastern Erg but because twice he had survived.

He told me he was first lost in the summer of 1957, when he and an assistant were hauling equipment south from Biskra to the newly discovered oil site at Hassi Messaoud. Rather than driving their truck the long way around across the hard gravel plains to the west, they decided to cut straight through the sand sea. It was a bad idea. Driving among dunes is slow and frustrating work, and requires scouting for soft sand; it imposes frequent turns and backtracking, and soon confuses even the best sense of orientation.

Neither Lag Lag nor his assistant was a navigator. They knew only that the sun rose from Mecca, soared high all day, and plunged into the west, and that it was chased all night by a universe of stars. And so they began to wander. Eventually they realized that nothing looked right, but they did not panic. For three days they struggled with the dunes, until they ran out of fuel.

Since they carried water, they were in no immediate danger. But the long-term prospects were not good. Walking out was unthinkable, and it was unlikely that anyone would come their way. The oilmen at Hassi Messaoud expected them, of course, but had no idea of the route they had chosen. The possibility of aerial search did not enter their minds. It was accepted then as now that people die in the desert.

The sun forced them into the shade under the truck, where they dug a shallow trench. Day after day they lay there, watching their water dwindle and waiting for God's will. They turned inward to Islam and talked about the afterlife. They had food, but did not eat, fearing it would magnify their thirst. Dehydration, not starvation, is what kills wanderers in the desert. And thirst is the most terrible of all human sufferings.

The physiologists who specialize in thirst seem never to have experienced it. This surprises me. You would think that some-one interested in thirst would want to stop drinking for a while, especially since for short periods it can be done safely. But the physiologists pursue knowledge, not experience. They use words based in Greek, which soften the subject. For instance, they would describe the Sahara—the burning sand and relent-less sky—as *dipsogenic,* meaning "thirst provoking." In discussing Lag Lag's case, they might say he progressed from *eudipsia,* meaning "ordinary thirst," through bouts of *hyperdipsia,* mean-ing "temporary intense thirst," to *polydipsia,* by which they mean "sustained, excessive thirst." We can define it more pre-cisely: since *poly* means "many," *polydipsia* means the kind of thirst that drives you to drink anything. There are specialized terms for such behavior, including *uriposia,* "the drinking of urine," and *hemoposia,* "the drinking of blood." For word en-thusiasts, this is heady stuff. Nonetheless, the lexicon has not kept up with technology. Blame the ancients for not driving cars. I have tried, and cannot coin a suitable word for "the drinking of rusty radiator water."

Radiator water is what Lag Lag and his assistant started into when their good drinking water was gone. They had been under the truck for three weeks, and no one had come to find them. They wrote good-bye letters to their families, and stuck them up in the cab.

The assistant sobbed.

Lag Lag was annoyed, and said, "When you die, you die." He lay quietly, preparing for the end.

Years later when he described his peace of mind to me, I admitted to him that I found it strange. Afterward, I would have my own experience with a stranding in the Sahara. But Lag Lag was the first to say to me that such a death is not complicated, that the Sahara overpowers its victims and offers no choice but acceptance, that Islam too requires acceptance, that the greatest God is the desert God.

They had drunk most of the radiator water before Lag Lag had his inspiration. It occurred to him that the truck's tanks might still hold dregs of diesel fuel, and that he might add engine oil to form a combustible mixture. Having passed from tears to hopelessness, his assistant refused to move from under the truck. Lag Lag ignored him, and drained as much oil as he dared from the engine before pouring it into the tank. He climbed into the cab, cycled the glow plug, and pressed the starter. The engine turned over reluctantly, but after several attempts rumbled to life. The assistant scrambled aboard. Spewing dense blue smoke, the truck rolled forward.

After a few miles they came to a rutted track. With no idea of where they were, or of where the track led, they followed it. Because they had drunk most of the coolant, the engine overheated and seized. But the desert spared them: a refrigerated van appeared in the distance, shimmering in the heat, and drove up the track to them, carrying water, fresh meat, and vegetables. It was driven by a friend. He broke the seal on the back, and built a fire. Lag Lag and his assistant drank and feasted. The specialists would say they rehydrated.

AFTER ALGERIA'S WAR of independence, Hassi Messaoud kept producing oil and gas for the new nation. Lag Lag kept driving the open desert, and allowed his memory of the sands to fade. He no longer willingly cut through the erg, but in 1964 he agreed to deliver a massive concrete cap to an oil site deep in the dunes. His youngest brother went with him. They drove to an oasis on an established track, then set out into the sand. By the end of the first day they were lost. They doubled back by scouting their tracks, which in places had already been obliterated by the winds. At night they slept. On the second day, through miscalculation, they allowed the truck to sink into soft sand.

Because sinking into sand is a routine part of driving the open Sahara, even outside the ergs, Lag Lag was not at first concerned. You shovel sand or dig it with bare hands from the dikes that build in front of the wheels, and drive on. In a bad case, getting unstuck might take a few hours. But this time the sand was different, so fine and soft that digging only caused the truck to sink farther in. They tried pushing the concrete cap off the truck, and when that didn't work they tried prying it off. The cap was too heavy; it was a weight dragging them to the bottom of the desert. By the end of the day, Lag Lag realized that again the erg had trapped him, and all his memories returned.

His brother volunteered to walk out. Lag Lag feared the futility of an attempt, and argued that if they rested in the shade of the truck and did not struggle they would have enough water for perhaps a week. If God intended it, someone would discover their tracks or happen along. If not, Lag Lag said, it would be better to meet death quietly, like men. When you die, you die.

The week passed, and they drank their last water. Lag Lag realized no help was coming. Only the radiator fluid remained. He felt proud of his brother, who prayed not for salvation but in acceptance of God's will. Lag Lag's own mood was fatalistic, but not to the point of inaction. He decided on the basis of his past experience that he was destined to find a solution.

Lag Lag's solution was not original; he had never been much of a thinker. But his thirst forced him to concentrate. With his brother's help, he bled the tires, and bled them further until they bulged like pancakes in the sand. I know today how their work sounded then—the sharp hiss of escaping air penetrating the desert of naturally broader winds. They waited for night, and dug sand ramps for the truck to climb. That work sounded like two desperate men breathing hard. Then they waited for light.

In the moments before dawn, when the horizon first promised the sun, they prayed. Lag Lag climbed into the cab. He started the engine, and as a diligent driver, let it warm. He shifted into compound low. His brother stood outside, adding one manpower to the strength of the diesel. Together, with the clutch sliding and burning, they drove the truck from the grave.

They were still in danger: they carried no pump to reinflate the tires, and the rubber would soon peel from the wheels. Their water was gone, and their tracks from the week before had disappeared. Flawless sand lay all around. They set off in what they hoped was the right direction. And fate was with them: after barely two miles, having crossed the tentacle of a star dune, they found below them the same little oasis from which they had started.

It was a quiet place with a mosque and a post office. The residents were unimpressed by the sight of two men emerging from the desert. A few might have noticed their beards, and the condition of their tires. Someone gave them water, someone sold them food. Lag Lag pondered the deeper meaning of their ordeal. They had lain nearly within shouting distance of the oasis, but as good Muslims they had not shouted. It was all quite mysterious to him, and only added to the glory of God and the desert. Years afterward, when I met him, the sadness of Lag Lag's later life was apparent to everyone at the campfire. Having exhausted an old story, he had nothing left to say. With time and wine, he had allowed the memory of his desert to soften.

MY OWN EXPERIENCE in the Eastern Erg was less threatening than his. I walked, grew thirsty, and imagined cool water. And where I thought I would find the abandoned road or the half-buried village, I found instead a farmer with a camel, tending his palms behind a palm-frond fence. He was dressed in pants and a shirt, and wore a loose turban. He seemed unsurprised that I had strolled out of the dunes.

"*Bonjour, monsieur,*" he said, in accented French. "You have enjoyed your walk?"

I said I had.

He offered me water, and I drank deeply. He watched this with interest. Saharans sip. He said, "We used to see a lot of Europeans here, just a few years ago, because we have the finest dunes in the entire Sahara. Did you know that Monod himself was here?" He meant Théodore Monod, the lyrical Jacques Cousteau of the desert. Among Saharan explorers I prefer Bagnold, whose austerity was truer to the desert itself.

I said, "I'm not French."

"I know. You're American."

"You can tell from the accent?"

"You came in the taxi from Biskra. My cousin rode with you."

I laughed. "What else do you know?"

"You don't like scorpions."

"That's easy."

"Last night you sat with the French couple at the hotel. They had scorpions in a box." He smiled. "I have a cousin at the hotel, too."

He felt like bragging. He said, "I also know that you posted a letter to the United States. The Parisians tried to telephone Paris, and couldn't get through. But you—you did not even try the telephone."

I did not ask how he knew. We walked back together to El Oued, to his community of cousins. All the next day I rode the taxis west and south, to Touggourt, an oasis on the edge of the sand sea, and on across a gravely plateau to Ouargla, the oasis where Ameur and Malika Belouard had lived.

6

A LESSON
ABOUT
LOVE

THIS IS A story by which to navigate Malika's desert.
They say long ago a king of Ouargla wanted to know if his subjects were obedient. He called all the young men of the oasis to
the palace, and said, "I have a test for you. To prove your loyalty
to me, you must go to your houses now and kill your fathers.
There must be not a single old man left in Ouargla by tomorrow, when you will return to the palace."

The men left, and when they got home they cut the throats
of their fathers. Only one son did not have the courage. He hid
his father instead in a great jar meant for storing dates.

The next day the men assembled in the palace courtyard. The
king asked, "Have you killed your fathers?"

"Yes," they answered. "And may God damn their souls."

The king said, "Now I'll see if you have lied to me. I want
each of you to return tomorrow with your king, your enemy,
and your best friend."

The subjects left the palace in confusion, desperate to fulfill the king's mysterious request. The young man who had hidden his father went home. His wife served him dinner. His father emerged from hiding and joined him for the meal. The young man was so nervous that he could not swallow the food.

His father noticed. "What worries you, my son?"

"Father, it is the king. He has asked me to bring to the palace my king, my enemy, and my best friend. But I don't understand the meaning of his words."

"Oh, my boy," said the old man, "eat, and do not worry. Tomorrow, when you wake up, put your son on your shoulder, take your dog in hand, and command your wife to accompany you.

"Show your son to the king, and say, 'Here, sire, is my king. When he cries, my heart breaks. I would give everything I own to console him.'

"Show him your dog, and say, 'Here is my best friend. Wherever I go he accompanies and defends me. When I feed him he is happy, and he wags his tail. When I beat him he doesn't get angry, or run away, but continues to serve me.'

"Then show him your wife, and say, 'Here is my enemy. She causes me constant trouble. When I bring something home, if I don't give her a share, she begins to scream and cry.' "

The young man felt reassured by his father's words. He finished his meal and went to bed. In the morning, all of Ouargla's men assembled in the palace courtyard. The king said, "Approach and show me. Have you found what I asked for?"

The crowd was silent. No one had been able to solve the king's riddle. But then the young man stepped forward with his son, dog, and wife, and he repeated the words of his father.

The king listened, and answered, "My friend, I can tell that these thoughts are not your own. They are so wise that only an old man could have uttered them. This tells me you have hidden your father. He is not dead after all."

The young man hung his head in shame.

The king said, "I will pass judgment on you now. Because you did not obey me, I hereby expropriate all your possessions. But because, out of love for your father, you alone have retained your sanity, I give you one-half of all my possessions, and appoint you as my successor to rule over these imbeciles who have neither minds nor hearts."

The king put the royal staff in the young man's hands, draped the royal robe on his shoulders, and sat him upon the throne.

Ever since then the men of Ouargla have venerated their fathers. They have loved their children. They have enjoyed their dogs. And their wives have perhaps been less fortunate.

7

THE
KING OF
OUARGLA

THE KING OF Ouargla was a driving license examiner, Malika's husband, my friend Ameur Belouard. He lived with Malika and their four children in Ouargla, and was sent by the Ministry of Transportation on a circuit to other oases to test new drivers. Whenever possible he rode Air Algeria. He loved airplanes, especially jets, wished he had been a pilot, and knew all the Air Algeria pilots by name. They knew him, too. He was a famous man. Whenever he flew they asked him to ride with them in the cockpit, and were genuinely delighted with his company, and flattered him by talking shop. It was the least of favors they could do for him. They would have liked to do more. Over time I learned not to be surprised by this. Ameur Belouard was admired throughout the Algerian Sahara. The extent of his reputation became clear to me only with distance, in settlements far from Ouargla, when strangers sought me out simply because Ameur had sent word.

He was forty-two then, a small man with swarthy skin, and impatient reflexes. Women found him attractive; men imagined him their brother. He was of course more than just a driving license examiner. He was street-smart, corrupt, and connected. A telephone nested in his hand. He would find you a black-market refrigerator or television, and expect nothing immediately in return. He knew the best sources for tires. He gave good exchange rates on foreign currencies, cash only, no records kept, and always carried a thick wad of Algerian dinars. He could be counted on for a loan, among friends, no interest asked. He knew a man at the telephone exchange who could repair a bill or cut through the interminable delay for service. He could book you a seat on an overbooked flight. He could book you five seats. People believed in him because he was a fixer.

His Ouargla was not a pretty place. At its core, it had a mud-bricked *ksar,* an ancient fortified village of twisted streets with a certain picturesque appeal, but farther out it grew in boulevards and shadeless slums into an oil and government town. I met Ameur during my first visit there. He was the older brother of a friend in France, an Algerian immigrant, who had insisted that I look him up. "*Sacré Ameur!*" my friend had said fondly.

This was during the opening days of the Islamic revolution, when Algiers was rioting over the price of wheat, and the army was machine-gunning the protesters. I left the capital's shattered streets, and flew south, expecting to find a peaceful desert. Instead, I found in Ouargla an army garrison on high alert. A soldier in a guard tower cocked his Kalashnikov when I walked by. As a foreigner, I was conspicuous; as an American, I was suspect. A captain of army intelligence questioned me, and sent watchers in leather jackets and sunglasses to shadow me around the oasis.

It was sort of comic. At the shabby government hotel where I stayed, the clerks downstairs breathed into my phone calls.

Ameur found out about the surveillance from army insiders who thought they owed him. He came to the hotel café to meet me, and said, "Do you know what these bastards are doing to you?"

"Of course."

"Do you know how they are treating you?"

"They have their jobs."

"I don't want you to worry."

"I don't."

"They're frightened," he said.

"I know. I've come from Algiers."

"It's because they're soldiers."

"I'm sure."

"The people will have no pity on them."

I didn't answer. I thought Ameur was talking too loudly.

"They could be dangerous for you," he said.

"I've got nothing to hide."

"You are my guest. I don't want you to worry."

"I promise, I won't."

"You'll see. I'll make a call. I'll take care of these bastards for you."

"I'd rather you wouldn't."

But he would hear none of it. He touched my arm. "There is no problem, absolutely no problem!" He said it a third time, and with emphasis. *"Il n'y a pas de problème!"*

I indulged him, as all his friends did. Anyway, Ameur was unstoppable. Confidence was his greatest asset. He came from a peasant family, and had the eagerness of a social climber. When he heard about the world beyond the Sahara he liked to remark,

"Now, *that!* That's *class!*" He wore pressed, pleated pants and patterned Parisian shirts. He would have looked at home in most of the world's biggest cities. Only his loafers gave Ouargla away: they bore the unmistakable indelible ochre stain of desert dust.

He stole me away from the hotel in his worn Peugeot sedan. My watchers were on foot, and could not follow; I doubt that they cared. We drove to Ameur's house, by a new mosque, where it squatted randomly in trampled dirt, without shade or vegetation.

Ameur had built the place with his own hands, of cinder block and concrete. It was a small flat-roofed bunker, typically poor and unfinished on the outside, offering few hints to the neighborhood of its inner comfort. Power and telephone lines burrowed into its side. Only one small window, barred and shuttered, looked onto the street. The other windows looked onto a courtyard hidden behind high walls. An air conditioner rattled and hummed. A television antenna stood on the roof.

We entered the courtyard through a metal door and were greeted shyly by the children, ages three to ten. I gave them small presents from Paris and a bag of bad chocolates from across town. We left our shoes in the entrance hallway. The house had two parlors, one for the male visitors, and the other, next to the kitchen, for the family and women.

But Ameur was a naturally open man. In a gesture of friendship, he invited me into the family's room, which was cool and dark and heavily furnished. I do not know where Malika was; I had not yet met her. Ameur and I sat in overstuffed chairs while his eldest daughter served us strong, sweet coffee. She brought in a French language exam, just graded, on which she had earned a perfect score. She brought in a map of the world, and asked me to point to my home. She pointed to hers.

In a wall-length cabinet stood Ameur's prized possessions—a stereo, a television, a video recorder, a multivolume Arabic encyclopedia, and a collection of Malian figurines, souvenirs of a trip south from the years before Algerians were imprisoned by their currency. His most prized possession, the telephone, stood alone on a brass tray beside Ameur. He dialed the number of an army intelligence officer, and worked himself into an indignant anger, speaking in French to allow me to understand. He felt personally insulted by the way his guest had been treated.

After he hung up, he said, "They will not bother you again."

I said, "I'm impressed."

He nodded and tapped his chest. "Ask anyone and they will tell you. Ameur Belouard is the king of Ouargla."

I never saw the watchers again. It was a short, strange period in Saharan history when soldiers and the political police hesitated.

WE DROVE TO a market street in the old *ksar*, where Ameur asked a butcher to hack the leg from the carcass of a lamb. The butcher tried to make a gift of the meat, but Ameur refused, and paid liberally from a thick wad of bills, without requiring change. The butcher joked with him to demonstrate their friendship. We bought carrots, potatoes, and tangerines. We drove the food home, and the children carried it inside. We returned to the car and kept driving.

Ameur drove with both hands on the wheel. He was the government examiner, a public example, a pillar of civic responsibility, and more than polite. When a donkey and cart blocked our way up an alley, he did not gesture, or gun his engine, but waited patiently. When a group of veiled women stepped off a curb, he stopped to let them pass. When a truck turned without signaling, he clucked. He did not drive fast, or brake hard, or accelerate aggressively. He did not take corners quickly. He was smooth, alert, and very safe. He felt every eye was upon him.

It took me a while to realize that he had no destination. We crossed the town, crossed back, angled off, and turned around, cruising Ouargla like country boys from Texas. We covered all the main streets from both directions. Other drivers cruised as well. Ameur tapped the horn in friendly hellos, and waved to his acquaintances. We stopped to talk to an air-traffic controller. People came up to us and crouched beside the car to pass the time. Ameur promised to provide one man with hard-to-find white house paint. No problem.

When daylight faded, the air cooled. We swung by Ameur's house and picked up his youngest daughter, a coy, curly-haired girl of four. He called her his princess. She sat on my lap as we drove north from town, following a paved road for miles into the desert. Ameur wanted to recite his evening prayers in the dunes. He said he had been a drunk and a sinner in earlier years, but had returned to the path of righteousness.

I asked when.

He answered, "Recently."

I asked why he wanted to pray in the desert.

"Because the sand here is clean." He went off alone to bathe his soul in it.

His daughter nestled in my arms against the night winds. She smelled of soap. We wandered into the darkness under stars softened by translucent clouds. Ouargla lined the horizon like a lighted thread.

8

SLEEPING

WITH

WOMEN

THIS IS ANOTHER story about Malika's desert. Long ago in Ouargla, when merely to see a woman was to have slept with her, there lived a powerful judge who had seen all the town's women except for the wife of the tax assessor. His problem was that she was rumored to be the most beautiful of all.

The judge asked himself, "How shall I go about seeing this man's beautiful wife?" Then he had an idea: "It's easy. I'll send the assessor on a mission."

He wrote a few letters, then called for the assessor, and ordered him to deliver them to an oasis called the M'Zab, days distant. He accompanied the assessor to the gates of Ouargla, and when he was certain he had gone, he went to speak to the assessor's neighbor, an old woman.

"Tell me," he said. "Exactly how does your neighbor the assessor knock on his door when he comes home?"

"That's easy," she answered. "He knocks like this. He taps with his finger."

The judge thanked her. From a jeweler he bought a beautiful gold ring. Then he went to the assessor's house, and tapped on the door exactly as the old woman had showed him.

Inside, the wife said to her black maid, "Get up. Go to see. Only one man taps so. Your master must have come home early."

The maid opened the door and found the judge. She returned to her mistress and said, "He taps like the master, but he is the judge."

The assessor's wife was as wise as she was beautiful. She answered the maid, "Show the judge into the parlor. We will prepare a lesson for him."

The maid led the judge into the parlor, and invited him to sit in the place of honor on the rugs. She went to the kitchen and, following her mistress's instructions, prepared a meal on covered plates.

When the meal was ready, the maid carried it on a tray to the guest. The judge was at first delighted by the hospitality, but when he lifted the covers he found on each plate a single cooked egg. "What is the meaning of this?" he asked.

"That women are like eggs," the maid said. "To some, God gives white shells. To others he gives black shells. But inside they are all the same."

As impressed by the wisdom of the assessor's wife as by her virtue, the judge abandoned any thought of seeing her. But when he stood to leave, he carelessly dropped the ring he had brought for her. The ring slipped under a corner of the rug.

When the assessor returned from the M'Zab, exhausted after a long journey through the desert, he sat on the rug. Feeling a lump under his thigh, he discovered the ring and drew the obvious conclusion. He called the maid. "Tell your mistress that I will never see her again."

For months afterward he refused to clothe or feed his wife. She became pale and weak, and fell sick. When her parents came to visit her, they were shocked by her condition. She told them about the judge's visit and the ring.

Now the parents went to the judge. The father said, "Your honor, we once had a lovely garden that we entrusted to a friend to fertilize and irrigate. But now we have discovered that he has allowed it to wither. We asked him why, and he told us that he discovered the tracks of a jackal there, and was afraid to return."

The judge called the assessor before him, and asked, "Why have you neglected your garden?"

"Your Honor, I discovered jackal tracks."

At first the judge was stern. "If you don't tend your garden," he warned, "I will tend it myself." But then the judge remembered the woman's virtue and her wisdom. He said, "The desert is home to jackals, it's true. You found tracks, so it is certain that a jackal visited your garden. But nothing was eaten. Nothing was damaged. Nothing was touched."

The assessor believed the judge. He took back his wife, clothed and fed her, and according to the legend lived as happily with her as before.

9

AMEUR
WAS A
MODERN
MAN

AMEUR WAS A modern man, and wanted me to meet his wife. We returned from the prayers in the sand. She came into the family living room before dinner that night, smiling warmly, drying her hands on an apron, surrounded by a protective gaggle of children. I thought she was lovely. We shook hands. Her palms felt rough from housework. She asked about my wife and young children, then studied the snapshots I showed her. "They are beautiful," she said. "You must miss them terribly." I admitted that I did. She asked about mutual friends in Algiers and France. I assured her they sent their love. This seemed genuinely to please her. Her voice was thin, gentle, pleasant to hear. I guessed she was a good mother, and by Saharan standards a good wife. She had vulnerable brown eyes. She was retiring. She was undemanding. So Ameur should have been a happy husband. But I admit that Malika made men restless.

She returned to the kitchen to finish preparing our dinner. Ameur and I ate in the living room. Afterward we watched television as the Algerian president, a military man, spoke to a somber assembly of party hacks in distant Algiers. Before the address, an invocation was offered by a child who recited verses from the Koran in a musical choirboy's voice, with his hand cupped over his ear. The president stood beside him, with his head high, his eyes ahead, and his hands extended, palms up.

A formally dressed man sang the national anthem. Ameur's children, who had come into the living room, sang along. Malika stood in the doorway, listening calmly. Ameur watched the television with growing impatience. The president spoke in the Algerian dialect, but his words were covered by a simultaneous translation into classical high Arabic.

Ameur swore. "They don't dare to talk plainly! Do they think people will be reassured by this circus? These are the same men who have driven Algeria into the ground. Do they think we are impressed?"

He switched off the television, and asked me to accompany him. "We will drive to the *ksar,*" he said. "I will introduce you to my friends."

I caught the expression of worry on Malika's face. When I sought her eyes, she smiled unconvincingly. I misunderstood, and thought her fear was political. I noticed again, when we left, the way she clustered the children around her.

In the *ksar* that night, off a dark alley, in an ancient mud-walled house, Ameur introduced me to his friends. We met in a windowless room, lit by a naked bulb. Sitting on Saharan rugs, we brewed tea on a butane burner and smoked cigarettes. The heavy trucks of a military convoy rolled nearby, shaking the neighborhood. We talked politics.

One man said, "We Saharans are great girl-chasers. We're famous for it. It's something we all do. It's in us. The desert heats our blood."

Another said, "We've heard that in America girls of sixteen will give themselves to a man."

"That's young," I answered.

He looked disappointed. "Then it's like here."

"Not exactly . . ."

Another said, "Here, the soldiers will always take the best girls for themselves."

But one of them refused to be discouraged. "It's a recognized fact that by the end of the decade there will be six times more women than men in the Sahara."

I didn't ask him to explain. He was a young man, thin and unmarried. He looked uncertain. I thought, give him his jackal's paradise.

AMEUR TOOK ME on an overnight trip to Touggourt, an oasis famous for its rugs. He had a driving test to administer there, and he told me after we started out that he had friends to see. It was afternoon. We drove for three hours through a pale desert of scrub and sand, and came to the oasis, with its date palms, donkeys, and mud-brick buildings.

At the shaded café in a park at the center of town I watched Ameur move easily among the other customers, knowing everyone, stopping to shake hands, to embrace, to smile and laugh. In Touggourt, too, he was loved.

A man with a goatee motioned for me to sit with him. He wore a leather jacket, and had heavy eyebrows and an alert expression. He wanted just to say, "I've known Ameur since he was a boy of four. Ameur is extraordinary. He has always been like this."

Ameur had booked me a room in the hotel. Because I was his guest, he wanted to pay for the night. The hotel clerk would not allow it. He suspected that we were changing money on the black market. He insisted that I pay for myself, and in officially declared dinars. He demanded the currency-exchange document that all foreigners were required to carry.

The clerk's demand was normal for Algeria at the time—in fact it was the law—but Ameur took it as an insult. He introduced himself, something he rarely had to do, but the clerk was a newcomer and had never heard of him.

Ameur began to shout. The clerk would not be swayed. Ameur stormed out of the hotel. I followed. We drove back to the café and drank espressos. The caffeine strengthened Ameur's resolve. An oasis is a small place. Because Ameur's reputation was now at stake, we set off again for the hotel.

On the way, by a small police station, Ameur pointed out the two plainclothes detectives standing conspicuously in the street ahead of us. One was fat and bald. The other, his deputy, had a thin, pockmarked face and the look of a country bumpkin. I thought they both looked a little dangerous. Ameur set his face to neutral as we drove by.

But then Ameur had an inspiration. He stopped the car abruptly, asked me to wait, and walked back to the detectives. I watched in the mirror as he shook hands with them, put his arms over their shoulders, and ushered them into the police station. They emerged a while later, and to my surprise came over to climb into the back of our car.

At the hotel, the chief detective did the talking. This time there was no argument from the clerk. He no longer demanded my currency documents, and he apologized for having to record my passport number. Then he offered the room for free. Ameur refused disdainfully, and dropped cash on the counter.

We all trooped down to inspect the accommodations. Ameur noted with satisfaction that I had been assigned the room numbered one. We crowded into it, while the clerk waited humbly in the hallway. The chief detective made a show of turning back the sheets to see if they were clean. He sat heavily on the bed to test the mattress. Ameur cycled the light switch. The deputy went down the hallway to flush the toilet and check the shower. Then we stood around awkwardly until I realized they needed an approval.

"Very good," I said.

"Impeccable!" Ameur said.

And we trooped out.

Ameur did not spend the night in the hotel, but went off to the house of a woman. He said he was a good Muslim. He had stopped drinking. He loved his children. But he said there was trouble in his marriage. We drove home to Ouargla on the second day, and did not speak about where he had spent the night. By mutual sentiment we did not speak about Malika.

THE WEATHER CHANGED overnight, so that one morning thick gray clouds lay over Ouargla. I met Ameur in the afternoon. We picked up his friend the air-traffic controller, and cruised.

The controller's name was Ishmael. He was a Haratin black, the descendant of slaves brought to the oasis by caravans from the south. Were it not for the fact that he had married another Haratin, that his children were Haratins, and that he lived in the *ksar*'s old Haratin quarter, I would have guessed that he rarely thought about his skin color. He had read about the difficulty between whites and blacks in the United States, but mentioned it just once, laughingly, as if to say that it had nothing to do with his own life. He said that the desert like death makes equals of all people.

Ishmael knew I had worked as a pilot, and he wanted to talk technicalities. He said that being an air-traffic controller in the Sahara means you wait for an airplane to radio in, then you say "Cleared to land," and you report the wind and temperature. This may happen four times a day. Since the same airplane will eventually depart, you also get to say "Cleared for takeoff." You can issue the clearances in Arabic or French—or in the international language of air-traffic control, which is English. Ishmael did not get many chances to practice his English in Ouargla, so he took the chance with me. He said things like, "I have certain you seem interesting to our airport." Ameur agreed hugely because in any language he loved to talk about flying.

Ameur, Ishmael, and I drove to Ouargla's airport. It had a small, dusty terminal building guarded by soldiers. We climbed the stairs into the glass-walled cab of the control tower. A controller, one of Ishmael's friends, slouched sleepily by the radio. He woke up to ask Ameur about the possibility of finding a rebuilt distributor for his car. Ameur was polite, but just now did not want to be distracted. Out on the tarmac, a crowd of passengers climbed down the stairway from an Air Algeria Boeing. Ameur recognized the pilots.

The clouds overhead had the airport people excited. Downstairs in the weather room, we found the meteorologist presiding over a vintage teletype and a rack of old instruments. He was a lanky young man with sloping shoulders and an academic disposition. The weather came from the north, he said. He called it an important atmospheric depression, and pointed to a cold front that had escaped from the Mediterranean and was swinging just now across the Atlas Mountains. He took us out a side door to squint at the overcast, which he called merely the leading edge stuff. He showed us the windsock standing straight out.

Back inside, the teletype rattled. The meteorologist stooped over the latest reports. "I have rain at Annaba. Rain at Constantine. At Bou Saâda, and Biskra." He looked up. "I have rain everywhere. It's coming this way."

Ishmael said, "The airport is prepared!"

Ameur said, "*Pas de problème.*"

The Air Algeria pilots walking across the ramp toward us seemed less interested. They regularly flew through the clouds of Europe, and saw enough rain even back home in Algiers. Their visit to the weather room was yet another routine. But they brightened when they found Ameur there. They embraced him. While the copilot indulged the meteorologist, the captain took Ameur aside to ask about an exhaust pipe for his Fiat. Ameur promised it within a week. The captain admitted he was short of cash. Ameur called the exhaust pipe a small gift, and insisted on peeling off a little extra to help the captain until the next paycheck. The captain felt profoundly grateful. That was Ameur's genius. In a land of drought, he knew how to seed the clouds. Moreover, he seemed never to calculate the returns. He was the warmest and most instinctive of men.

From the airport we drove to an outlying village, to a farm market, where Ameur and Ishmael heaped sacks of vegetables into the back of the car. Under darkening midafternoon clouds, we started back toward Ouargla. Several miles out, near a small

palm grove and a cluster of houses, we came upon an old turbaned man standing beside the road, and sitting beside him, a
boy of about ten. The old man was tall and thin. He gestured for
a ride. Ameur slowed, but raised his hands in helplessness, because the car had no room. The old man waved his understanding. We drove past.

Ameur looked at me. "I wonder if that boy was sick. That
boy looked sick."

He turned the car around and drove back to the hitchhikers.
Indeed the boy had a swollen throat and a fever. The old man
was his grandfather. He squeezed into the back beside Ishmael
and the vegetables. The boy sat wordlessly on my lap up front.
We set off for the hospital. The old man said he cultivated dates,
and was too poor for a taxi.

Ameur prodded the boy gently, touching his neck and cheek.
"I just had a sense, you see, it's not normal for a boy to sit. I
thought he had to be sick."

The hospital was a modern government building, the last
outpost of Algeria's once-hopeful socialism. I asked Ameur if
the doctors were competent.

He shrugged. "Among the old ones, some. Not among the
new ones."

"What's the difference?"

"It's like everything else. They don't give a damn."

But Ameur did. He went with the boy into the registration
room as if he owned the place, and went behind the counter.
From the nurse, he extracted a promise that the doctors would
not keep this boy waiting. Before leaving, he slipped money into
the callused hands of the old man. He never introduced himself,
because it was enough that God was his witness.

THE RAIN STARTED as a drizzle. We dropped Ishmael off in the *ksar,* and drove home. Ameur's children dashed about excitedly in the still-dusty street holding their hands up to touch the drops. Malika stood inside the courtyard feeling the coolness against her face, looking calm and relieved. Ameur felt so good that he wanted to telephone the United States. I gave him a number. He got through, and said, "It's America!" and handed me the phone. Afterward, we drove the children to the municipal zoo.

The zoo was playground size. It stood in a nationalized palm grove on the outskirts of town. The rain had turned the dirt there to mud. In an open-sided thatched-roof shelter, a zookeeper sat watching insipid Algerian variety shows on a black-and-white television. He lowered the volume when we walked in, and announced that because of the weather the admission was free. In a glass case beside him two small vipers huddled near an electric bulb. They were the color of sand, horned, and still.

"They're dangerous," I said.

"*Very* dangerous," Ameur said.

The zookeeper nodded. So we all agreed.

A collection of scorpions infested another display case. The zookeeper reached in with a scrap of metal and prodded one. It curled its tail. The thatched roof had rotted away directly overhead, and was letting in the rain, which was falling harder. I had crushed a scorpion that morning in my hotel room. I wondered why the zoo bothered to collect them.

The zookeeper kept poking the scorpion, daring it to strike. When it did not, the zookeeper said nastily, "Watch the rain hit him now. The scorpion is a desert creature. You'll see. He can't stand the water."

He was wrong. The reason scorpions populate the oases is that they seek water, and thrive where they find it. Some species can survive submersion for up to three days.

I sloshed with the children across the muddy yard to see the animals. They lived miserably on concrete pads in wire enclosures—ostriches, monkeys, foxes, and two mangy lions who refused to look at me. We returned to the car and drove away. Ameur mentioned that the place always saddened him.

The rain continued. Ameur's wipers, which had been chattering and screeching across the windshield, shed their blades. Ameur was annoyed. Wiper blades were perhaps the only car part he was not prepared to come by. Who would have thought of the need? There had been no rain in Ouargla for years, and nothing like this for a lifetime.

Ouargla was set up to live on groundwater alone. By nightfall, the residents had grown worried, because the rain had not let up, and most of the neighborhoods were without power, and the roofs were leaking, and the mud walls had begun to melt. Ameur's telephone had failed. We ate by candlelight. The entire family joined us. I watched Malika in the flickering light. After dinner, Ameur and I drove with the children through the dark, empty streets of the oasis. The water forced Ameur to drive at a creep. In places it came almost to the car's doors. Soldier sentries stood miserably at their posts. A new river flowed through the marketplace.

Ameur commanded his children, "Look! Look!" meaning, "So you will remember!"

And they did.

Only months later, on a desert road, Ameur, the driving examiner, was in a car accident. He was not behind the wheel or in his own car, but was with a woman to whom he had long before given a license. Because he was in love with her, he had forgotten to attach his seatbelt. When she lost control and the car rolled, Ameur struck his head and went into a coma.

After it was clear that he would never return, his friends deserted him. Eventually they deserted even the memory of him. They said that God had punished Ameur for his sins. I try not to blame them. They were growing older in a puritanical desert. They sought distance from their own indiscretions. By condemning Ameur, they could repent. And there was something else. After a strong man dies, cowards may forget that once they needed him. Ameur's friends were cowards, and he could not help them now. Far away in Algiers he spent his days staring mindlessly at the walls of his mother's ruined house. Eventually word came back to the Sahara. What Malika said to me in Algiers was true. If you told Ameur the sky is blue, he would answer, "Yes, the sky is blue." But if you told him the sky is red, he would agree with that, too. Nothing was left of his kingdom.

10

THIS IS NOT a legend. Ameur's mistress lived in an oasis 150 miles west of Ouargla. She was a career woman, a gynecologist named Fatima. By the age of thirty, she had not married, which was unusual because she was neither ugly nor poor. She met Ameur and decided she loved him. He allowed her to be a strong woman, and he did not fear her. In return, her dedication was absolute. There were nights when she gave Ameur a taste of paradise. Malika found out because Ameur, in one of his secret rages, punished her with a declaration. She later told me that he was a tormented and sometimes cruel man. His affair with Fatima lasted several years, during which he made Malika pregnant with her fourth child. Fatima did not get pregnant because Ameur did not want her to, and because she knew about contraception. She could offer Ameur her passion with none of the immediate consequences. Moralists say she also offered him self-destruction. They blame her as well as him. That's probably fair. Fatima was driving on a well-paved road when she lost control.

Word spread quickly through the desert: Ameur lay unconscious in some roadside oasis, breathing shallowly, bleeding from the head. Fatima was unhurt but wild with sorrow, refusing to leave his side. Malika had gathered her children around, and would not go to him as long as Fatima remained. It didn't matter to her that Fatima was the only doctor for many miles. Fatima was her demon.

The impasse was broken by an old friend of Ameur's in Algiers, a wealthy merchant who, sensing the gravity of Ameur's condition, chartered a private jet to evacuate him from the Sahara directly to Paris, where Ameur was put in the intensive care unit of Saint-Sulpice, a hospital near the city's center.

Fatima arrived in Paris within hours, went to the hospital, and introduced herself as Ameur's wife. She stuck fiercely by Ameur's side, and after several days began to quarrel with the French doctors, accusing them of neglect. It is true that they wasted little time on him. He was an "Arab," another would-be immigrant. When his condition stabilized, they took him off the respirator, and left him alone. He lay in the ward, still deep in a coma.

Malika left the children in Ouargla to the care of her old Berber mother, and rode Air Algeria to Paris. Her ticket was a gift from the pilots at the airline. At the hospital, having revealed herself as Ameur's true wife, she demanded that Fatima be kept from visiting him.

Fatima argued that she was Ameur's second wife under Islamic law and she may almost have believed it. Fatima was very much the outcast then. She had sacrificed her family, her friends, and her career to be with Ameur. She was smarter than Ameur, but trusted him when he promised marriage. She made herself his public woman. Then in a moment of weakness, with a shift of her eyes and a move of the steering wheel, she sacrificed him as well. It was a fate too terrible to accept, even in the Sahara. And so she had married Ameur in her heart.

Nonetheless, under Islamic law the marriage was illegal. A man may take a second wife only if he does not neglect the first one. And for years Malika had been neglected. The hospital administrators did not know that, but they were pleased not to recognize polygamy.

Fatima tacked. She claimed to be Ameur's physician, and demanded the right to attend to him.

The French asked for her credentials.

She said she had left them in the Sahara.

The French answered, then go get them.

They underestimated her. She had the money and devotion. She flew back to Algeria, hopped another flight to the desert, and within a day returned to Paris with her documents.

The two women crossed once in a hospital hallway.

"Haven't you done enough?" Malika asked. "Won't you leave him alone now?"

"Who else can heal him?" Fatima snapped. "Can you?"

"Have you no shame?"

"Have you no feeling for him?"

"I've come to be with my children's father."

"I've come to be with my lover."

They worked out an arrangement, unspoken, by which they would not have to meet again. Malika stayed with Ameur during the hospital's visiting hours, sitting quietly beside his bed. Fatima came afterward, as Ameur's doctor, and spent the nights with him.

It is said that comas may be pierced—that through the intensity of the sleep, some patients may hear and feel the world around them, though they cannot respond to it. Upon recovery, some may even remember the details of their experience. But Ameur was not among them. If in some dreamlike state he was aware of the vigils held beside him, if he heard Malika's soft voice or felt the breath of Fatima, his solitude was no less absolute. He had made a mess of things. The coma was an escape. With every day he slept, he drifted further away.

FATIMA COULD NOT accept that Ameur might never return. Malika knew Ameur better. Years before she had discovered inside of him an uncertain core that no one else suspected. It was the reason he stayed within the oases, and never ventured far into the open desert, and felt uncomfortable without a telephone nearby. It was the reason he kept Malika pregnant. He was terrified of thirsts—of his own, and of hers when she was alone. Now Malika could sense the depth of his abandonment.

Ameur had not prepared her for this freedom. He had left her with four young children, an old Peugeot with bad wipers, a small house in Ouargla, and a kingdom of fickle friends. Ameur's employer, the Algerian civil service, would not be of much help, since Ameur had not been injured on the job. No doubt there were debts to be called in, but from whom? There was a bit of cash hidden around the house, but already the oldest boy wanted sneakers and a basketball, and the oldest girl needed school supplies. There would be medical bills. Eventually there would be the question of caring for Ameur. To make matters worse a civil war was brewing. Malika had no idea how the family would survive. Still, she neither cried nor sought release; she had long ago learned patience and acceptance. And she was learning new lessons now, even if she could not yet appreciate them. The desert teaches by testing.

Time imposed its order. Malika's first battle was with Saint-Sulpice, the hospital, where an administrator threatened to discharge the still-comatose Ameur because the Algerian government had not answered the formal request to accept financial responsibility for him. Malika asked for more time. The hospital gave her another two days. Malika pleaded for understanding, and promised that the Algerian government would eventually get the paperwork in order. The hospital responded with indifference.

I WAS PASSING through Paris. It was a typically gray and wet afternoon. Malika waited for me on the street outside the hospital. I recognized her even from a distance with a sort of jolt. She was dressed like an elegant Parisian in a scarf and tailored dress. She led me inside, but not to Ameur. To my surprise, she took me instead to the cramped fourth-floor office of her tormentor, an overthin blonde with a ring for every finger, whose title was "social worker." The social worker must have been confused by my presence, which I myself did not understand. Malika may have hoped I would intervene, or she may simply have wanted my company. I said nothing. The social worker avoided my eyes.

Malika promised her again that Ameur was insured by his employer, the Ministry of Transportation, and that eventual payment was guaranteed.

The social worker was unmoved. "I regret, *madame,* that your word alone does not suffice."

Malika answered simply, "*Oui, madame,*" because she had run out of ideas.

The social worker said, "You would find it useful to remember that you are not in Algeria now, but in France."

"Oui, madame."

Rain blew drearily against the office window. The social worker picked up Ameur's file, and began, once again, to read through it. She had decorated her walls with posters of modern dance. She had a radio, two lamps, a computer screen, a keyboard, and a collection of serious novels, some in translation.

I did not know the woman, but silently constructed a world for her. I imagined a small apartment in the suburbs, and a long metro ride home each day. I guessed she followed the movies, and intended still to enjoy Paris, but I doubted whether in practice she went out much anymore. In a city that exalts youth, she had started wearing too much makeup. Now she lived trapped in a new Europe, shuffling hospital papers at a level beneath her education, remembering her schoolgirl ideals, but obviously unable to shake her anger with foreigners.

For years now she must have seen these Saharans parading through her office, pleading their cases in thick-tongued French, with the old-fashioned uneasy attitude of the peasant, servile and insolent. No matter how firmly she described hospital procedures to them, they asked for exceptions, implying that she had the power, as if all the world were corruptible. Malika was not the first she had warned of the differences between Algeria and France.

I don't think she saw Malika so much as catalogued her. Down in Ward Five, on the second floor, lay some Saharan in a coma. Malika was his wife. He had a second wife here too, squabbling over love. There were Algerians who had fought with knives in the hospital halls. There were many more who had sworn to pay their bills, and had not. So in denying Malika, she was on familiar ground. And of course she was right.

"Algeria has hospitals of its own," she said.

Malika sat looking down at her hands. "Please. He has four children. You don't know Algeria. You will kill him if you send him back."

The social worker frowned and studied the file again. I may have misjudged her. She shrugged. Her superiors were pressuring her, but she would argue Ameur's case, for all the good it would do. Malika said nothing. The social worker mentioned that she had been to Tunisia and had visited the desert. What she needed now was a document, a telegram perhaps to show that efforts were being made, a scrap of paper with an official seal, anything really.

Malika and I walked away from the office. I expected she would be grateful, but found instead that she had turned angry. The anger robbed Malika of her softness and seemed to surprise her, as if she weren't used to the emotion. And rather than fading, it grew stronger. "She is nothing but a racist!" she said furiously. "Did you see how she hated me? A foul racist, did you see?"

I did not answer, because Malika must have known that the problem lay deeper.

Malika said, "I won't humble myself again!"

This was closer to the truth. Malika had begun to leave the desert.

IN A MUSTY ward of a dozen beds screened by curtains, Malika led me to Ameur. I would not have recognized him. He lay on his back, breathing shallowly, pale, emaciated, and mostly naked. His eyes rested half-open, but were milky and unseeing. Tubes ran into his nose and arms, and a heart monitor was taped to his ribs. His mustache had been shaved off, and replaced by the stubble that spread across his chin. The bruise on his head still looked large and raw. I laid a picture book of Cape Cod on his bed, an offering to his former life. He had talked of visiting the world. But when I squeezed his hand, it felt as rubbery as the hand of a corpse. I thought he stank of death.

A male nurse strode in and slapped him on the chest. "Wake up, Monsieur Belouard, you have a friend from America!"

But he would not wake up. I watched Malika. She sponged him down and neatened his sheets. She spoke firmly to him, as if he were a child. She stood quietly. She did not love him, but loved his children. This understanding passed between us.

Afterward we sat together in a brasserie crowded with evening customers. We shared a table at the front of the establishment, by the sidewalk windows. Outside, the rain had turned cold, and the city's lights reflected on the pavement in colors that slowly grew richer with the night. We drank tea. Malika told me about her stay in Paris.

"Afternoons I go to the hospital. Mornings, I spend at the Algerian embassy, trying to get them to finish Ameur's paperwork. But it's just like Algeria in there: the officials are arrogant, and nothing gets done."

I asked where she was staying in Paris. She said, "With old friends, a family that lives here now." She was proud or brave, and did not want to complain. Only after I pressed her did she admit that they were ten, crowded into a two-room apartment in a tough neighborhood below Montmartre. In her spare time she helped with the housework, and she wrote letters to the children at home in Ouargla. "Already I've been gone two weeks. The two youngest ones don't understand—how could they?"

"And if Ameur remains in the coma?"

"It's very difficult for me. You know I have a duty as mother as well as a wife."

But beneath this burden, I heard Malika's relief. She seemed to be discovering a duty to herself as well. There was a special radiance to her. In the way she angled her legs, in the way she shifted her body, in the line of her neck, she carried her beauty with subtlety and grace. Men watched her. She was vital. She leaned forward and touched my arm in secret celebration of her freedom. She was in no hurry to leave the brasserie. She carried the picture book of Cape Cod. Like Ameur, she wanted to talk about the world.

Each afternoon I met her at the hospital, beside Ameur. Each evening at the brasserie I watched her shed the Sahara. Sometimes she seemed obsessed with Fatima, against whom she could rail for minutes in tight, bitter monologues. Then she would fall silent, and visibly shake herself free. She was fighting an elemental fight—this dwelling on Fatima, so closely connected to her old life with Ameur, followed by the rising above it, which was new. I don't think she analyzed it, because in Paris, under the shock of change, she was operating mostly by instinct.

When I asked her about Ouargla, she answered with unfinished thoughts. "The Sahara is no place for a woman," she said. She meant a desert neither of sand nor gravel, but of life contained within a cinder-block house in a certain part of town.

She did most of the talking now, sounding at times like an effervescent girl but more often like an angry wife. She said that a woman in Ouargla, once she is married, lives under house arrest. A woman is allowed out, but only under veil. She may scurry to a neighbor's house, or visit her sisters, or with other women slip furtively to the market. But even this she must not do frequently. Her desert is occupied by her husband and his brothers.

When one evening Malika mentioned that Ameur had beaten her, I did not interrupt to ask why or how often, or why she had stayed with him afterward. There comes a point in conversation beyond which there are no limits to intimacy. I had my own impulses to fight.

The following night, Malika spoke again about Ameur. She said he was born too late to fight the war of independence, but not too late to share in the victory. He moved to the Sahara because of its oil, to become a modern man. He did not think of himself as a real Saharan, and never intended to cloister his young wife. But the oases taught him that all women are weak. When Ameur saw Malika through the eyes of his new friends he felt a poison inside. He began to make requests about her clothes and behavior. He veiled her. The veiling did not help, and the poison spread farther. Malika was not to be trusted. Ameur's affairs with other women only confirmed his fears and made him more angry. He wielded Fatima like a weapon. He taunted Malika with her. When he sought salvation in Islam he could stop drinking, but he could not stop this.

Malika's talk at times disoriented me. I watched her emotions, and heard her words, but could not pretend to see things as she saw them. I myself judged Ameur as another man, in that sense like myself. Did Malika not understand the irony of talking about her life, like this, to me? I studied her face and her body. I was hardly a neutral confidant.

Lying in his hospital bed, Ameur drifted on. The French doctors told Malika that even if he emerged from his sleep he would probably require care the rest of his life.

Malika had to return to her children. I had to go to Algiers on business. We flew from Paris together, on Air Algeria. Malika still played the good wife. She said if Ameur was returned to Ouargla, she would grow old beside him here, and if he was returned instead to Algiers, she would move with him into his mother's house, to live under the domination of his family. She seemed resigned to this fate.

During the flight I offered no opinion because I had none that could possibly matter to her. Sympathy without action is a cheap emotion, and it can sound like a promise to help. But of course I could not help Malika. Most people live in hard places in hard times.

Bitterly Malika said, "No one is concerned with our lives as women. We serve our husbands, our brothers-in-law, our mothers-in-law. If we are unfortunate and have an unhappy marriage, there is nothing we can do. That is just life. I am here for my children."

When one of the airline stewards, a man who knew Ameur, scolded her for the way she was dressed, she looked chagrined. As we crossed the Mediterranean, she drew a scarf over her head.

MONTHS LATER, AMEUR emerged from his coma. He was paralyzed, speechless, disoriented, unresponsive. Never having received payment, the French deported him. The Algerians sent him to a military hospital in Algiers. I went to see him there. He squeezed my hand, but did not recognize me. When he grew agitated, an orderly strapped him down. The hospital could do nothing more for him. He went to live with his ancient mother in a ruined farmhouse in the slums of Algiers.

Malika had spent the time thinking. She closed up the house in Ouargla, locked Ameur's car into the courtyard, and took the children to Algiers. She took them to see Ameur in the ruined farmhouse. But then, rather than moving in with him as expected, she took her children to live across the city with her sister Zora. She said the farmhouse was too small for the entire family, but no one was fooled. Her in-laws were outraged. On what grounds did she take this act upon herself? Where was the daughter they had known? They demanded her labor. They demanded her obedience. They demanded the car in Ouargla. When Malika looked away, they damned her. By the standards of the desert they were right, but Malika refused to submit.

OUARGLA REMAINED UNFORGIVING. On my final return, by taxi from El Oued on the long way south, I found sand piling against a corner of Ameur's house. The cracks in the courtyard wall had grown wider. Ameur's old car sat on flat tires. The television antenna had toppled.

Out of habit, the hotel clerks still listened in on my phone conversations. I called Ishmael, the air-traffic controller; he took me to a late-night session with Ameur's old friends in the *ksar.* They wanted as usual to talk about women. The same one said, "We Saharans are great girl-chasers." The same one said, "Someday there will be six times more women than men in the Sahara." Ishmael wanted to talk about Malika. He called her a bad wife, because by the standards of Ouargla she had become a public woman. He talked about her as if she were available for his satisfaction. He never once mentioned Ameur. I had no patience for him, and kept checking my watch. For me Ouargla was already a memory. Later that night I took a taxi deeper into the desert.

11

THE ROAD THAT night stretched across black stony flat-lands, swerved, and stretched again. It went on hour after hour. The taxi was old and slow, but durable. It rattled through the darkness. I sat beside the driver, a gruff, silent man with a lined face lit by the reflection of the headlights. Behind us, the passengers slept. We came to the oasis just before dawn, when the road started down into a narrow, steep-walled valley. We took another turn, and the valley spread below us in a sprinkling of electric lights. It was the famed M'Zab: five walled towns, the home of 100,000 people and twice as many palms, where wells strike water at a hundred feet, and gardens will grow.

The M'Zab was settled a thousand years ago by an Islamic sect fleeing persecution in the north. They spoke a distinct Berber dialect, married among themselves, and developed recognizably sharp-faced features. They became known as Mozabites. Though eventually they became traders, opening shops

through all the oases, they never gave up their feeling of sepa-
rateness. During the war against the French, they let the fighting
pass them by. The attempt by independent Algeria to sell the
M'Zab to tourism never quite worked. Even today the Mozabites cling to their traditions. Old men wear antique pan-
taloons, and women of all ages, when they venture out, swaddle
themselves in white woolen shrouds, allowing only a single eye
to show. Islamic radicals recently attacked and killed a group of
foreign pipeline workers here. One of the towns still closes its
gates every night against strangers and infidels.

By the day's first light our taxi passed through an army checkpoint, and on into the valley. We overtook a man on a donkey cart
hauling firewood from the palm grove to the market. We turned
around a traffic circle and a concrete monument to national independence, swerved once to avoid a pickup truck, and swerved
again to avoid a horse. The oasis was coming to life. At dawn the
valley's walls echoed with amplified exaltations of Allah, the
haunting calls to prayer. We arrived at the marketplace of
Ghardaïa, the M'Zab's main town. The Mozabite on the donkey
cart arrived later in the old-fashioned way, by beating his beast.

The M'Zab is the diving board for the deep Sahara, the point
from which the bus sets off into the wilderness. The bus follows
a route called the Trans-Saharan, which is shown on maps in
bold ink, as if it were an established highway. You might expect
gas stations and the occasional motel. But the maps reflect ambitions that have never been realized. A road from north to
south across the Sahara would have to cross 2,000 miles of the
most tormented land on earth, conquering drought and flash
flood, canyon and mountain, salt, sand, mud, rock, and war.
And then it would have to be maintained.

Attempts have been made. In the early 1990s, just before the outbreak of the Islamic revolution, the Algerian Army built and rebuilt the Trans-Saharan in sections as far as the geographic midpoint, in the mountain town called Tamanrasset. But as always the desert quickly took the road back. By the time I arrived in the M'zab, the ruin was nearly total. Only hours south of town, the pavement of the Trans-Saharan broke apart, and forced buses into the open desert, which fed them sand and shook them apart. Because the Ministry of Transportation had no money for bus repairs, the once-ambitious schedule had been reduced to the occasional departure. I discovered that I would have days to linger in the M'Zab. There are worse ways to wait for a bus.

I FOUND A friend of friends, a Mozabite named Hassan Hamim, who owned the state concession for the M'Zab's movie theater. Hamim was a placid clean-shaven man in slacks and Italian loafers, which he dusted insistently. He knew his customers, who tended to be young men frustrated by the smallness of oasis life. Hamim gave them cheap love stories and karate productions, and made a good business of it.

Like other successful Mozabites, he had two houses—one in town for nine months of the year, and another in the shade of the palm groves for the worst heat of summer. The house in town was three stories tall, and had thick mud walls and traditional rooftop courtyards for sleeping in the coolness of night. He invited me to stay with him.

We sat before lunch in an upstairs salon sparsely furnished with rugs and cushions. The walls were papered with murals of alpine lakes, and with verses from the Koran. Hamim introduced me to his young daughters, though not to his wife. The daughters disappeared into the family quarters, the harem, where unrelated men were forbidden to go. Hamim told me that the cloistering was as much his wife's choice as his. I believed him. Within the extremes of a hard desert, it made a certain amount of sense. Had Malika truly cloistered herself, Ameur would never have seen her through the eyes of strangers. There are Saharans, women as well as men, who would call that freedom.

Hamim's friends arrived—a shy postal clerk, a date farmer, and a cynical commerce inspector in a three-piece suit. Work was over until evening. Hamim's daughters served us. We shared a bowl of couscous, followed by oranges and tea. The men did not know the desert beyond the M'Zab. They wanted to talk, but had little to say. They dozed. They gossiped. They said it had been years since they had seen an American. They said now even the French were staying away.

At the time the only foreigners in the M'Zab were those who had come with a Saudi prince to hunt gazelles with rifle and falcon. The prince had arrived the week before in a private airliner, and had set up camp north of town. His pilots, whores, and retainers had taken over the hotel, where they passed the nights in drink and dance. Hamim's friends disapproved. As Mozabites, they resented hedonistic displays. As Algerians, they resented claims to royalty. I sympathized. When after a polite delay, they asked what had brought me to the M'Zab, I said I was waiting for the bus.

The bus to where?

"To Tamanrasset," I said. Far to the south.

They stared. Hamim spoke for them all. "The bus is not a bus," he said. "It's a Safari."

I did not understand him. I thought he meant an exotic trip.

The date farmer said, "The Safari is not for you. It is only for Malians. It is like hell."

"I don't mind."

Hamim had seen the same movies I had. He said, "It's not what you think." He explained that the bus from the M'Zab did not go all the way. "Safari" was the name for the hard-sprung truck to which eventually I would have to transfer to cross mountainous central desert. He said, "Why don't you fly?"

"Because I want to see the desert up close."

"Buy a postcard."

"But I want to feel the desert."

"It feels bad."

IN THE EVENING Hamim took me to his movie theater. We entered by a side door, and stood near the screen, watching the show. It was a steamy Los Angeles mystery dubbed into Arabic. I forget the title and plot, but remember bared breasts and love scenes, an audience entirely of men, an atmosphere thick with sexual frustration. Hamim told me he had seen the movie before; but I noticed now that he intended to see it again. I wanted to leave, but Hamim was his own good customer. We stayed to the end.

In the morning we strolled through town. Shrouded Mozabite women scurried close to the walls, like nervous one-eyed ghosts. One of them came toward us. At first she seemed like just another figure, as anonymous and uninteresting as she was meant to be. But then we exchanged glances, she and I, and I discovered an eye of the most exquisite beauty—oval, almond-colored, lightly made up, with long lashes and flawless skin. The eye was warm, lively, and inviting. I didn't need to see more.

I asked Hamim if he had noticed. He smiled and said, "But she is married."

"You know her?"

He shook his head. "That's why she veils herself."

"And your wife, does she wear a veil?"

"Of course!" I had gone too far. He was offended that I had asked.

Later I pointed to an unveiled woman crossing the street in a tailored suit. "And who is she?"

"A whore."

"You know her?"

He shook his head.

I said, "Maybe she works in an office." I thought of Malika's sister Zora, and of women workers I had seen in other oases.

Hamim was emphatic. "She is a whore."

It was like talking to someone about his faith. I said, "Okay, but why?"

"These are loose women who become known. They screw for the pleasure of it. Afterward, no one will marry them."

About that, he was probably right. Oases are the smallest kinds of towns. People are stained indelibly by their reputations. There is little mercy. A girl who succumbs too easily to love may become a woman who knows no love at all.

ONCE AT THE outskirts of an oasis, around midnight, I was sitting with a group of men by a campfire when two women appeared in the firelight. They were unveiled and unescorted, and they wore tight jeans. One was a schoolteacher, the other her best friend. I saw in their brazenness that they were outcasts. The men, my friends, despised them openly. They introduced them to me as "bad women, hungry for men." When the women did not leave, the language escalated. In their presence my friends called them dogs in heat. They said I would not have to pay them, then said the women would pay me. And still the women would not leave.

When later they allowed two of the men to take them into the desert, it was not for love or pleasure, but for self-loathing. The men were done quickly. The women came back to invite the hatred of the others. They did not take money. They had acquired the defensive habit of submission.

On another occasion, in West Africa at a riverbank market, I saw a young woman with crippled, twisted legs, who swung along by walking on her hands. She wore a torn dress hiked up around her hips, and had a sweet and lively face, and matted hair. A band of market boys began to taunt her, calling her a "goat," reaching down to fondle her breasts. She did not seem afraid or angry. She even smiled. Then one of the boys put his foot against her shoulder and kicked hard. The girl rolled sideways into a puddle of fetid mud. I started toward her, but stopped when she came up coated with filth, and laughing with her tormentors. Walking on her hands, swinging her twisted hips, she disappeared into the market crowd with a final backward look, not of horror but of satisfaction. She seemed to feel she had won something. People everywhere are confused by the oases they inhabit.

HAMIM WAS NOT in the movie business by chance. He was a good Muslim, but had a vicarious fascination with sin. One evening he took me to dinner at the hotel, which stood on a hill above the M'Zab like a mud-walled citadel of forbidden pleasure. The Saudis had come in from the hunt, and had begun a long night of drinking. They were not good Muslims. They sat at tables heaped with food and wine, and were entertained by musicians with drums and horns.

Hamim and I sat in a corner with two of his acquaintances— a former farmer employed by a German company to collect scrap metal in the desert, and a wiry architect in a beard and sports jacket, more grandly employed in the study of traditional Saharan houses.

During a pause in the music, the architect told me that the houses of the M'Zab are renowned for their starkness and practicality. The French modernist Le Corbusier had come here to learn, to confirm his theories, to find a connection to the past.

I was interested, and asked the architect if he liked Le Corbusier's work.

He said, no, and changed the conversation to women.

The women with the Saudis were young Italians, starker and more beautiful than any building. The architect said something lewd about them, which rang hollow.

Hamim forced a worldly smile. But I could see by the stiffness of his expression that the women bothered him. They were lively and vain, and openly sexual; they were entirely unveiled. And it was obvious that natives like Hamim hardly existed for them.

Wine flowed heavily. Eventually the Saudi men rose from the table, and danced among themselves. The women urged them on. Then from the back reaches of the restaurant a young, lithe, curly-haired man, a stranger, leapt forward and joined the dance. He was like a woman himself. He danced the dance of a loose-limbed satyr with his arms upraised and delight on his face. He was decadent, anarchistic, and entirely sober. Hamim had to look away.

The women laughed. The Saudis were unamused. One of their bodyguards, a huge man in a turban who had been standing with his arms folded, now shooed the satyr away. The satyr got around him and kept dancing. The bodyguard moved on him more firmly, and blocked his attempts to return. The women laughed. The Saudis were amused. The satyr slinked past our table looking aggrieved. The architect remarked wryly, "He's unemployed, but manages to live here at the hotel." He did not know how.

There was more drinking upstairs. Hamim and I went to the room of an Air Algeria captain spending the night because his Boeing had broken down. He was a tight-tempered, sinewy, mustang of a man, sitting in an undershirt sharing whiskey from airline bottles with his flight crew. He liked Buffalo, New York, where he had taken his flight training. He bragged to me about being a real Saharan, the descendant of nomads. But he did not romanticize the desert. He talked about the oasis airports, and said, "V.I.P.s, there are always V.I.P.s. They make the entire airplane wait for them. I feel like telling them, 'Me—my father was killed by the French! I throw you to the dogs!' "

The pilot did not need to be a Muslim. He was a natural moralist. He drank a lot of whiskey. He curled his lips and snarled, "If I had my way, I would stand all those kinds against a wall and shoot them. Like that! And have no second thoughts about it."

He included the Saudis downstairs in his plans.

Hamim was heartened. We left the hotel. By the certainty of his stride, I saw that he felt again like a man. The Air Algeria captain had been a fighter pilot. Saudis dance, but Saharans are soldiers.

HAMIM'S BEST FRIEND was a Mozabite named Moustafa
Oukal, who was as blustery as Hamim was timid. Oukal had
driven once for Texan oilmen, and had admired them, and was
thereafter known as "L'Américain." When we met he grinned
and said in French, "We Americans are not afraid to get our
hands dirty!" He was bald and beefy, and had muttonchop side-
burns, a tweed cap, and rough outdoor clothes. He told me he
had given up an earlier career as a photographer. He still had a little photo shop near the market, but said he could not find film,
and in any case no longer had time for such small pursuits. No
matter who won the civil war, he was certain that ordinary Mozabites would continue to suffer. But he himself would prosper—
he pretended to be certain of that, too.

Oukal was a Saharan survivalist. His hope lay in a patch of
desert about twenty miles out of town, where he had dug a well
and planted the first palms. He called it his ranch, and promised
to take me there, but first wanted to do a little drinking.

We drove in his Volkswagen van, tools rattling in the back, to
buy wine at the end of an alley. The wine was Algerian, originally intended for export to Europe. It was sold unlabeled from
a doorway by a woman in a veil, doing a steady and furtive business. As we clattered up in the Volkswagen, an old man slipped
down the alley, tucking a bottle into his robes. But Oukal was
never bashful. He greeted the woman loudly, introduced me to
her as his dear friend, and loaded up with two dozen bottles. He
wanted to throw a party in honor of America.

He held the party that night, in the concrete courtyard of his
house. Already I recognized most of the men there—the architect, the scrap-metal farmer, the commerce inspector, the clerk
from the hotel, the rug merchant from the market, the police-

man, the sly, hooded plumber, good for a wink and a smile, and of course Hamim, ever the voyeur of sin. Oukal was in a fine humor. He apologized for the clutter in his house and made excuses for a wife overwhelmed by two young children. I guessed she might disapprove of her husband's friends.

It was all very American. Oukal cooked. He built a big fire directly on the concrete patio, and after it had settled into a glowing heap, he roasted skewered lamb over the coals. The night air became chilly. We huddled close to the fire, chewed the meat, and set to drinking. At first the mood was jovial. When the concrete below the fire exploded, shooting embers across the courtyard, the policeman somersaulted backward in surprise, and we laughed. But the wine was strong, and the conversation flagged. I wanted to talk about the oasis, but the others had done their complaining and their bragging, and had exhausted the easy things to say. The drinking grew humorless and isolating. Only Hamim, the good Moslem, remained sure of his future. Hamim could dream. He wanted to keep the evening going. But for the others, the party had turned sour.

ON A BRIGHT afternoon, Oukal drove me to his homestead south of town. It lay in a desert depression, on land available to anyone willing to work it. Oukal had claimed ten acres of level ground, and an equal amount of hill. He had drilled a well and hired two nomads to clear the rocks for him. The nomads were illegal immigrants, Tuaregs from the highland deserts of Niger, to the south. The Tuaregs are Berber nomads, fierce camel riders who controlled the Sahara's mountainous core for thousands of years. These two were typically tall and gaunt, and wore the *chèche* of the hard desert, a long cotton turban wrapped first around the head, then forward across the nose and mouth and neck. The *chèche* protects against the dryness and dust of the hard desert, but more important still, it gives its wearers the power of anonymity. Tuareg society was built on raiding and war. Tuareg men were so convinced of the *chèche*'s advantages that until recently they never showed their faces to strangers. Tuareg women, by contrast, do not veil themselves. Europeans excited by this apparent liberation have misunderstood the *chèche* and its context. The bareness of the women's faces is in fact an expression of their vulnerability. The men's *chèche* is not a veil but a mask.

Oukal's Tuaregs were the losers in a war against modern times. They lived in a roofless straw enclosure equipped with a wooden front door. Oukal had provided them with one shovel, one bucket, and a wheelbarrow. Today he brought them a week's groceries, with which they retreated hungrily into their dwelling. Oukal chuckled and said they had found their door out in the desert. Smoke from a cooking fire soon rose above the enclosure.

Oukal took me across the property to the well, which was 120 feet deep and sheathed in concrete. He started the diesel pump and offered me water from a gushing hose. I praised the water as sweet. He showed me the first date palms, tender chest-high infants planted in rows at the base of a hill. He explained where he would grow his vegetables. He said he would have chickens, goats, sheep, and maybe a horse for taking Texas-style rides in the hills. The water would make it all possible. He walked me over to where his house would be, and predicted that his wife would be less distracted here than in town. He predicted success for his children. He said they were young, and would learn to love the open horizons away from the oasis. He vowed to give them that freedom. Like a good American, he even paced the outline of a swimming pool.

But his enthusiasms could not endure the drive home. We both felt the change—the suspicion of defeat that overcame him like a slow fatigue, the thought that already his history could be written. He was not a young man anymore. He stopped the Volkswagen where the dirt road overlooked the valley of M'Zab, and sat silently behind the wheel. I waited for him to speak. Gazing out over the roofs of the oasis, he swore that he had no respect for the people who lived there. He called them lazy, and fearful. He called them Africans, although he was one too. He looked into the distance. He brooded.

Hamim had told me already that Oukal's ranch would fail, as his other ventures had. His well was sweet but weak, and could be pumped only an hour a day. He implied that Oukal was a dreamer.

But Oukal was not a dreamer. Faced with the frustrations of a life in the M'Zab, he had simply refused to surrender. If this made him foolish, I admired his strength and his courage nonetheless.

Hamim had said, "Oukal's life is like this: he has a dog and a goat. The dog chases the goat. The goat chases the dog. They stir the dust."

But Hamim's life was like this: he went to the movies.

12

THE

MECHANICS

OF ESCAPE

IF YOU'RE LUCKY, you just take a bus. Mine was an old oily Nissan with bald tires, heading south from the M'Zab one sunny morning. I crowded up to the door, waved a ticket, fought my way on board. The other passengers were silent, watchful men in turbans and *chèches*. I made my way past their unsmiling stares, and found a broken seat in the back. The driver climbed on looking unshaven, unalert, overweight, surly.

His assistant, the conductor, surveyed the passengers sternly. He was a small and self-important man, infused with the drama of his mission. We were headed for a town called In Salah, 400 miles deeper into the desert, down the disintegrating Trans-Saharan, in a decrepit bus, with a driver who didn't give a damn, in a time of revolution. The conductor's job was to keep the passengers under control. He seemed to look forward to the possibility of dissent.

For most of the day the Trans-Saharan resembled a road—a rough but drivable strip of black pavement stretching into the distance across gravelly plains. On level ground, the bus gathered speed, but hills threatened to defeat it. I write "hills," and re-member hummocks; they were in fact mere ripples on the sur-face of a vast and level desert. But for our feeble engine they rose like mountains.

The steepest climb was a contest so difficult that the driver leaned forward sympathetically over his wheel. Blue smoke rose through the floorboards. The conductor scowled, daring the passengers to notice. We crept over the crest and began to accel-erate down the far side. Somehow, the engine had endured. Now speed threatened to shake the bus apart. The passengers re-mained impassive. Windows popped open. The breeze purged the smoke.

In an oasis called El Golea more passengers boarded, and crowded the aisles. Among them was a veiled woman accompa-nied by children. The conductor shouldered his way into the back, and with obvious satisfaction ordered two men to give up their places. Then he shoved his way back to the front, and went outside to slam the popped windows.

The sun set, and the night turned sharply cold. The bus was unheated. I huddled on my broken seat above the engine, ab-sorbing the warmth and fumes, listening to the driver grind the gears. A crescent moon rose among the stars. Dunes forced the bus to slow to a crawl. Once we braked so hard for a herd of camels that the luggage on the overhead racks slid forward in a cloud of dust. The conductor glowered. The driver lit a cigarette.

We came then to the first roadblock—a line of stones beyond which the pavement had disintegrated into rubble. The driver shifted down and swung over the shoulder, out into the open desert. But for the rest of the night we seldom touched pavement. Stopping, considering, backing, we traveled out in the sand and rock flanking the road, at times quite far from it. The windows popped open again. The air swirled with dirt. Breathing was difficult, sleep impossible.

I passed the hours watching the driver work. He had wrapped his face in a *chèche,* and was like a new man out here, guiding his unwieldy beast with concentration and skill. He was superb. He was proud. He was temperamental. When one of the passengers leaned forward and questioned the route he had taken, he braked to a stop, opened the door, and switched off the headlights. He wanted the moon to illuminate the horizons.

The driver said nothing.

The passenger hesitated.

The conductor looked triumphant. He said, "You can walk if you prefer." He would have stranded the man with pleasure.

The passenger retreated into his seat. We set off again. The moon set.

We came to the end of the line, In Salah, in the bitter blackness before dawn. I went into the ruined cinder-block station, where groups of men stood in the gloom. Melancholic Arabic music drifted through the air. A baby cried quietly. From far away came an early call to prayer. Huddled forms slept in blankets against the wall: it was so cold that a bucket of drinking water had iced over. I crouched with robed strangers around a paper fire. The smoke floated against the ceiling. I spread my hands to the feeble flames. Beyond In Salah the land rises into the Sahara's wild and mountainous center. No one knew when the Safari, the passenger truck for Tamanrasset, would leave. The schedule called for one trip a week, God willing. I waited at the station because others waited.

13

THE
INFERNO

I ONCE WENT to the Sahara during the high heat of summer to write about water in a provincial capital named Adrar, which lies west of In Salah, and is a place known even here for the severity of its climate. In Adrar, out of some 4,100 hours of possible annual daylight an average of 3,978 hours are filled with direct sun. This is steep-angle sunlight, powerful stuff. In the winter, when the air temperatures drop to freezing at night and rise to 90 degrees by noon, soil temperatures fluctuate so brutally that rocks split apart. In the summer, the Sahara is the hottest place on earth. The world record is held by El Azizia, Libya, where on September 13, 1922, the air temperature was measured at 136 degrees. Death Valley claims a close second, with 134 degrees in 1910. More recently, in 1994, the temperature in Death Valley hit 131 degrees, and the *New York Times* wrote: "An observer reported that even in the shade he could not hold out his open hand against a strong wind because the burning sensation was too painful." In Adrar this would not have made the paper. Death Valley is just one little heat trap. The Sahara is a heat trap on the scale of a continent; its air will burn your hands from one ocean to another, across plains too large even to imagine.

I could have gone to Adrar in the spring, or waited until fall, but I chose July for its intensity. My only compromise was to fly. I sat in the cockpit behind the pilots. The airplane was a stodgy turboprop, a forty-passenger Fokker droning at 18,000 feet on a roundabout three-day run from Algiers to the oases. It was midday, and the Sahara stretched in naked folds to the horizon, brilliant, and utterly still. The land was blanketed by a haze of dust, suspended not by winds but by heat. The Trans-Saharan had appeared as a fading scar. Below us, a canyon had cut through the downslope of the central highlands. Now we passed across featureless plains along the northern edge of the vast and terrible Tanezrouft, where for hundreds of miles nothing lives.

The captain, who was not a desert man, had pasty skin and the look of an experienced pilot: bored, dissatisfied, underexercised. He flew with sloppy control motions, as if he could barely endure the job. For him the Sahara was a tough assignment. He said he suffered at night in the oasis hotels. "There is nothing out here," he complained. "You let a sheet of paper fall, and it takes forever to hit the ground. It's the heat."

He tried to be polite. He asked me where I had been and where I was going, and why. He seemed worried that I had a one-way ticket only, and would have to find my way out on the ground. He called Adrar hell.

THE HEAT AT the airport was brutal and disorienting. Somehow I caught a ride into town and checked into the hotel on the main square. The square was barren concrete. The hotel room was unbearably hot. I went down to the lobby, sat under a ceiling fan, and like the rest of Adrar, waited for night. It was so hot that even that did not help. After dark, people came onto the streets more out of necessity than relief.

I had the phone number of a local man who had volunteered to show me around. He was a young merchant named Moulay Miloud. Moulay is a title of respect, indicating descent from the Prophet. The family, if it can be called that, has been extraordinarily prolific. I have heard the Sahara called, only half-jokingly, The United States of Moulay.

This particular Moulay, Miloud, was stuck in Adrar for the summer because, as it was explained to me, he was still too poor to escape. However, he had wealthy cousins in Tamanrasset, whom I had met and knew to be generous men; I thought they might have given Moulay Miloud an air conditioner. I dialed his number in hope.

The man who answered said his name was Ali, and that I had the wrong number. He would not let me hang up. He said he had heard of a Moulay Miloud, and would help me to find him. He wanted to meet me immediately at the hotel. I felt too hot to refuse. He asked how he would recognize me. I told him without getting into details that it wouldn't be hard.

Minutes later, Ali pulled up to the hotel in a decrepit four-wheel drive Lada. He was a middle-aged man with a brisk manner. He loaded me into the car, clattered through the dark streets of Adrar, and within a few stops found Moulay Miloud's apartment, in a sprawl of ground-level duplexes. A neighbor told us that he had gone into the desert, to an outlying village, to visit a brother who had returned from Mecca. He would be back in the morning. Ali insisted that I leave a message on the door. He was the rare Saharan who left nothing to chance.

Ali invited me home, to the oldest part of town, for late-night coffee. We sat on rugs under a bare bulb in a high-ceilinged room. The room's walls were painted in two tones, in green and white. Ali's young son brought in an electric fan, but the air that it stirred was stale and hot, and sweat streamed down our faces. We drank the coffee strong and sweet, and sat mostly in silence. It occurred to me only toward the end that Ali expected nothing from me.

At dawn a haze of dust and heat veiled the central square. Moulay Miloud sent word that he would meet me there at noon. He turned out to be a thin, fastidious bachelor, in a pressed white robe and sandals. We went to his apartment to talk. He did not have an air conditioner, but had a fan and an evaporative cooler that lowered the temperature in his apartment to, say, 100 degrees Fahrenheit. We sat on the floor of his living room, and waited out the midday hours, drinking brown water from a plastic jug.

The water was brown because Miloud had mixed in cade oil, which smelled of pine sap and tasted of clay. The cade is an evergreen bush that grows far to the north in the Atlas Mountains. Saharan nomads value its oil, which they use to seal the insides of their goatskin waterbags. Miloud did not have a goatskin, but he came from a long line of desert travelers, and cade oil was his heritage. He bought the oil at the market in small bottles and added it to his water for flavor and good health. He was pleased that I liked it. But I would have drunk anything, because in the morning I had gone for a walk.

During the walk the air was still, the sky nearly white. There was no shade. The streets were deserted. The heat had sharp edges that cut at my skin, eyes, and lungs. An hour was all I could endure. I felt threatened, weakened, overwhelmed. I retreated to the hotel lobby and sat very still, questioning my judgment for having come to Adrar.

Now Miloud said, "It's raining less. And every year it's hotter. Nomads can no longer survive in this climate."

I believed him.

The living room, like Miloud, was immaculate and small. It was furnished Saharan style, with mattresses, pillows, and color- ful rugs. Black-and-white enlargements of nomads hung on the stucco walls, and a guitar stood in one corner. *The Cosby Show* played soundlessly on television. Miloud put on a cassette of screechy Saharan music. In the hallway by a portrait of Bob Mar- ley was a postcard of three naked women. They were grotesquely fat. I did not understand why Miloud had put them there, if this was humor or hatred or both.

Maybe it was cabin fever. Miloud said, "In the summer even the mind shuts down. You get tired of television, music, and books. There is no stimulation. There is little to say. You are too much indoors."

LATE ONE AFTERNOON, with the air temperature settling below 128 degrees, Miloud and I drove a borrowed Renault to an outlying oasis, south along the ancient caravan route that leads eventually to distant Gao and Timbuktu. The road left Adrar across a rolling plain of sand and dirt, past neglected palm groves. The western horizon was lined by the dunes of the Erg Chech, an uninhabited sand sea extending 600 miles into Mali and Mauritania.

Miloud was thinking closer to home. He said, "In the winter all this is green."

Translation: In the winter a bit of moisture may sneak in from the Mediterranean, and if some of it falls from the sky, a few translucent grasses may sprout. But the average annual rainfall in Adrar is less than an inch.

Still, there is water underground. Adrar's two dozen oases sit at the receiving end of the largest dry watercourse in the Sahara, an ancient riverbed called the Messaoud. It is a long, shallow depression where water still collects close to the surface. The water lies on gradients, sloping with the land. To tap into it, the people of Adrar centuries ago borrowed a technique from ancient Persia: they built their palm groves and villages at the low points, then dug their wells uphill.

Known locally as *foggaras,* these upward-sloping tunnels are self-filling aqueducts, designed not only to find water but to deliver it in a constant and effortless flow. They extend for miles into the higher terrain, and are marked by regularly spaced excavation mounds like the diggings of giant moles. Although they are marvels of ingenuity, most are slipping into disrepair. One reason is the danger and difficulty of maintaining them: they clog up and cave in, and require constant shoring, and ever since the abolition of slavery—in the nineteenth century, under the French—there has been no ready supply of volunteers to do the work.

Our destination appeared as a green line against the dusty sky. The line became a palm grove and a medieval fortified village of about a thousand people. In searing heat, we walked through the streets—a warren of baked mud, and dark, built-over passages just wide enough for a loaded camel to pass. The inhabitants were Haratin blacks, the descendants of the slaves who had once maintained the *foggaras.* A band of dusty children followed us out into the desert to examine a decaying tunnel. They were surprised by my interest in it, as if the collective memories of digging were still too fresh to allow any Haratin to appreciate the engineering.

The Haratins had their own slaves now, electric pumps housed in cheap concrete shacks, requiring little companionship. The electric pumps drew water stupidly, vertically, from drilled wells. The modern world had arrived, and no one but a visitor could complain.

Still, the system of distribution was the traditional one. We followed the ditches that carried the water back through the village. Upstream the water was drawn for drinking; downstream it was used for washing and sewage. There was no treatment plant, and no need for one. The water that finally flowed into the palm grove was rich in nutrients. It was also precious. Water rights in the oases are inherited, bought, and sold, and are more valuable than the land itself. Within this grove, the water was divided and metered through finger-width gateways into an intricate branching of channels. In the end it spread into individual plots, separated by dikes and protected against wind and sand by adobe walls. There the date palms grew.

Date palms are well adapted to the Sahara. They thrive on sun and heat, and will produce fruit in water that is ten times as salty as that which humans can tolerate. Though they require copious irrigation for the first few years, they sink deep roots into the groundwater and become self-supporting. They become, in a sense, their own *foggaras*. They also shade the irrigated vegetable crops, mostly of corn and tomatoes.

The grove was small by Algerian standards—about a half-square mile of junglelike vegetation. Miloud and I strolled through it on dirt paths between the plots. The shade was dense, as was the heat. Dead fronds draped from the trees and littered the ground. Miloud pointed to them and said that when he was young the farmers would have been ashamed. Yellow butterflies flitted about. Ants carried oversized trophies. A turbaned man hacked at the earth. A ditch gurgled with polluted water. I stopped to list the other sounds: the distant music of Arab horns, a dove cooing, a donkey braying, a cricket, birds trilling, children laughing, the *thunk* of a woodchopper, a sharper hammering, a rooster, flies buzzing, a chanted prayer.

THERE IS A limit to the insulating qualities of adobe construction, a temperature extreme beyond which the walls go critical and begin to magnify the heat. Airborne dust makes things worse because it traps the heat radiated by the soil, and does not allow it to escape on summer nights. I have studied this: the walls do not cool down at night; at dawn the inside surfaces are hot to the touch; the next day they are hotter still. The houses become solar ovens. Concrete is worse—it gets hotter than adobe in sunlight, and no less hot after dark. In the big concrete buildings built with the help of the Soviets you can burn bare feet on upper floors.

During the peak months of summer, people move outdoors. In the morning and late afternoon they sit in the shade cast by the walls. At midday they hide as best they can, under an awning or a tree. Strangers flock to the hotels, where the lobbies have fans and high ceilings. Secret police flock there too, for the same reasons, and to investigate the strangers. Everyone waits. At night, while hotel guests lie trapped in their rooms, the Saharans eat and sleep in the gardens.

Miloud and I went to dinner in Adrar at the house of Nouari, a bookish construction engineer. He had also invited a tall, shy hydrologist who the next day was to guide me through an irrigated "experimental farm" north of town. The four of us sat on carpets in the sand behind the house. It was a sweltering night, with the temperature still over 100 degrees. The stars were blackened by dust. The meal was lit by kerosene lanterns on a barrel. Nouari's wife and mother cooked for us, but did not appear. I made no mention of them. Nouari poured water from a pitcher, and we washed our hands.

We started the meal with warm milk and dates. Nouari said, "The Prophet recommended dates."

Miloud added, "Milk and dates make a complete meal. They are all a person needs to eat."

Nonetheless we also had tripe, couscous, and melon. Afterward we drank tea brewed by Nouari on a butane burner. The discussion returned to dates.

Saharans eat dates directly off the branch; they dry them and eat them; they bake, boil, and fry them and eat them. They are date gourmets and can distinguish hundreds of varieties by taste, texture, and color. They know date facts: that a thousand dates grow in a single cluster, that half the weight of a dried date is sugar, and that dates are rich in minerals and vitamins. Nouari listed them, taking care that I note every one: "Vitamins A, B, C, D, E."

He described the yearly pollination performed by the farmers. He recited the line from the Koran that is read while this is done. "In the name of God, mild and merciful." And he wrote it down for me:

بِسْمِ اللهِ الرَّحْمَنِ الرَّحِيْمِه

The hydrologist added, "Dates help against cancer. Research is being done in the United States at a big university."

Miloud observed that the tree itself is a wonderful resource. With help from the others, he went through its uses. They are too many to list here, but they can be summarized as follows: things that can be made from palm wood and fronds.

The hydrologist finished by saying, "The Prophet loved the tree too." It is not surprising that the neglect of the groves in the Sahara has added to sympathy for the Islamic revolution.

The hydrologist's name was Sollah. In the morning he took me to see the irrigated farm, which he called a model. It sprawled across 800 unshaded acres in virgin desert—an American-style operation, privately owned, with a bright green tractor and a crew of Haratin workers. Circular irrigation systems stood over wheat stubble. There were greenhouses, and plots of tomatoes, peppers, pimentos, cucumbers, melons, and cantaloupes. There was plenty of mud. This was modern agriculture—energetic, productive, and perhaps wasteful. I told Sollah that it reminded me of the farming in California. He looked pleased, and asked why. I answered, "Cheap water." This pleased him even more, because it was *his* water. He had directed the government crew that had drilled the first well.

We went to drink the results. Two pumps drove a heavy flow into a holding tank. The water was sweet and cool. Sollah and his crew had struck it with an Oklahoman rig at a depth of 450 feet. The well had run brown with sand and mud for two days, and afterward had turned clear. The project had taken a month to complete, which was average. There were several crews like Sollah's in that part of the Sahara. Between them they were drilling forty-five wells a year. Every well had produced.

Most of the Sahara is too dry for drilling. If you do hit water, either there is too little, or it is too salty, or too expensive to pump out. Although it might sustain a few settlers, or people passing by, it is not worth the cost of getting to. But here in the northern third of the desert, large reserves of fresh water lie under the parched surface.

The shallowest reserves are the ones that for centuries have irrigated the oases. They are immediately susceptible to drought and overuse: the water table falls, crops fail, and the oases must be abandoned. But if rain falls, even far away, eventually the shallow reserves are replenished.

Of greater importance for the near future are the deep reserves, whose discovery was a by-product of the search for oil. The mere knowledge of their existence has had a profound effect on life in the Sahara. Known as confined aquifers, they are pools of fresh water trapped in permeable rock strata at depths of 300 to 6,000 feet. They hold as much water, according to one estimate, as the Amazon River discharges in two years. That is a lot of water. What's better, much of it is under pressure. Once tapped, it rises to the surface and forms artesian wells. Geysers have shot hundreds of feet into the air. Wells have been capped to keep villages from flooding.

The new water works powerfully on the souls of Saharans. Muammar Qaddafi launched an agricultural revolution in Libya, and began building gigantic irrigation projects. He spoke of transforming the sands. If for no other reason, he was respected for this. Other Saharans have equally grandiose dreams: miles of tomatoes, famous potatoes, rice paddies, fish farms, horizons of grain—the United States of Moulay. If there is water in the desert, anything is possible. Sollah, by nature a quiet and rational man, was suffused with the glory of his mission. He spoke then not as a hydrologist, but as a Saharan. Even the taxi driver who took us out to the farm had an opinion. He believed that irrigation would eventually bring rain. Call it reverse desertification, the trickle-up theory.

But there is a problem. If you measure a desert by the amount of heat at the surface versus the amount that would be necessary to evaporate the annual rainfall, the excess evaporative power of the Sahara ranges from a factor of ten to infinity. Of course these so-called dryness ratios are high partly because there is so little rain—in places no rain at all. You might reasonably expect some level of man-made rainfall to fill the need. But even in the wettest parts of the Sahara the air is so dry that regardless of the heat, evaporation rates are the highest in the world—twice those of the Californian and Australian deserts. The average relative humidity is 30 percent, and it has been recorded as low as 2.5 percent. In the Sahara it is not only the ground but also the sky that is thirsty.

In any case, the deep aquifers are being recharged very slowly, if at all. They contain mostly fossil water, deposited long ago when the Sahara was not a desert. The water that Sollah and I were drinking was perhaps 5,000 years old. In western Egypt, well water may be five or ten times older. My comparison to California was only partly accurate, because so much of the irrigation water in the American desert comes from rivers and reservoirs—short-term, renewable surface supplies. Some waste is therefore affordable: you suffer drought, you change your laws, you wait, you drink again. But the deep water of the Sahara is different: you pump it here for keeps. Like oil, it is not renewable.

Another problem is that, despite the large reserves, only a fraction of the stored water can be extracted economically. There are many reasons for this, including lowering water tables, loss of artesian pressure, expense of drilling, expense of pumping, and increasing salinity. Thoughtful people caution that new wells should be drilled sparingly, and the water used wisely. They use terms like "practical sustained yield"—meaning you take out no more than is going in. They say an aquifer is like a bank account—if you must draw it down, the reason should be to build a return in the long run. They warn about unchecked exploitation, and talk about the end coming as soon as 2025.

But their advice passes unheeded. Saharans are as greedy as anyone. They dream of green. It is the color of Islam. In Algeria now, the revolutionaries have vowed to make a garden of the desert, though of course they never will.

14

THE

SAFARI

THE SAFARI ROLLED into In Salah after dawn, when the chill was off the air. It was a high-clearance truck, a tough three-ton Mercedes that had been modified for passengers by the addition of a narrow door at the front of the cargo box, and a row of small windows along each side. The windows were opaque with dirt. A ladder climbed the rear to an overhead luggage rack. Up front in the cab, the driver and his assistant sat smoking in self-important isolation, as sober and concentrated as pilots headed into a storm. The condition of the truck—its crumpled fenders, cracked windshields, and wired-on hood—hinted at the rigors ahead. Oil dripped from under the engine.

Twenty-five of us boarded, a full load. The air inside was stifling. We sat shoulder-to-shoulder on metal benches and looked each other over—the typical collection of tight-lipped and dusty men. The only woman was an unveiled Malian cradling a baby who, over the grueling trip to come, uttered hardly a whimper. The mother and child were accompanied by two men in filthy robes and *chèches*. I later learned that they came from somewhere near Timbuktu, had been working for years in Libya, and were struggling home. Other passengers were laborers and traders, black Africans returning south across the Sahara to the nations of Niger, Burkina Faso, and the Ivory Coast. Only the poor traveled this way. The driver's assistant made a quick count, then locked us in from the outside.

There was no road now, only the scarred and rutted desert. The first bump threw us from our seats, and some of the passengers laughed. The next bump threw us hard against the ceiling, and the fun was over. One of the young men landed badly, taking a seat corner in the ribs; he shouted in anger and pain, but shouted in vain. The driver could not hear him, and would not have cared anyway. His driving was unflinching. Because from the back we could not see the ground ahead, we never knew when the next blow would fall. Crouching to protect ourselves from serious injury, we hung grimly to the seatbacks and endured the passage of time. Imagine being blindfolded, baked, and beaten.

Every few hours, when we stopped for a rest, the driver's assistant would unlock the door. The woman and child would remain inside. Emerging into the brilliant sunlight, the men would spread into the desert, turn their backs to the truck, and kneel modestly to urinate. Sand and rock then extended with brutal clarity to the horizons. But the real Sahara was a tangle of Africans on the inside of a long-distance truck, the stink of their unwashed bodies, the poison of diesel exhaust.

The day passed in a haze of sweat and injury. The open side windows, high above eye level, let in clouds of dust. Once, as I

floated above my seat, I spotted a Mercedes sedan laboriously
picking its way south. The land climbed. In the afternoon we
urinated on an upsloping desert of a mountain.

The roughness of the ride forced temporary friendship on
the passengers. We first shared our hatred of the driver, then
shared our bread. We stopped for the night in a gorge called
Arāk, a funnel through which all Trans-Saharan traffic passed.
Arāk had a roadhouse—a café and a few of the traditional straw
huts known as zeribas. The establishment was run by a wizened
Frenchman, emaciated and deeply tanned, who draped a scarf
around his neck. He said he had lived in Algeria for thirty-five
years, as a teacher, and later here in Arāk, and he didn't give a
damn about the first Algerian revolution or the second.

He took me for an adventurer and a fool. "You'd better get
yourself a zeriba," he said. "It'll freeze tonight. These Africans,
they can sleep anywhere. I've lived here long enough so I can
too." He squinted at me critically. "But you—you might not
survive the night."

Resisting the impulse to prove him wrong, I rented a zeriba.
I paid him the equivalent of three dollars, six times the normal
rate. He pocketed the money, and afterward left me alone. We
did not speak again.

I borrowed a greasy blanket from his help, an Algerian hustler
with a permanent smirk. "Keep an eye on your suitcase," he
said. "These niggers will steal everything." He wanted me to
change French francs with him, or sell him my razor, or my
watch, or give him batteries—he was alert to any possibility. I
said I had nothing for him. He lost interest and moved away.

One of the Malians warned me against eating the couscous.
It had been cooked days before, he said. The café at Arāk was

known throughout the desert to make people sick. The Malians shared their tea with me. I gave them the last of my food, two oranges, and ducked into the zeriba. Wrapped in the blanket, I lay in the dirt and listened to the wind rustling the walls.

The next morning, I saw the Trans-Saharan from a hillside. We had stopped for a brief rest. It was eight o'clock, rush hour on the desert highway. An empty basin stretched below, twenty miles from rim to rim, crisscrossed by tracks. Far in the distance, a cargo truck inched northward raising dust.

In the afternoon we came to a sudden halt. The engine revved. The assistant did not emerge to free us. We stood on our seats and peered outside. A tractor-trailer crossing an *oued* ahead had mired to the top of its wheels in mud. Rare autumn rains had fallen on the mountains; the *oued* looked dry, but was not. The truckers now were trying to dig out.

I thought we should stop to help them, or offer a ride, or check their water supply. But not a word was exchanged. Having surveyed the trucksters' misfortune, we chose another crossing point, and with brutal speed rocked and slithered through the mud. On solid ground again, we hesitated for just a moment before hurrying on to the south. The stranded truckers, who had put down their shovels to watch, seemed not to mind.

PART II

THE CENTER
IS A WAR

15

TAMANRASSET

IT IS THE desert of more so: drier, fiercer, and wilder, an emptiness of stony basins and barren volcanic peaks, of buttes, cinder cones, and confused black rock. The land is as mesmerizing as a night sky. The canyons give it depth; the nomads give it scale. You can gaze into it for hours absorbed by the drama of desolation and distance. The sense of Africa, of ancient roots and shared history, is inescapable. Then you turn around and find Tamanrasset.

Tamanrasset is not an oasis. It has no date groves, few trees, and little water. Perched nearly a mile high in the Hoggar Mountains, it is the Sahara unimagined. Forty-five thousand people live in these mud-bricked neighborhoods which spread along a dry riverbed. You can walk from one end of town to the other in fifteen minutes, and around the entire thing in an hour. Travel-weary trucks list through the streets. Women duck out of sight when strangers approach. Masked Tuaregs in twos and threes ride by slowly on their camels, or haughtily stride down the sidewalks. Soldiers linger in the stark cafés.

Few towns in the world are so remote: there is no telephone connection, no good road, and no decent postal service—only a municipal downlink for national television. Groundwater is in such short supply that new households are not allowed to hook up to the municipal system, and old households are severely rationed. The middle class lives on deliveries from private water trucks that scavenge supplies from distant wells. The poor live by the bucketful. Once there was a plan to pipe in water across the hundreds of miles from In Salah, but no one expects it to be completed now. Despite all this, Tamanrasset is growing fast.

Some growth is due to troubles in the Sahel, the parched savanna along the Sahara's southern edge. The troubles are ecological and political: recurrent droughts have shoved traditional enemies against one another, and a widespread rebellion has broken out through much of the central Sahara, which pits Berber Tuareg separatists against the new black national majorities of Niger and Mali, and has little to do with the Islamic revolution in the north.

Refugees from all sides of the conflict filter through the desert across the international borders, and camp loosely for miles around Tamanrasset. No one knows how many are out there. They live in scrap-shacks and discarded army tents, which quickly take on the color of the earth. Like illegal immigrants elsewhere, the men look for day-work, and the women take in laundry. The smallest children go naked and hungry. Dressed in rags, young boys slip into town to hawk cigarettes and to shoplift. There are no schools for them, and no doctors. The neglect is intentional. Tamanrasset's police chief once said to me, "The drought is over. It's time they left." But on both subjects the refugees disagree.

The other reason for Tamanrasset's growth is commerce—the old-fashioned chance to buy low and sell high and trade goods across the Sahara. Tamanrasset sits at the heart of the desert. Linked to the north by 1,200 miles of the Trans-Saharan, it dominates a web of unmarked trading routes stretching equally far into Mali, Niger, and Libya. Because the local currencies have little international value, and "hard currencies" are rare, the commerce works mostly by barter. Tamanrasset traders export Algerian food and livestock in exchange for hard-to-find durable goods—car parts, electronics, guns. The merchandise moves not by caravan, but by truck. It is a difficult business of bypassing import tariffs and greedy government officials. Serious risks are involved; the traders are threatened by army patrols, Tuareg rebels, bandits, breakdowns, and death by thirst. By the standards of international smuggling, their profits are small. Nonetheless, behind the plain mud walls of Tamanrasset's compounds, they manage to support their families in some luxury. They make connections as far away as Lagos, Accra, and Dakar. War and famine swirl around it, but Tamanrasset endures. Saharans call it the new Timbuktu.

I HAD FLOWN there before, and thought I knew the place. But only now, arriving bruised and exhausted after weeks by ground from the north, did I understand the extent of its geographic isolation. The Safari pulled into town around sunset, and with a final rattle settled into silence. I nodded to the Malians, who slipped away toward the outlying refugee camps. Shouldering my suitcase, I headed through the camel market and into the center.

Tamanrasset's oldest building, which dates from the First World War, is a small adobe fort with crenelated walls, like a set piece out of a Foreign Legion movie. It was built by Charles de Foucauld, a French aristocrat and army officer turned desert monk, who moved to Tamanrasset in 1905 to live among the hostile Tuaregs.

Foucauld was an early example of the modern visitor, a runaway who came to the desert for reasons that had more to do with himself, and with Europe, than with the people he intended to help. Tamanrasset then was a fragile encampment of fifteen straw zeribas clustered around a well in the mountains. Foucauld chose it because of its isolation and poverty. In his diary he wrote, "It does not seem possible that there could ever be any garrison, telegraph, or European here, and there will not be a mission for a long time. I chose this distant spot where I want the only model for my life to be the life of Jesus of Nazareth."

Foucauld never saw the Sahara squarely. His desert was at first just a place far from France; his Tuaregs had value mainly as a dangerous people among whom he could express his Christian ideals. Much as he sought to live humbly among the natives, he was inescapably a European, with the full force of Europe behind him. His refusal to understand the power he wielded was not without consequence. It led ultimately to his murder, and to the French reprisals that followed. More important now, it predicted the confusions afflicting the desert today. Does it matter that Foucauld meant well?

He was a short, gaunt, heavily bearded man, uncompromising in his humility. For decades he had wandered the Sahara under the most punishing circumstances, walking in sandals when he could have ridden, denying himself food and wine, thinking about Christ when he might have been sleeping. Now he intended to show the Tuaregs the path to Catholicism, and to found a new and ascetic monastic order. At both efforts he was unsuccessful during his life. Though he compiled a four-volume dictionary of Tamachek, the Tuareg language, and collected two volumes of Tuareg poetry, he converted not a single man or woman. The Tuaregs learned to stay away from the wells of Tamanrasset to avoid his sermonizing. His appeals to other Catholics to join him in the desert went unanswered. His only unambiguous achievement was the martyrdom he yearned for. He wrote, "If I could be killed one day by the pagans, what a fine death! My very dear brother, what an honor and what a joy if God would only listen to my prayer."

He got his wish during the First World War, which awoke the Frenchman in him. About the Sahara he now wrote, "Progress is possible only by means of a *French,* a truly French administration, which natives will be permitted to join not only when they have French citizenship and have received a French education, but when they think like Frenchmen!"

It would be easy to misread this. Foucauld was a man of his time, and not of ours. He did not abandon his earlier spiritualism, but faced with the threat of national annihilation in Europe, he widened his perception of the path to salvation.

During the war Foucauld continued to live in a zeriba in Tamanrasset. Sensing the new vulnerability of their colonial masters, certain factions of the Tuaregs rebelled. Foucauld felt personally betrayed: how could these people, his brothers, have forgotten the love and understanding he had shown for them? The French army had stationed soldiers in the plains below the Hoggar Mountains, about thirty miles from Tamanrasset. Foucauld began to send them reports of the rebels' activity. He offered them military advice. As the rebellion spread, he employed the locals to build him a little fort in Tamanrasset, into which reluctantly he moved. He saw the desert now in terms of good and bad Tuaregs. He encouraged the soldiers to exile, and in one case to execute, the natives who had gone wrong. But he tried still to live the life of a good Christian.

On the night of December 1, 1916, he was alone in his stronghold when someone knocked on the door. Foucauld asked who was there. A muffled voice answered that it was the army mail. Foucauld opened the door, stuck out his hand. He was yanked into captivity. Catholic texts still go wild over this treachery. In an otherwise contemplative biography published in 1972, one author wrote, "The leader of these rogues was that El Madden who had been particularly well cared for by Père de Foucauld. This Negro had a diabolical, degenerate appearance, for his skull and face looked as if they had been crushed, and he had hardly any nose."

Foucauld was bound, and forced to kneel by the door while the fort was looted. The rebels carried off food, weapons, and ammunition, and scattered Foucauld's precious manuscripts. There are several versions of the final moments, all Catholic. One has Foucauld answering the Tuaregs' shouted interrogation in biblical language: "I say to you, unless the grain of wheat fall into the ground and die, itself remaineth alone; but if it die, it bringeth forth much fruit. He that loveth his life doth lose it, and he that hateth his life in this world shall keep it into everlasting life." Another version has Foucauld staring ahead in silent forgiveness, preparing to die for his murderers as Christ died for him. This fits. But it is of course also possible that Foucauld was silent because he was angry and upset.

Just then two soldiers, Saharans working for the French, happened to ride up on camels. The rebels ambushed and killed them both.

Foucauld may have tried to warn them. In the excitement his fifteen-year-old guard shot him in the head. Foucauld toppled into the ditch at the foot of the walls, and drifted out of Tamanrasset on the way to sainthood, a formal status he has now nearly attained.

After the war, the boy who shot Foucauld was captured and executed, as were five of his accomplices. The French built a larger fort beside the first one, and settled in to stay. The Tuaregs never did convert. But Foucauld's hoped-for monastic order, a self-sacrificing group called the Little Brothers of Jesus, was founded in the Sahara in 1933, and joined later by an equally austere order of Little Sisters. When ugly El Madden was an old man, he was finally court-martialed, in Libya in 1944. Tamanrasset got a telegraph and an airport, and grew into a town. When tourism still flourished there, Catholic pilgrimages accounted for some of Tamanrasset's prosperity. I remember the frustration of the Saharans who liked the business but still thought of Foucauld as an agent and a spy.

Today the two forts flank the town's main street. The street is crooked, shaded, and lined with adobe buildings stained ochre, and backed by the clear sky. Black stone mountains mark the horizons. Every evening when the high-altitude air turns cool, people meet to stroll and to sit and talk in the cafés. Traders trade over sweet tea. African women in colorful print dresses balance baskets on their heads. Drafted soldiers walk in twos and threes, holding hands. Small stores sell clothes, hardware, and Tuareg jewelry. There is a well-kept marketplace, a movie theater, and an arcade outside the post office.

The style of the street is not entirely spontaneous. During the tourist boom, a German architect was brought in to spruce up the place. He stayed five years. Citizens now criticize his intrusions. Particularly galling to them is a garish administration building in mock-Saharan style, and a public square with cement columns that cast no shade. The centerpiece of the square, in this town without water, is a fountain. It has never been connected, and has slowly filled with garbage.

THE LOCAL ARCHITECT chosen to protect the city from such mistakes in the future is at thirty-eight one of the most admired men of Tamanrasset. His name is Salah Addoun. Tall and athletic, he has close-cropped black hair, dark Berber skin, and a charm that wins him many friends. He is not, however, a flexible person. Call him a traditionalist. By Western standards, he is a Muslim fundamentalist. I have known Addoun for years, and have listened carefully as he has grown more convinced with age.

I found him now with friends on a street near the center of town. We embraced, and he insisted that I stay with him at his uncle's compound, as I had in the past. He asked neither why I had come to Tamanrasset, nor how long I would stay. I mentioned that I had arrived on the Safari. He made nothing of it. He hurried me to a wedding feast, where with other old acquaintances we talked through the night, waiting for word of the marriage's consummation.

In the morning, as Addoun and I walked through town, I mentioned that I needed his help. I was headed south along the Trans-Saharan to Niger, but wanted first to make a side trip to the east into the remote deserts along the Libyan border, where the cliffs and overhangs hold one of the world's great collections of Neolithic rock art—a half-million etchings and paintings chronicling 8,000 years of Saharan history.

Addoun looked worried. "I'll take you instead to the rock paintings here, close by, tomorrow."

I insisted on the east. "I thought you might know of someone headed over there."

"You've heard about the Tuareg troubles?"

I nodded. "But in the other direction—toward Gao and Timbuktu."

"We've had raids right up to the edge of Tamanrasset."

"Who do they hit?"

He shrugged. The violence was opportunistic. Someone had been murdered out behind the airport. Someone had been robbed on the way out of town.

I said I did not intend to wander alone.

Addoun agreed to ask around for my ride.

It had been nearly two years since my last visit. Addoun was still waiting for the licenses that would allow him to open the town's first independent architectural studio. In the meantime he worked for his uncle's construction firm. He took me to his office to show me the drawings of a house in Tamanrasset he had designed for the Algerian consul to Agadez, Niger. The office was the same cement cubicle he had occupied before—a noisy, dusty room, with an inclined school desk, and a bare bulb. Interrupted often by questions from the yard crew, Addoun labored there without complaint. His designs were works of art—well proportioned, austere, built of stuccoed adobe, suited to the desert in which they stood. I sometimes thought he would succeed in Arizona or New Mexico—but then I thought better of it. We walked up the street to the house in progress, where he showed me a floor plan whose main purpose was gently to keep men and women apart.

Addoun was hardly a prude. In his younger years he had mixed with many women, romantic Europeans who used to fly to Tamanrasset to make love in the desert with desert men. "Ah," he said to me, laughing, "if the stones could talk!"

But he had since become sterner. Late in the afternoon, we brewed tea in the desert outside of town. The marriage of the night before was working on him. He said, "These weddings are not trivial affairs."

"You look concerned, Salah."

He studied the horizon. "There is always the worry that the bride has already lost her virginity. No matter what the families believe, you can never be sure until the wedding night."

"Does it sometimes happen that she is not a virgin?"

"Oh yes, it happens."

"And then?"

"It's very serious. The marriage may be off. Did you see how nervous the bridegroom was last night?"

I said I had not. "He was worried about his bride?"

Addoun nodded. "His friends spent the ceremony trying to keep his courage up. He had other worries too, of course. For the bridegroom there is also the pressure to please his new wife, to perform before the night is over."

"Does it happen that he can't?"

"There are weddings where the families have to wait for two or even three days."

Addoun had all that to look forward to. He had found a future wife for himself, a distant cousin who lived with her parents in In Salah, and he had gone through the difficult business of negotiating a formal engagement, but as a proud man he wanted to start his own studio and build a proper house before the wedding. He kept waiting for the architectural license.

"My fiancée understands," Addoun said. "I'm lucky. she is very patient, and writes to me regularly."

"I'm sure," I answered carefully.

To my surprise he took out his wallet, and plucked out a snapshot of her—a young and pleasant-looking woman, with curled hair and an open smile.

I nodded without comment.

Addoun put the picture away and mentioned that he had never showed it to anyone before. He called me his brother, and invited me in advance to his wedding. I accepted awkwardly, knowing I might never meet his bride or learn her name.

He called me his brother, but knew I was not. My awkwardness may have sounded like criticism to him. He was a sensitive man. He wanted to admit our differences, but on safer ground. So he told me the story of a political scandal that had rocked Tamanrasset when the provincial government, in a belated attempt to encourage tourism, had commissioned a statue of a Tuareg warrior for the entrance to town. Addoun and others on Tamanrasset's architectural committee had objected to the plan. The government had built the statue's foundation anyway. Rallying support from the citizens, the committee had taken to the streets. Faced with more serious rebellions, the government had backed down.

Addoun knew I would ask why he had bothered. He explained it was because of the Islamic proscription of statues— a tradition whose origin is Mohammed's crusade against idol worship in heathen Arabia.

"But this was a statue of a Tuareg," I said. "What connection to idolatry did it have?"

Addoun answered, "You understand, our traditions run deep."

ADDOUN AND I spent the evening with friends, watching television in the open courtyard of his uncle's compound. We sprawled on pillows and chewed oranges. An American movie, dubbed in French, showed a bikini-clad actress on a California beach. I asked Addoun what he thought, was she a whore to exhibit herself?

He grinned at me. "Why, because of the bathing suit?"

"Your Islam would ban them."

"For our women, not for yours."

"What's the difference?"

"The difference, my dear friend, is purely cultural."

Later, maybe to change the subject, he said, "You can tell an American movie by the cars."

I pointed to the screen. "That's a Volkswagen."

"It's how they *show* the cars—they advertise them. You wait, there'll be a car chase."

There was.

He said, "In French movies, they advertise food. There's always a scene where they're eating dinner."

He thought for a while. "In Arab movies, they show weddings."

It was not a happy evening. Addoun's neighbor had died in the desert. He was a young man named Boucenna, who caught a ride with a driver heading south down the Trans-Saharan for Niger. Near the border, the car broke down. The driver hitched a ride with a passing truck and returned to Tamanrasset to fetch a part, leaving Boucenna to guard the car. Boucenna knew the desert. He had water, and should have been comfortable. But after only a few hours alone, he set off on foot. He walked twelve miles before he collapsed of thirst and died.

"He must have panicked," I said.

Addoun shook his head. "Boucenna was not a coward. And he was not stupid. But for every man there are two times that are inescapable—the time of birth and the time of death. Boucenna walked because his time had come."

I balked. "You mean death is everyone's destination."

"I mean there is a time, and it is predetermined."

We left it at that, unresolved, because faith defies argument. The world is not as small as it appears on television.

Addoun's own father died in the desert. He was a native of In Salah, an Air France ticket agent who turned against the French and was imprisoned by them during the war for independence. In 1962, as a free man again, he set off from In Salah with five friends, all experienced desert travelers, to drive to an oasis two days away. The route was unmarked; they missed their destination, realized they were lost, and kept driving until they ran out of gas. Addoun's father wrote farewells on his *chèche*. He survived a month, and was the last to succumb to his thirst. The next day the bodies were discovered. Addoun was six.

So Addoun was the desert's child. He grew up in an overwhelming land, and began to travel himself. Once he set out on a trip at sunset, to avoid the heat of day. After a full night of driving he came to some lights, and found himself back where he had started. He concluded that God did not choose for him to die just then. If that seems hard to understand, you might try substituting the word Sahara for God.

More recently Addoun was a passenger in a desert taxi heading across the sands, southwest bound from El Golea to a village called El Homr. After a while one of the passengers said to the driver, "Where are you going?"

"To El Homr."

The passenger said, "No, El Homr is toward that star there." He pointed to the left. The driver was unsure. The passenger took the wheel and followed the star to safety.

These are the skills of the nomad, and they require an encyclopedic knowledge of the land and stars. An old Saharan explained it to me this way: "Yes, by the stars at night. In daylight, by local knowledge of the desert—this soil, this tree, this ruin, these tracks, these shadows before sunset. It is passed down from father to son, and spoken of among friends." We were discussing the way across a thousand miles of open desert, where a compass is of little help, and mistakes are all the more dangerous because they are not obvious at first.

Even along the main desert routes, navigation is a worry. The tracks are braided, eroded, obscured by dirt and sand. The braiding occurs when one driver gets stuck, and other drivers detour around the signs of softness, making new tracks. Still others follow, mire down in turn, and pick new ways through. The Oregon Trail once braided the same way. In the Sahara every truck, every car, every motorcycle leaves its trace. People take shortcuts. People take long cuts. People go wildly wrong. This repeats itself over the years until the routes consist of ill-defined bands of crisscrossing tire marks, perhaps twenty miles wide. Bandits, smugglers, and army patrols leave their tracks, too. Intersecting routes lead off to unknown destinations. Seen from the air, the tracks might make sense; on the ground they can become hopelessly confusing. People follow them until they die.

Concerned about the number of drivers lost in the desert, the Algerian government marked the main routes with metal pylons every ten kilometers. Ten kilometers is about six miles, a long way, and drivers still get lost. For marking the Trans-Saharan south of Tamanrasset the government decided on something more certain, since this is the route that causes the most trouble. It is where Addoun's neighbor Boucenna died. For 260 miles it descends across infernal badlands to the border with Niger. There are no wells, and few natural landmarks. Drivers take days to negotiate it.

During my first visit to Tamanrasset, the route had just been marked with 451 white concrete pillars, one for every kilometer from Tamanrasset to the border. Addoun's uncle won the contract, and gave the project to his nephew. It was spring. Addoun left Tamanrasset on foot, followed by a three-man crew in a Land Cruiser carrying supplies and topographic charts. Over two weeks he walked the entire distance, surveying thirty kilometers a day and driving stakes at the prescribed intervals. He did this as casually as others might go for a weekend stroll, without photographers or expedition flags. After driving the stakes he returned to Tamanrasset, gathered a larger crew, and set off in trucks carrying steel molds. Pouring the concrete took an additional three months.

Thinking of his father, I asked him then if the walking had been a pilgrimage of sorts.

He smiled and said he had needed the exercise.

I asked if his markers would make the driving easy.

He said no, he was not a dreamer. Smugglers and adventurers would still get lost. People would take shortcuts, break down, and get stuck. The tracks would braid.

THOSE WERE TAMANRASSET'S last tourist years. For a while there was even a once-weekly flight directly from Paris. Most of the visitors were French. Addoun quietly resented them. He told me that the memories of the war were still too fresh. But in fact he had more recent reasons: he read back copies of *Le Monde,* and watched French television, and saw the French loathing of Algerians. He heard panel discussions in which his religious beliefs were openly despised and feared. He read accounts in which Algerian immigration was depicted as an assault on the French soul.

In bitterness he said to me, "The French occupied us for a hundred and thirty-two years. We've had only thirty-two years since independence. That gives us another century to occupy them."

As an army officer, he had gone to visit friends in Paris and Marseilles. I saw pictures of him on the trip, standing upright in a jacket and tie, looking like an Arab sophisticate. He told me about staying with Parisian acquaintances on Isle St. Louis in an elegant town house with linen napkins and fawning servants. The luxury offended his Spartan tastes. "What do they *do* in those bathrooms?" he asked me.

He fled south on the train, and suffered the hostility of the passengers. On the Côte d'Azur he was thrown out of a café. The experience soured him; upon his return to Tamanrasset, he found the French tourists even more difficult to accept.

When he overheard them criticizing Algerians he would draw himself up and in elegant French ask them whose country they thought it was. When he overhead them trying to haggle with shopkeepers, he would intervene to ask them if they did the same in France. I thought it was beneath his dignity. But it was his habit.

The French in Tamanrasset were joined by Germans, Swiss, Italians, and sometimes Japanese. They arrived on the airline, and wandered the streets in cautious groups. Most stayed a few days on packaged tours. They bought souvenirs, rode camels through the outlying desert, and were taken in four-wheel-drive caravans to visit the hermitage built by Charles de Foucauld high in the Hoggar Mountains.

The hermitage had five stone huts and a stone dormitory where visitors could sleep on the floor. It stood at 8,950 feet on the Assekrem Plateau, amid desolate and windswept peaks sixty miles from Tamanrasset. I drove there one afternoon with Addoun in a hired Land Cruiser. We walked to the top of the mountain and sat quietly, watching the sun set. The wind turned cold. We climbed down past the chapel, where prayers were being said, to the dormitory, where a group of Swiss tourists had just arrived. They talked about trekking. They had been to Peru the year before, and had learned to dislike each other. We ate with them at a long table by the light of lanterns.

"Peru was marvelous," said a middle-aged woman. "We actually lived among the Indians."

"Shit," said the old man next to her.

They were not religious. They offered to share their whiskey with us. Addoun glanced at me as if to say, "Do you see the decadence of the West?"

But also sitting at the table was a gray-bearded Californian with a gentle smile and bright, feverish eyes. He said he was a retired lawyer with a house in La Jolla. He admired Foucauld, and had come to the Hoggar Mountains to fast and to meditate. For thirty-one days he had gone without food, living in a one-man tent by a spring below the hermitage. He had talked to no one and had read only the Bible. This was his first meal and human contact in a month. I asked him if he had come to any conclusions. He said yes, he would devote the rest of his life to alleviating hunger. He was, I thought, a true ascetic. Addoun distrusted him anyway because, he said, he was not born to the desert.

A DIFFERENT TYPE altogether were the Europeans who came to Tamanrasset along the Trans-Saharan. For them the town was merely a stopping point on the long way south. The ones remembered were the lone eccentrics, the walkers, wanderers, bicycle riders, and lost souls of the sort who drift through all the lonely corners of the world. One man had come through pushing a wheelbarrow. It was said later that he had finished the desert crossing, and had pushed deep into equatorial Africa before dying of disease.

But most of the Trans-Saharan tourists—the ones you saw daily on the main street—were motorists. They traveled in groups of four-wheel-drive vehicles, usually to Dakar or Abidjan or some other famous place with a beach. The vehicles were equipped with colorful decals, with placards proclaiming EXPEDITION, and with gas cans, tires, shovels, and steel tracks for the sand. The drivers were dashing and self-conscious, mostly Germans and French playing the explorer. If they were brawny, they rolled up their sleeves to show off their biceps. If they were fat, they grew beards. They wore bandannas around their necks, and swaggered around the hotel, smelling of sweat and dust, talking loudly. Addoun called them "chichi." They seemed to have seen too many cigarette ads.

But those tourists are gone now, chased away by the fighting. The Europeans who still drive through Tamanrasset are different again. Crossing the Sahara is their business. They drive luxury sedans, preferably big Mercedes, to be sold in Niger, or Nigeria, or points beyond. In the cities of Africa a Mercedes-Benz is seen as the ultimate earthly good, and the class of traders, politicians, and soldiers that floats on top has earned a new name—the Wabenzi. Many of these cars on the Trans-Saharan were said to be stolen, provided with papers to satisfy the Algerian police.

I talked to one Frenchman who had made the trip fifteen times before. He was barrel-chested and balding, with a drooping mustache and strong arms—a tough guy right off the docks of Marseilles. I asked if he worried about losing his way. No, never, he said. He did only this now for a living. I did not ask what he had done before. He took me to see the BMW he was ferrying south. Under the dust and mud it was gleaming black and very new. It had a digital radio and a burglar alarm. I asked him if he ever had trouble. No, never.

There are others for whom driving a car, stolen or not, is a one-time adventure. They operate on the assumption, probably correct, that if they keep moving, the Islamic revolution will not catch up with them. They are willing to gamble on the Tuaregs. Most are young, middle-class, and studiously care-free—thin Germans, and tangle-haired Frenchwomen. In Africa they have rejected the constraints of European society. They wear Ali Baba pants and sandals, and have the kind of self-congratulating conversations you might hear between cruising yachtsmen in warm waters. They have neither the money nor the desire to invest in satellite navigation. These are the people who still get lost. It happens most often after they leave Taman-rasset, somewhere on the way to the border of Niger, or in the hundreds of miles of wilderness that lie beyond. Addoun was right—his concrete markers have hardly helped.

Recently, four young Germans—three men and a woman—left Tamanrasset in a Mercedes. They drove south to within 60 miles of Niger, then turned east, probably to avoid the border police. They got lost. They wandered 400 miles to the Libyan border, turned around, wandered back, and ran out of gas. Their families came to Tamanrasset to search for them, and distributed a poster with photographs. Absurdly, the poster was written in German. In bold print it read, "LOST IN WEST AFRICA!" Weeks later, the Mercedes and three male corpses were found. The woman was presumed to have been eaten by jackals or buried by blowing sand.

I saw the poster tacked to the wall at La Source, a hostel built around a spring of bubbling mineral water three miles outside of town. I went there for a drink with Addoun and his friends. The poster was in the entranceway; the photographs had been slashed with a knife. When I remarked on this to my companions, they seemed unsympathetic.

"They're dead anyway," one said, as if that explained the slashes.

"They brought it on themselves," said another.

Addoun was more expansive. "The families blamed us for not finding them alive—but how could we have? Just look at the emptiness here. It is something Europeans just cannot understand."

THERE IS AN old sign still standing beside the track leading south from Tamanrasset. In crudely lettered French and English, it warns drivers about the dangers of crossing the desert, and advises them to take precautions. But even during the high years of Tamanrasset's tourism, the sign made little difference. Drivers who got to the central Sahara were either fully prepared to start with or not inclined to take precautions.

The Belgian family probably went by it without a second look. They were husband, wife, and five-year-old boy, driving an old Peugeot sedan for resale in Burkina Faso. At first their trip went fast, from Algiers through the northern oases to points south. Eventually the pavement ended. They were prepared to spend nights in the desert, but the driving was slower than expected. They were encouraged when they arrived in Taman-rasset. After resting there, and refueling, they pushed on, planning three days to the border with Niger. They tried to follow Addoun's markers, but many already had disappeared.

Partway to the border, as the desert descended into the great southern flats, the Belgians took a wrong turn. When they understood their mistake, they still had plenty of gas, and they set out to retrace their route. This was not easy, since the ground was hard-packed and rocky. But getting lost was part of the adventure, a memorable game for carefree Europeans. We know this because the woman later wrote it down. People dying of thirst in the desert often leave a written record. They have time to think. Writing denies the incredible isolation.

The Peugeot broke down. The Belgians rationed their water and lay in the shade of a tarpaulin. The rationing did not extend their lives; they might as well have drunk their fill, since the human body loses water at a constant rate, even when dehydrated. The only way to stretch your life in the hot desert is to reduce your sweating: stay put, stay shaded, and keep your clothes on.

The Belgians hoped a truck would come along. For a week they waited, scanning the horizon for a dust-tail or the glint of a windshield. This was in a place, more or less, where the maps still insist on showing a road. The woman felt the upwellings of panic. She began to write more frantically, filling pages in single sessions. The water ran low, then dry, and the family grew horribly thirsty. After filtering it through a cloth, they drank the car's radiator fluid. They had arrived at the danger stage.

Water is the largest component of our bodies, but we have little to spare. In the hottest desert we lose it, mostly by sweating, at the rate of two gallons a day while resting in the shade, or four gallons a day while walking. We are hardy animals. Because our sweating keeps us cool, we function well in extreme heat as long as we replenish that water loss. If water is available, we naturally maintain our fluid content within a quarter of a percent. But what happens when the supplies run out?

Thirst is first felt when the body has lost about 0.5 percent of its weight to dehydration. For a 180-pound man, that amounts to about a pint of water. With a 2 percent loss (say, two quarts), the stomach is no longer big enough to supply the body's needs, and people stop drinking before they have replenished their loss, even if they are given ample water. This is called voluntary dehydration, though it is hardly a conscious choice. Up to a 5 percent loss (about one gallon) the symptoms include fatigue, loss of appetite, flushed skin, irritability, increased pulse rate, and mild fever. Beyond that lie dizziness, headache, labored breathing, absence of salivation, circulatory problems, blued skin, and slurred speech. At 10 percent, a person can no longer walk. The point of no return is 12 percent (a three-gallon deficit), when the tongue swells, and the mouth loses all sensation. Because swallowing becomes impossible, a person this dehydrated cannot recover without medical assistance. In the Sahara it may take only half a day to get to such a condition.

Now the skin shrinks against the bones and cracks, the eyes sink into the skull, and vision and hearing become dim. Urination is painful, and urine is dark. Delirium sets in.

As the body dehydrates in a hot desert climate, a disproportionate amount of water is drawn from the circulating blood. The blood thickens, and finally can no longer fulfill its functions, one of which is to transport heat generated within the body to the surface. It is this heat that ultimately kills. The end comes with an explosive rise in body temperature, convulsions, and blissful death.

After the radiator coolant was gone, the Belgians started sipping gasoline. You would too. Call it *petroposia*. Saharans have recommended it to me as a way of staying off the battery acid. The woman wrote that it seemed to help. They also drank their urine. She reported that it was difficult at first, but that afterward it wasn't so bad.

The boy was the weakest, and was suffering terribly. In desperation, they burned their car, hoping someone would see the smoke. No one did. The boy could no longer swallow. His name was Maurice. His parents killed him to stop his pain. Later, the husband cut himself open and allowed his wife to drink his blood. At his request, she broke his neck with a rock. Alone now, she no longer wanted to live. Still, the Sahara was fabulous, she wrote, and she was glad to have come. She would do it again. She regretted only one thing—that she had not seen Sylvester Stallone in *Rambo III*. Those were her last lines. She had lost her mind, but through her confusion must have remembered the ease of death in the movies.

The family's remains were found, and returned to Tamanrasset. I arrived later on a flight from Algiers, and was shown the woman's journal by the provincial judge. Her handwriting grew difficult to read toward the end. My own son, who was an infant then, has since turned five. I have not taken him to the Sahara. I cannot stop grieving for the Belgian boy.

AFTER A WEEK, Addoun found a man who was driving east to Djanet, an old oasis near the wild Libyan border. This man would allow me to accompany him, and then for a price would take me farther—into the infamous Tadart, a vastness of sculpted stone where the rock art endures.

I was not cautious enough. I simply asked Addoun if he knew this man. He said he did not, but knew of his family. The ride had been arranged by a merchant who from a distance had helped me before, Moulay Lakhdar Abderhadim, the most successful businessman of Tamanrasset. I had never met him. But the day before my departure, he invited Addoun and me to lunch at his house.

Abderhadim lived beyond the camel market. To the unaccustomed eye, it was a dismal neighborhood. Chickens and goats picked through garbage in the rutted streets. There were long, monotonous compound walls, crumbling and neglected, stained brown with mud and blowing dust. Only the vehicles hinted at money: Range Rovers and Land Cruisers, worth two to three times their price in Europe.

Addoun knocked at a metal gate. After a delay, while the women scurried out of sight, we were let in by an old Haratin in a robe and a turban. Addoun greeted him warmly and introduced him as a friend of the family, though clearly he was a servant. We entered a lush garden of fruit trees and flowering bushes. The house was sprawling, single-story, made of stone and adobe. Addoun knew his way and led me into the sitting room, where Abderhadim reclined on a mattress watching a soccer game on television. Plump and soft-looking, Abderhadim was a middle-aged man with a round face and thinning hair. He wore a blue running suit zippered up tight around his throat. A blanket was draped over his legs. He excused himself for not greeting us at the door; he suffered from rheumatism, and it had flared up in his knees. Addoun and I sat on cushions on the floor. The doorway gave onto a lush courtyard, brilliant with desert light. Other men arrived. The servant came with a bowl of couscous, and sat with us.

Abderhadim had an affable but impatient manner, with a decisiveness that hinted at his authority. He waved aside my thanks for arranging the trip to the east, and asked me to come to lunch again when I returned. He mentioned in passing that he himself did not know the driver who would take me. Most of his own business was with the south.

We talked about commerce. He described himself as a trader in food and car parts—and in other goods as the opportunities arose. I asked him to explain. Modestly, he called himself a simple shopkeeper who had become an importer by default. "Niger is very poor. But you can find everything there."

I asked if he found business difficult across such distances, with no roads, no telephones, and nonconvertible currencies.

He smiled and said, "We are all Muslims."

An older man, dressed in a white robe and turban, told me a story about this. His uncle had been a trader in Tamanrasset, who for years had run camel caravans to Niger and Mali, carrying dates and salt to the south, and returning with chickens. His name was Salem Ben Hadj Ahmed. In 1953, on the way to Agadez, Niger, he and his men came across the encampment of a nomadic Tuareg family. The father and older sons had gone off to hunt, leaving the mother and her youngest children alone. The woman made the caravaners welcome, gave them water, and prepared to slaughter a sheep in their honor. But Ahmed stopped her, since his men had killed a gazelle and had fresh meat. They roasted and ate the gazelle, shared the meat with the family, and in the morning moved on. It was Ahmed's last trip; he was getting to be an old man. Afterward he stayed in Tamanrasset and sent out trucks to do his business. He died in 1968. News of his death spread by word of mouth through the desert. One day a letter arrived for his son. It was from Niger, and it said that his father had forty-five sheep there; he should come get them. The son had never heard of these animals. He checked his father's will and found no mention of them. However, he set out for Niger and eventually found the old nomad whose wife had offered the sheep so many years before. The sheep was Ahmed's, the nomad said, and so were her offspring.

The story seemed true. But fraternal love between Muslims is a fiction that has always been hard to maintain. Abderhadim was a subtle man, and he may have been embarrassed by the attempt. He brought the talk back to the present by criticizing his trading partners to the south. "Look at the poverty just in Mali. People are starving there. I know a merchant in Gao, a Muslim like us. He is a wealthy man. A beggar comes to his door, begging. He takes a date—one date!—and he does this." He cupped his hands and touched them to his forehead. "Then he gives the beggar the date. He thinks he has fulfilled his duty. In Algeria we feed our goats better than that!"

Over tea, Abderhadim described his work more carefully. Some of the commerce is legal. Dates from the northern oasis are exported; camels, goats, and chickens are imported. Since the exports exceed the imports, over the course of the year the merchants of Tamanrasset build credit in the neighboring countries. Then, every spring, a fair is held here during which the government relaxes import restrictions. Consumer goods, mostly Japanese, flood across the borders. The fair is an exception to the regulated Algerian economy—a sanctioned experiment in free trade. In Tamanrasset, the balance sheets return to zero. The goods are sold to buyers from the north.

But the real profits are in smuggling. Abderhadim admitted it reluctantly, and only because others were in the room. After pointing out that he himself never broke the law, he explained how it is done. The driver who imports a load of declared Malian goats into Algeria might on the next trip south head out with an outlawed cargo of wheat bought at subsidized prices. The truck that hauls dates down the Trans-Saharan to Niger may return by a less public route with a load of precious car parts.

"Electronics are the best," one of the guests said. "They are small and light and easy to hide, and they don't spoil in the heat."

And you can mark them up 1,000 percent.

Governments have fought back with expanded border patrols and stiff prison terms. They have regularly declared a war on contraband. People in Tamanrasset are not concerned. The Sahara is a big place.

I mentioned the Islamic radicals. They claim to be economic liberals. Might they not do away with import restrictions altogether? And wouldn't this undercut business? Abderhadim urged me not to worry. His logic went like this:

A free-market economy, though of course desirable, is a remote possibility.

Islamic radicals are moralists, which of course is also desirable. They have plenty of reasons to ban imports.

Look at Iran. Look at Sudan.

Mohammed himself was a trader.

Thanks be to Allah and the desert, business prospects in Tamanrasset remain excellent.

We stood to leave, and I asked Abderhadim a final question, whether the Tuareg attacks had not complicated his work.

He looked up at me languidly, and said, "Oh yes, you're aware of that, then."

16

THE JACKAL AS usual was wandering from one waterhole to the next, hoping to find a stray lamb or kid goat, or carrion left by some more discriminating carnivore. To his delight he spotted a beautiful young sheep who was grazing on a green plateau some distance from her flock and shepherd. The jackal was famished, but a coward by nature, and willing to attack only if he could lure her closer to him. After some thought he decided he had the solution. He crept to the base of the plateau, and from below he called, "Hello, my big sister sheep."

The sheep ignored him and continued to graze.

"Hello, my big sister sheep. Have you heard the good news?"

"What good news?" she answered.

"Why, ever since yesterday, there is complete peace between all creatures. If you would only come a little closer to me I could tell you many wonderful things. Come closer, big sister sheep. I am small and I have been running so hard all morning that I cannot climb up to you."

The sheep looked away at the horizon, and was apparently intrigued by what she saw there.

"What do you see over there?" asked the jackal. "Come, I'm in a hurry. I have to get the great news to all the other villages."

"Wait a moment, little brother jackal, wait."

"But what do you see over there?"

"I see the shepherd coming, with his four dogs. Wait until they arrive, and we can all talk together."

The jackal did not wait, but began to run away.

The sheep called after him, "Little brother jackal, why are you running away?"

"Because I don't get along with shepherds or their dogs."

"You told me there is now total peace between all creatures."

"Yes, but never between jackals and dogs. Good-bye, good-bye."

17

LESSONS

IN

HISTORY

Iɴ ᴛʜᴇ ᴍᴏʀɴɪɴɢ the man named Aissa stood in a walled dirt yard barking unnecessary orders to immigrant Malians who were loading goats into the back of two Toyota pickup trucks. Dust swirled in the sunlight. The goats stood flank-to-flank so tightly packed that they had to crane their heads upward to breathe. I would like to think that from the beginning I did not trust Aissa, but the truth is I suspended judgment. He was a wiry sharp-faced man, about thirty, barefooted, in a billowing shirt and black-and-gold embroidered pants. He draped a pure white *chèche* dashingly over his shoulders, like an aviator's scarf, and wore rings on several fingers. I know now he was the type of man who would watch himself in any reflection. This morning the reflection would be me. He watched me watching, and after a suitable delay, came over to hear himself speak.

He said that later, if it still pleased him, we might visit the rock paintings of the Tadart. But first we would drive three days east to Djanet, across 500 miles of rough desert, and some of the goats would die. There would be other passengers, too—Tuaregs who spoke only Tamachek. But I did not need to worry. I would accompany Aissa in the lead truck. He told me he was an excellent driver, and also the son of a powerful man. They were a family of Chaamba Arabs, authentic nomads from the vicinity of Ouargla. I would find this fascinating. If I had any questions, he would know the answers. He spoke many languages. His close friend was the crown prince of Belgium. He had girlfriends in every major city of Italy.

We started off. The other truck was driven by Aissa's servant, a masked Tuareg of the black lower classes. His name was Abdullah. He seemed friendly, and perhaps a little stupid. He drove too close behind us, deep in Aissa's dust. Nonetheless, only an hour out of Tamanrasset, I had begun wishing for his company.

The route took us north of the Hoggar Massif, across a desert of black oxidized sand and gravel. The track was unmarked— easy to follow where it narrowed through canyons and passes, more difficult where it spread across plateaus. We passed a hamlet of stone huts. Aissa played a tape of Beethoven sonatas, and impressed himself by listening.

The wind was hot. We crossed sand dunes. Aissa asked me to notice that he rarely engaged the four-wheel drive. I admitted that he was a good driver. For a brief stretch across salt flats he hit 80 miles an hour. Abdullah lagged behind.

We stopped for lunch and a rest in the shade of a stunted acacia tree. In the afternoon we entered a desert of basins and ranges. A herd of gazelles leapt away from us. We descended and the air grew hotter. Creeping across a dry riverbed, we blew a tire. Aissa allowed Abdullah to catch up and mount the spare. The spare was flat. Abdullah inflated it with a bicycle pump.

"Don't worry," Aissa said. He held two fingers together. "This is how I am with the desert. If you love a woman, she can never hurt you. The desert is my woman."

Oh, I thought.

A goat in the back lay down to die. Aissa twisted its ears, forcing it to stand again. He seemed to take pleasure in this. He said, "As long as the goat stands, he will survive."

"Maybe he needs a drink."

"I told you not to worry."

"I don't. I won't. He's your goat."

Aissa looked hurt. I regretted my irritability. We drove on in silence. The goat died. We abandoned its carcass to the shade of thorns.

Aissa said, "You see, he lay down."

I surrendered. "You were right."

Aissa nodded. Reminded of himself, he asked, "Did you notice that I have drunk no water today?"

"Tell me," I said wearily.

"You—you drink whenever you get thirsty. I have trained myself not to, so I don't need water like you do. If we had to survive out here, I would last longer."

"I'm glad."

The day ended. The night exploded in stars. We settled on a sandy shoulder between piles of volcanic rubble. The Tuaregs walked away to say their prayers. They returned, and squatted close to the fire. Abdullah cooked a stew. Over tea, Aissa showed me snapshots of his women. "These are not all," he said. "I have thirty in France alone."

"I can only imagine."

He paused. "But I have never loved a woman."

He had composed a poem to explain why, and he recited it to me. It addressed the moon rising over the Sahara, veiled by cloud, too shy to show herself because on earth there was one person more lovely still, the only woman Aissa could love.

I asked Aissa to describe her.

He couldn't, but mentioned green eyes.

I wandered into the desert until the campfire became a flicker. The wind blew softly through the mountains. I lay rolled into a blanket, listening to the shifting sand. After the wind faded, the grains settled, and the desert became absolutely quiet. Past midnight, the cold interrupted my sleep. I huddled until dawn, absorbing the solitude.

THE TUAREGS INVADED the central Sahara from the north perhaps 3,500 years ago, and eventually established a nomadic existence based on the camel and the goat. Converted to a nominal form of Islam during the Middle Ages, they were known for the autonomy of their women, and more generally for the fierceness with which they clung to their ancient traditions. The Hoggar Mountains stood like a fortress at the center of their territory, which stretched for a thousand miles through the core of the desert. The land was wild and utterly poor, but it occupied a strategic position between the rich civilizations of black Africa and the Mediterranean. The Tuaregs survived by taking advantage of the trade that crossed it. Their isolation was a façade.

The advantage of the camel is not just that it endures drought, but that it carries heavy loads. The first camel caravans plodded through the Sahara around the time of Christ. By the Middle Ages the caravans had become large and regular. The biggest business was in salt, which was mined by slaves in dry lake beds, and hauled short distances to ports on the Niger and Senegal rivers. But for the Tuaregs the most important caravans were the long-distance ones that spanned the desert. The largest such caravans could carry as much cargo as a modern freight train: fortunes in grain, gold, ivory, and slaves for the north, and in metals, beads, and trading goods for the south.

The Tuaregs themselves were not traders. They were camel breeders, desert guides, toll collectors, bandits. They were opportunists. By siphoning wealth from the caravans, they managed to break free of the nomad's hand-to-mouth existence. They built a hierarchical society in which light-skinned aristocrats ruled over black slaves and serfs, whom they forced to settle around the wells, to cultivate their crops. The aristocrats continued to herd and to raid. They taught their sons to stand straight and tall, and to hide their faces, and treat others haughtily. They thought of themselves as noble warriors. They had a reputation as killers.

Their tactics were sly. The caravans were loose groupings of independent merchants, involving thousands of pack camels strung out unprotected for miles, lacking cohesiveness and organization. Small groups of masked Tuaregs would appear quietly out of the desert and ride along for days, searching for the weakest and most unattached members. The bandits might demand a few tributes, or small charities, but they remained generally friendly and even helpful. The caravaners knew what the Tuaregs were about, but were unwilling to assist one another. When the time was right, the Tuaregs would cut their victims out of the caravan, to rob and kill them in private. They counted on the remainder of the caravan simply to ride away. If the Tuaregs did not overreach, they could chew like this at the same caravan for weeks.

Then came the French. By the mid-nineteenth century they controlled the big oases to the north, and much of West Africa to the south. But the central Sahara remained untamed, and to the French largely unknown. The Tuaregs wanted to keep it that way, and may have believed that the French were afraid. The truth was that the French were too busy with more promising parts of the continent. In a world before cars and airplanes, the central Sahara simply remained too hard to get to. But empires abhor a void. In 1879, the French government, frustrated by British control of the lower Niger River, decided to explore the possibility of supplying its West African colonies by building a railroad directly across the desert. The man chosen to survey the route was an experienced Sahara hand, a lieutenant colonel named Paul Flatters.

Flatters led two expeditions into the central mountains. He knew about the scattered killings of lone adventurers and missionaries over the previous years, and he suspected correctly that the Tuaregs would resist the threat posed to the caravan trade by any railroad. From the start, he was afraid.

The first Flatters expedition left Ouargla in March 1880 with a hundred men, most of whom were Chaamba camel drivers. A month later, they entered the mountains, and encountered a small group of Tuareg warriors. Over the following days, the Tuaregs shadowed the surveyors, appearing and disappearing on the crests of the rising country, and spooking Flatters into the feeling that out there just beyond sight he was being surrounded. The Tuaregs had long experience in judging their enemies. In typical fashion, they entered the Flatters camp and listened to the grumbling of his native troops. They learned that Flatters was a weak and uncertain leader. When the time was right, they lined up with their shields and swords, and refused him permission to proceed farther. Flatters retreated all the way to Paris.

The next year, he left Ouargla at the head of a more heavily armed column, again of about a hundred men. This time the Tuaregs offered to serve as guides. They led Flatters deep into the desert north and east of the Hoggar Mountains. The country grew steadily drier and more difficult to cross. Days now lay between the wells and watering holes. Camels died. The Tuaregs began demanding gifts. In places the ground was dense with fresh camel prints, as if a large force of hostile riders were gathering just out of sight. But this time Flatters refused to be intimidated. He forced his way south from one well to the next.

By February 16, 1881, more than two months out of Ouargla, he knew he was in trouble. The expedition had marched several days since the last water hole, and men and camels alike were growing desperately thirsty. Now where there should have been a well, there was only dry desert. At midday the guides admitted that they had made a mistake, but said they now knew where the well lay, several hours away.

Flatters angrily ordered the expedition to make camp, and he set off immediately for the water with an advance party of five Frenchmen and twelve Chaamba soldiers and camel drivers. The other camels were to follow as soon as they were unloaded.

It was, of course, a trap. When Flatters and his companions got to the well, at the bottom of a narrow valley, two hundred sword-swinging camelmen rode down upon them. Flatters and his entire advance party were annihilated. Flush with victory, the

Tuaregs then backtracked, killed the camel drivers, who were strung out from the baggage camp to the water hole, and seized almost all of the expedition's camels.

When the men at the camp learned of the ambush, they shoved the baggage into a defensive bulwark against an attack that never materialized. That night, the fifty-nine survivors abandoned the supplies they could not carry, and began their retreat on foot.

The Tuareg followed, and picked off the stragglers. The expeditionaries found water, but no food. On the fourth day they ate their dogs. Later they killed and ate their last camels. The Tuareg toyed with the starving men. They offered them a meal of poisoned dates, which killed several. They sold them a flock of sheep, then slaughtered the soldiers sent to collect them. They taunted the men. They shot at them. They made camp within their sight, and ate well. They showed no mercy.

One month into the retreat, thirty-four Chaamba troops and one French sergeant remained alive, but barely. In desperation, they began to eat one another. They started by eating corpses, but soon turned to murder. The French press later assumed that the sergeant had resisted, as if only Africans were capable of cannibalism. The sergeant was shot and eaten late in March. On April 4, 1881, the twelve survivors arrived in Ouargla, and found that, because news travels fast in the desert, knowledge of their defeat had preceded them.

The Flatters massacre bought the Tuaregs another seventeen years of isolation. But in 1898 a large military expedition left Ouargla, marched defiantly through the Tuaregs' Hoggar homeland, and fought its way to Agadez, on the desert's southern edge. From there it went on to conquer the people of Lake

Chad, then marched south, and by late 1901 floated down the Congo River and returned to France. In all the history of the desert, nothing like this had ever been seen before. Meanwhile, north of the Hoggar Mountains In Salah fell to the French in 1900. The Tuaregs' future now was clear.

That future came in the form of a new style of colonial soldier—camel-mounted Chaambas commanded by Frenchmen, freed from the disciplines of garrison duty and encouraged to live as nomads in the open desert. A column of these soldiers left In Salah on March 23, 1902, and rode to the well at Tamanrasset. Their formal mission was to find and punish a band of camel thieves, but in practice they had Flatters and revenge in mind; they wanted to provoke the Tuaregs to come out and fight, and they did. Fifteen miles north of Tamanrasset, along a barren oued called Tit, hundreds of Tuareg warriors assembled. There are two versions of the ensuing battle. The old version envisions a desperate and heroic stand, in which outnumbered French troops managed to hold off and then defeat hundreds of fanatic rifle-bearing tribesmen. The new version wonders why the French lost only three men, and the battle-wise Tuaregs lost several hundred. It calls the battle not a battle but a massacre. This of course is the version now promoted by the Tuaregs. It should be no surprise that the modern French, who tend to romanticize the Tuaregs, are the first to agree.

The fight at Tit decimated a generation of Tuareg aristocrats. Afterward the French army effectively took control of the central Sahara. Merely three years later, in 1905, Charles de Foucauld could establish himself safely in Tamanrasset. His own killing in 1916 was an unimportant miscalculation.

The same in fact was true across the highlands in Niger called the Aïr, where a larger Tuareg rebellion broke out between 1915 and 1918. It was led by a man named Kaocen, who is still revered today by Tuareg separatists. Kaocen was armed by the Ottoman Turks in Libya. He marched on Agadez, took it, and held the town for nearly a year. Confused by his success, the French thought that he was not Tuareg at all, but rather an agent named Adolf Kraus—the German equivalent of Lawrence of Arabia. But Kaocen was an authentic Tuareg—the first to dream of a modern and independent Tuareg state. He told his followers not to trust any foreigner, whether French or Turkish. That was the easy part. But when he told the Tuaregs, on the other hand, to trust each other, he ran against the traditional disunity of the desert. Members of his own clan, the Kel Gress, were hired by the French to hunt him down. Forced to retreat to the east, Kaocen was executed by his old allies the Turks, who knew that he had betrayed them.

After World War I, the French turned their attentions again to their colonial holdings, and brutally suppressed the remnant rebellion in the Aïr, and similar Tuareg disturbances in Mali, near Gao and Timbuktu. It is said that 30,000 Tuaregs fled the central Sahara. A similar exodus has occurred in recent years. Bad memories have been awakened. Normally this would have nothing to do with me, but history in Africa lies on the land like a trap.

AISSA KNEW ALL about history. Two nights out of Tamanrasset, he said, "There is a woman behind every war."

"Behind Vietnam?"

"Madame Kennedy."

"And the Persian Gulf?"

"Ah, I'm glad you ask." He started with the birth of Mohammed, never got to the woman, and after a long discourse said, "There is much more, but I cannot tell you everything tonight. I will tell you more every night. By the time we return from the Tadart you will know enough to write a book." So I had something to look forward to.

It had been another rough day, and two more goats had died. In the afternoon we had come to the Tassili escarpment, a craggy mountain wall rising along the eastern horizon. But instead of turning toward Djanet, which now lay only a hundred miles away, we had nosed into a barren settlement of cinderblock shacks. Children ran up to us, and trotted the surviving goats off to water. Aissa told me the village was home to Abdullah, his black Tuareg driver. Abdullah's wife and children had gone off, and his windowless one-room house was empty. We went inside, and sprawled on the dirt floor to the buzzing of flies.

Abdullah kept flicking the light switch and giggling. "It's not working," he said in Arabic. I noticed that the light socket was empty. I doubted anyway whether it had been hooked up, or whether the village had a generator.

Men masked by *chèches* stooped through the doorway, slipped off their sandals, and sat with us. Abdullah knew them by the folds of their *chèches*. I had to resort to the cruder technique of watching their feet: he with the splayed toes, or the decimated nails, or the mottled skin. The children came back with a jug of water and a bowl of carrot stew. We ate. Abdullah lay along the wall and began to snore. I asked Aissa the name of this place, and he answered nastily that it had none. The air was stale. I went outside into the afternoon sunlight, and walked through the settlement. The children followed silently, stopping when I stopped. I could not get them to smile. The settlement was treeless, relentless, dismal. It had an open well with a bucket and a hand-crank, and a vegetable patch where carrots grew. I found our goats perched on rubble in a ruined yard. I wanted to drive on for Djanet, but accepted my fate when the sun fell and darkness softly settled.

We walked into the desert to cook dinner in the dunes. With wood scavenged earlier, we built a fire. Abdullah made the unleavened bread called *tagela,* by kneading water from a goatskin into flour, forming the dough into a circular loaf, burying it in sand by the fire, and shoving hot embers over the top to bake it. After about an hour he dug it up, and with a knife began the slow ritual of scraping and banging the sand from its crust. Baking and scraping *tagela* occupies many nights in the open Sahara; it marks the tedium of desert time. You simmer a sauce while waiting. When most of the sand has come off, you pull the *tagela* apart and shred its hot flesh into the pot. You rinse your fingers in goatskin water, then use them to eat from a communal bowl. If there is meat, someone throws fatty scraps one at time onto your little pile of food. You chew slowly through the gristle.

Toward the end of our meal, an old nomad in a bulky *chèche* came out of the darkness to join us, and Aissa introduced him rather stupidly as a "master of the desert." The man was tall and light-skinned, and had the erect bearing of a Tuareg noble. He wore a dagger. His hand, which I shook, was as cracked and hardened as a hoof. He spoke a little French, but used Tamachek to name a confusion of stars.

In the morning we loaded the goats back into the trucks and drove across a sand sea called Admer. The dunes were 300 feet high. I noticed again Aissa's aggression, and his skill in driving. He assaulted the slopes, jamming the truck at full throttle up each dune, counting on momentum to carry him across the crests, and gravity to pull him down the steep slip faces. Never did he get stuck. Abdullah worked more cautiously, relying on the four-wheel drive to crawl across the dunes, hesitating on the crests, sometimes bogging down.

Finally we got to Djanet, a town at 3,600 feet built on terraces above a dry riverbed. Aissa had business there, which would take a few days. Afterward, he and Abdullah would together, for the price of one, drive me south into the Tadart. I took a room at the Djanet hotel and settled down to wait. Having endured one trip with Aissa, I guessed I would endure another.

I should have made different arrangements. The Tassili plateau, rising to 7,000 feet just east of Djanet, is a greater repository for rock art than the Tadart, and less risky. It holds 400,000 Neolithic paintings and engravings in a national park the size of Yellowstone. The Tadart lies farther from Djanet, and offers less. But that is precisely why I wanted to go there—because the Tadart is the desert's desert.

And Djanet was a pleasant place to wait. Built of pale stone, the town scaled steep valley walls above a green palm grove. On one hill stood the ruins of a fort from which the Tuaregs had once driven a small French garrison. On another hill stood a whitewashed mansion with a satellite dish—an old presidential retreat, still maintained. There was an airport ten miles out of town. Along the shady main street, Tuaregs and Arabs mixed easily with immigrants from the south. At the market, long-distance Saharan trucks nestled under trees.

Outside the small army base, soldiers relaxed between desert patrols. Their responsibilities included policing the remote borders with Libya and Niger. They drove groups of battered Land Rovers years past normal retirement. I saw Soviet-made helicopters flying in loose formation. At the shaded café I heard talk of a skirmish somewhere the week before. Smugglers, Tuareg separatists, Islamic revolutionaries—I knew enough not to ask. The storytelling did not worry me. I've heard lots of it. I thought Djanet swaggered like other border towns.

WHEN WE LEFT Djanet, Abdullah drove, and Aissa sat beside him in the front of the pickup truck. I crouched on the jump seat in the truck's extended cab. The hot desert air blew forward through the sliding rear window. In the back we carried supplies under tarpaulins—blankets, food, a shovel, a spare tire, jerricans of fuel and water.

South of Djanet we followed the well-worn track to Libya through a desert of scattered acacias. We were stopped by an army patrol driving a Land Rover in the opposite direction. It was like a meeting of friends on a small-town street: no one bothered to get out. We handed our identity cards to the driver, who handed them across to the sergeant, who was surprised to find an American passport, and said something about Dallas, by which he meant the television show. I smiled. Abdullah acted obsequious. The sergeant asked Aissa where we were going, and why. Aissa answered that I was an important scholar interested in the rock art of the Tadart.

Later, I asked him why he lied. He said, "Because the army thinks all reporters are spies." But Aissa lied because he liked to.

We spent the hottest midday hours in a canyon by a spring where Tuareg nomads had made camp. Their tents were dark and low-slung, made of animal skins and burlap. The nomads had camels and goats and an old Land Cruiser with a faded tourist agency emblem on the door. Clothes hung from the trees. When we arrived, the women ducked out of sight, pulling the youngest children after them. The men were tall and thin, and wore *chèches* of course. They strode up swinging their arms, and stood with their heads held back looking down their aristocratic noses. One wore wraparound sunglasses and a digital watch. They invited us to sit with them in the shade of a tarpaulin stretched between two acacias. We shared our fruit and bread. They built a fire for tea. Their talk was spare, and in Tamachek. I realized with a start that one of them was the old master of the desert from the village without a name. He gave no sign of recognition now. The younger men deferred to him. Children escaped from their tents and came over to watch the strangers. The goats bleated. The high sun passed. We left the camp and drove south and east, across rough ground, locked into four-wheel drive.

The most surprising characteristic of the Sahara is the speed with which it changes. Here is the desert of just that one afternoon: pink and yellow dunes, blue craggy cliffs, black volcanic rubble, gravel plains, gray boulders half-buried in sand, an eroded gulch, two dry rivers, a cone, a canyon, many badlands. The track we followed forked, faded, and disappeared.

At night we made camp on a mesa. I asked to whom the land belonged. Abdullah looked at me blankly. Aissa said, "It belongs to no one. It belongs to the government. It belongs to God." We contemplated this for a while. He said, "There is often no government, but God is everywhere."

Even then he was not honest. There are various reasons not to believe in God, but Aissa's was the most selfish. At the age of thirty he was still his father's pet, and far too spoiled to submit to any higher authority. As a Saharan he could not admit this, of course, but religion was external. He kept revealing himself unintentionally.

I made a vicious sport of asking questions. Abdullah had the servant's habit of answering in the affirmative. Aissa had the opposite habit.

Were these sands made by water? No, by winds.

Were they made by winds? No, by water.

He could not help himself. If I wanted to stop, I suggested we go; if I wanted to go, I suggested we stop. And because Aissa was not stupid, he began to resent me for it.

He was a terrible braggart, pathologically unable to admit weakness or failure. Even when he appeared to admit a fault, it was only to brag again. Two days from Djanet he said, "I am a very cruel person."

I heard the implied threat, but couldn't tell if Aissa himself was aware of it. The night before he had pulled a .45 caliber pistol from his robe, and on a blanket by the fire, had cleaned it and checked the loading. Abdullah had giggled. The joke was on the army sergeant, who would have arrested us had he known. I asked Aissa how he planned to use the gun. He smiled and said, "To protect you from bandits."

When Aissa said he was cruel, he meant he was strong. He told me a story about family life back in Ouargla. "I have a little brother who is only six. One day a cat scratched him. It was a small scratch, but my little brother cried. Me, I took the cat and, like this, I snapped her neck. Then I took my brother and said, 'Now you see little brother, do not cry.'"

We came to the Tadart's entrance—a searing canyon that cut and turned through a scorched plateau. It was noon. Leaving the truck on the canyon floor, we climbed searing rocks to a prehistoric painting of a four-headed woman, and beyond, to scenes of copulation and hunting. In the shade of an overhang we drank warm goat milk heavy with fat, and chewed a mix of crushed dates and bitter desert herbs. The canyon was yellow and brown and violently bright, and so infernally hot that the winds blew upward and sand dunes mounted the walls to escape.

The rock art reminded Aissa of women. He said, "In 1992 in the United States, scientists discovered that exercise is bad for women. I could have told them that."

I laughed.

He didn't like that. He asked about the American women I knew.

"They still exercise," I said.

Aissa hated them for it. He said, "Someday you will introduce me. I will ravage them. I will make them beg for my love."

I doubted it.

THE SAHARA HAS not always been such a desert. Over the course of geological history, it has gone through wet spells that transformed it into woodland and savanna. *Homo erectus* first arrived during one of these spells, maybe 500,000 years ago, while following game north from the Niger River, or east from the Nile, or both. By 100,000 years ago, the center was inhabited by people living in small groups, hunting abundant game, scattering bones and stone tools widely about. The desert returned later as it had returned before, sometimes convincingly. The timing remains uncertain. Perhaps 50,000 years ago, a fishing

village stood near present-day Djanet, on the lake that left the sands of Erg Admer.

The haze begins to clear about 8000 B.C., at the height of the last great wet spell. Lake Chad, which is today mostly swamp, was an immense inland sea that reached to the Niger River and emptied into the Bight of Benin. At the core of the Sahara, the Hoggar Mountains were forested with oak, walnut, and elm, and the Tassili was forested with pine. To the south, the land descended into the rich grasslands of an African savanna. The Tadart teemed with wildlife. Rivers flowed through its canyons.

A culture flowered. Artists began to paint and etch the rocks. The largest of their images stood fifteen feet high. The artists imagined gods with round heads, and drew a Sahara roamed by African mammals—giraffe, elephant, rhinoceros, hippopotamus, zebra, buffalo, wart hog, and antelope. Catfish, perch, and turtles swam in the lakes. Crocodiles idled in the rivers. The people hunted on foot, with spears and bows and arrows. They made pottery, lived in villages, and buried their dead. They hoed the grassland and ground its grains. They did not farm.

Around 5000 B.C., a new people of obscure origins arrived. They were long-bodied herders of cattle, possibly from the distant mountains of Ethiopia. They introduced the finest period in Saharan art, the Bovine, characterized by its graceful depictions of a pastoral life. It seems likely that they were the ancestors of today's Fulani nomads, herders of the Sahel: the similarities extend beyond bone structures to include details of hair-weavings, clothes, and village construction. These herders had a long stay in the central Sahara. The period from 4000 B.C. to 2500 B.C., roughly contemporary to the Old Kingdom of Egypt, has been called the Golden Age of Saharan pastoralism.

THE CATTLE HERDING was so successful that it spread south from the mountains. Speculation that the herdsmen invited the desert through overgrazing is unfair. Older and larger climatic forces were at work. Around 2000 B.C., the weather simply shifted. A dryness settled tentatively across the Saharan lowlands, and crept into the mountains, and slowly deepened. There were years then as now when the rains returned and the vegetation thickened. But the desert was on its way.

You might expect people not to have noticed such gradual impoverishment. But these people lived surrounded by their art, the now-ancestral celebrations of a bountiful land: etchings scarred the rocks for hundreds of miles; paintings endured in the indelible burnt-orange of laterite and iron oxide. The old creations must have forced people to confront their loss. Did they fight each other, hunt witches, find new ways to pray? It made no difference anyway. The lakes and rivers shrank. The big wild animals drifted south. On a cliffside near Djanet, someone drew a weeping cow, which still looks like a declaration from the end of time.

Around 1500 B.C., with the drying-out well under way, a race of light-skinned Berber warriors invaded from the north. They drove chariots pulled by galloping horses, and soon became the masters of the central Sahara. Eventually they gave up chariots for the horse and saddle. They made their own drawings celebrating strength and aggression—key attributes for success in the deepening desert. These warriors were ancestors of the Tuaregs.

Not all of the original herders fled the desert. Those who remained became the Tuaregs' serfs, the original Haratins. Over more than 3,000 years, they never freed themselves from their captivity. Black African captives mixed with them at the bottom of a rigid Tuareg hierarchy based on skin color. By the mid-nineteenth century, 90 percent of central Saharan society was made up of black serfs who were permanently excluded from a true Tuareg identity. This is the traditional society that today is too easily idealized. The concept of equality came from the outside—from Islam and later from Europe—but it never thrived here. The Tuareg aristocrats did not need to rule oppressively because their serfs refused to rebel.

I saw it in the Tadart. Abdullah was a serf at heart. He had the sympathy of a prisoner for his guard, and seemed to like taking orders from a man like Aissa. He was a Tuareg, but a Tuareg in confusion. Days from Djanet, despite my objections Aissa ordered him to unwind his *chèche* for me. Abdullah did, and grinned about it. His face surprised me. He had long uncombed hair framing wide cheeks, flared nostrils, a sparse mustache, and buck teeth—the features not of a Berber or a Fulani, but strangely like those of an Australian aborigine. The episode unsettled me. Aissa watched with satisfaction. He wanted to demonstrate that Abdullah would do his bidding.

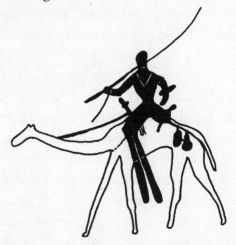

THE CAMEL FIRST came to the Tuaregs as a domesticated beast of burden. The short story of its journey starts in America with the Eocene rabbit-sized Protylopus, whose descendants crossed the Bering Strait and evolved into an early cold-climate camel, probably two-humped, that subsequently spread across Asia and into North Africa. This prehistoric camel was a shy and defenseless animal that lived in brushland, and relied for survival

on its ability to roam far from the watering holes of its predators. Apparently this strategy was not good enough. In a Sahara
also roamed by lions, wild dogs, and early human hunters,
camels became extinct sometime before the first rock paintings.
It seems likely that the species faced similar extinction throughout the Middle East. One branch may have retreated north into
the cool isolation of Iran and central Asia, where it evolved into
the two-humped, long-haired camel that lives there today. The
more important branch seems to have retreated into corners of
the Arabian Peninsula, where an intensifying desert protected it
from its predators. Over time it developed into the short-haired,
light-colored, one-humped animal capable of enduring ex-
tremes of heat and, to a lesser extent, of drought.

Camels do not store water in their humps. They drink furiously, up to twenty-eight gallons in a ten-minute session, then
distribute the water evenly throughout their bodies. Afterward,
they use the water stingily. They have viscous urine and dry
feces. They breathe through their noses, and keep their mouths
shut. They do sweat, but only as a last resort, after first allowing
their body temperatures to rise 10 degrees Fahrenheit. As they
begin to dehydrate, the volume of their blood plasma does not
at first diminish. They can survive a water loss of up to one-
third of their body weight, then drink up and feel fine. Left
alone, unhurried and unburdened, they can live two weeks between drinks.

Protected from predation by the Arabian desert, the wild
camel was relatively docile. Around 2000 B.C., Arabian nomads
began to tame it for its milk and meat. Later they got the idea of
riding it, and better yet, of using it to carry their cargoes. Do-
mestication of the camel eventually spawned changes of the

most dramatic kind. It shifted power from the cities to the desert, brought wealth and prominence to the nomad, and because of the desert mobility the camel provided, it helped give rise to Islam.

In fact the Arabian camel was so successful that in time it supplanted horses and ox-drawn wagons through most of the Middle East and North Africa. Across a wide swath of the earth, it replaced the wheel. In his pioneering exploration of this subject, *The Camel and the Wheel* (Harvard Press, 1975), Columbia historian Richard W. Bulliet explained why. He wrote that a camel can carry nearly as much as a wagon, but breaks down less often. A wagon is pulled by two oxen and requires a driver. Worse yet, a wagon rolls on wheels, which require roads, which must be built and then maintained. Pack camels walk in strings, on paths or open ground. They climb mountains, cross sand dunes, progress thirty miles a day, eat sparingly, drink deeply, don't fear the dark, respond to whippings, and live long lives. They can't offer riders the speed and impact of a battle horse, but then battle horses can't stand the hard desert. And camels do gallop.

Bulliet is a camel proponent, but also always fair. He explains why the camel never flourished beyond its natural range, and he makes the point that even within Arabia its advantages became apparent only slowly. The problem was the hump, which is made of fat and cannot bear a load. For over a thousand years, the saddles went on behind the hump, because the first camels did not have enough space in front. But the rear was weak and wobbly. The solution, engineered in north Arabia several centuries before Christ, was a new kind of saddle that straddled the camel's hump with a frame of inverted V's. By moving forward off the rear end, it provided the rider with a high, comfortable ride, and a stable perch from which to swing a sword and thrust a spear. More important, by distributing the weight, the new saddle allowed the camel to carry heavier packs. This was the saddle that defeated the wheel.

The wheel was already in decline. On the fringes of the Roman Empire the roads were not being well maintained. And since chariots had been surpassed in war by mounted horsemen, the wheel had lost its luster. Nonetheless, only in the land of the camel did the wheel actually disappear. With few exceptions, the Middle East and North Africa became wheel-less societies. The banishment was so complete that in some of the Saharan oases even the memory of the wheel was lost.

When the new camel technology arrived in the Saharan highlands, around the time of Christ, the Tuaregs seized on it first for its military uses. In the extreme desert climate, fierce horsemen could become even fiercer camelmen. The match was so good that the Tuaregs soon became the world's greatest camelmen. For riding and making war, they bred the ultimate camel, the mehari, a tall, thin animal with a back so long they could put their riding saddles *before* the hump. This placed the warriors low, within the upper reach of an opposing horseman, but improved the camel's handling.

The Tuaregs still love their camels. When they ride them they nestle their bare feet against the camel's neck, and direct them with gentle pressures. They speak tenderly to them and brag about owning those that are fast and white and beautiful. They are camel romantics. But even they must suspect that the camel is obsolete. Again the rocks tell the desert's story; interspersed among the ancient drawings are newer ones, of trucks and automobiles. The Tuaregs now forge their swords from the good steel springs of Toyotas. They idealize the past, but fight in four-wheel drive. The chariot has returned with a vengeance.

IN THE TADART we worked through an uncharted desert of sculpted buttes and blowing sand. We climbed to rock paintings, hid in caves from the noon sun, slept under the bright stars. Aissa navigated purposefully. When we came across tire tracks he got out to study them, and called them old, an army patrol's. They put him in a good humor. He said he would take me to a real Sahara where even nomads do not go. I accepted. It lay in hidden valleys choked by dunes too soft and steep for Abdullah's driving. With bare hands we dug the truck through. By evening we drove into a gray, rock-strewn moonscape. At the head of a canyon, under black walls, we stopped to make camp. Aissa and Abdullah abandoned me there.

It happened this way: we unloaded blankets and some food, a jerrican of water and a jerrican of fuel. Aissa said they would search for more wood, and they drove away. Night came. After an hour I walked to a promontory, and looked out into the darkness of the lower canyon, and saw no headlights. After three hours I realized something had gone wrong.

I thought the truck might have broken down or had a flat. How far would they have driven in search of wood? They had food and water of their own, and would probably wait for day-light before making repairs. I wrapped myself in a blanket, and lay thinking late into the night.

The Sahara's silence engulfed me. The sky slid slowly by. I dozed until a wind drove sand into my face, returning me to the desert. I felt strong and clear-minded. Carefully, I thought through the previous days—the fragmented conversations, the changing moods, the boasts and veiled threats. The truck was too new to have broken down. I remembered one of Aissa's stories, a lesson he had taught his young brother.

"Who am I?" Aissa asked him.

"Aissa," his brother answered.

"No. *Who am I?*"

"I don't know," his brother said.

"That's true, little brother. And you cannot know."

But I knew. Enough almost to pity him. Aissa was an unlucky fellow, not stupid, but addled and greedy. He was a killer. I think he had wanted to be my friend.

I knew now why he had agreed to drive me here, and why he had driven away. What better reason for wandering the Sahara than the pursuit of art and history? Aissa had confused me by accepting payment, and I had served him perfectly. For what he had to do now, I would have been an embarrassment. Because I might serve him again, I figured he intended to return. But this was a dangerous business, and with every hour my chances diminished. By dawn I was angry.

The sun drove me onto the canyon wall, into the shade of overhanging rock. From my perch I spent the morning looking beyond the lower canyon into the endless desert of sand and stone. Nothing moved. Under other circumstances the isolation might have seemed interesting, but it did not seem that way to me now. After all the warnings this desert had given me, after all I had written, I had allowed it to trap me. Worse still, I had gone out of my way to get here. The Sahara is not a natural destination, and it never will be. A writer writes about it, as a reader reads about it, to satisfy his curiosity about an unseen part of the world. Imagine abandoning life for no better reason. If the Sahara killed me, I would die stupidly. By afternoon, I had to face that possibility, and it surprised me.

About such strandings, Salah Addoun had at various times said to me:

"When you break down, you have to be calm, because the desert is calm."

"Tourists panic and drive aimlessly. They are afraid of the lion before the lion."

"When you are lost, you should sit. Wait. One hour, two hours, a full day. Sit. You will find your orientation."

He was right. By pushing other thoughts aside, I found I could patch together the route we had taken from Djanet. I thought in theory I could reverse it through the maze of the Tadart. So technically, maybe I was not lost.

The problem as always was drought. I had nearly thirty gallons of water, but could not expect to walk out carrying even half of that. Fifteen gallons weigh 120 pounds. From reading Edward Adolph, author of the classic *Physiology of Man in the Desert* (1947), I knew that any water I could shoulder would more than compensate for the additional sweat it demanded. Nonetheless, a person is not a camel. Walking by day, carrying as much as a strong man can carry, I might make 30 miles before collapsing. Walking by night I would triple that distance only to lose my way. Djanet lay more than 200 miles away, and the Tuaregs' springs almost as far. Fight as I might, the desert would overwhelm me. I could almost smile about it. I thought again of Addoun. "For every man there are two times that are inescapable—the time of birth and the time of death." If by tomorrow Aissa had not returned, I might get around to calculating mine.

The alternative to walking was, of course, to stay put and hope for rescue. In the shade of this overhang, with afternoon air temperatures rising to 110 degrees, I might make the water last several weeks, and after it ran out, survive perhaps another two days. But I knew already the horror of such passivity, the helpless anticipation of death by thirst. Saharans have the comfort of God, but even they may lack the courage to endure the suffering.

A friend of Addoun's died during one of my earlier trips to Tamanrasset. He was a young trader working alone, without the money yet to afford a reliable vehicle. I remember a thin, shy man with a face like a boy's. He drove the desert as far as Niger and Mali in an old Peugeot sedan. The car broke down often— he was used to fixing it. But the last time, only a hundred miles from Tamanrasset, the engine seized. His friends in Tamanrasset later wondered how long he had lasted. They believed in the end he drank gasoline. That much was normal. His body was discovered by passing truckers. The corpse was unusual because it was burned.

The next evening I had met with Addoun and others, and had suggested that their friend had preferred self-immolation to the final stages of thirst. The Saharans disagreed. Their friend was a religious man, and would never have killed himself. Suicide is immoral not because of the sanctity of life, but because it appears to preempt fate and God himself. They insisted instead that he had made an innocent mistake. Crazed by thirst, with gasoline on his breath, he had lit a cigarette. The fire had burned him from the inside. And that was his fate.

I must have looked skeptical. Addoun said, "He was alone in the desert. He had no water. In the end he understood his destiny. Why would he kill himself? He had no more worries."

Nonetheless, I decided in the Tadart to burn my fuel before I finished the water. I had matches in my pocket. The fuel was diesel, which is presumably less thirst-quenching than gasoline. I would burn it off slowly, starting in the morning, by soaking it into sand and feeding a small fire. The fire would smudge the sky. I did not imagine that I would be found. If Aissa had left an itinerary in Djanet, he had left a false one. Nor was anyone likely to happen by. I was stranded, not by chance, in the Sahara's most uninviting corner.

In the afternoon, I drank deeply. The water was hot. I swirled it in a cup, and admired its beauty. By evening I had decided on my course. I would wait in this canyon, burning the fuel, drinking the excess water, eating enough to stay strong. I would fashion a backpack, and experiment with water loads. I would write long good-byes to my wife and to my children. And when the only water remaining was the amount I could carry, I would set off to the northwest, hoping not for Djanet, but for nomads, or an army patrol, or a spring, or a well. My chances were small, but I would walk at night and keep walking until I died. I am not a patient man. The certainty that I would leave this canyon elated me. Addoun once said to me, "As you believe in life, you must also believe in death." I agreed, for once like a Saharan. But the mood did not last; late into the night I remembered the tears of my children.

THEN AISSA AND Abdullah returned. I heard the growl of an engine, and saw the headlights approaching. Too angry to feel relieved, I melted into the blackness of the canyon and watched. They parked by the campsite, made a fire, ate, and slept. At dawn I went to them. They lay by the ashes, with blankets over their legs. A tarpaulin held in place by deadwood covered the truck's cargo bed. The situation remained dangerous. I let my anger show through.

"You found your firewood," I said.

"We got lost," Aissa answered.

I shook my head. "Where have you been?"

"Oh, you know, out there somewhere." He smirked and waved his hand toward the desert.

Abdullah giggled.

Furiously, I told Aissa to stand. An emotion like hatred flitted across his face. We walked away from Abdullah. Controlling my anger, I said, "No more lies, Aissa."

"You're right. A man does not abandon his friends." He apologized insincerely.

"I want you to tell me how far into Libya we've come."

He smiled and never gave me an answer.

I have gone over the maps since, and still I don't know.

My ignorance reminded Aissa of his power. He said, "Are you sure you're not a spy? I should warn Abdullah."

I told him not to threaten me.

Abdullah fueled the truck and loaded it. We dug across the dunes, and in the afternoon headed northwest toward Djanet by a new route. We drove for days. We lingered over a few rock paintings, because even ignoring them would have brought too much into the open between us. Aissa still needed my help. If we encountered an army patrol, I would again serve as his excuse. This went unsaid. We kept a sharp eye out. The mood kept getting tenser.

Nights, beside the cooking fires, Aissa bragged about smuggling black Africans into Libya, and spoke about a newer business in automatic weapons. He spoke about the Tuareg rebellion, and the Islamic revolution. He said my government would be interested in such information. I answered that my government did not care, but I could no more shed my nationality than a man can escape his skin.

Abdullah giggled stupidly, but he had changed, and seemed less the serf. Aissa kept coming back to spies. He said, "You can lie among vipers, and they will not strike you unless you move in your sleep." I detested him.

One day we joined a track that led across gravel plains to a lonely well. The well had a stone and cement casing, a bucket with a rope, and no lid. The water lay about fifty feet down, dimly reflecting the brightness of the sky. No drowned bird marred its surface. Abdullah dropped the bucket, let it fill, and harvested a crop that was clear and cool. We drank, replenished the jerricans and goatskin waterbags, and poured bucketfuls over our heads. We drank again. We drove on.

The last afternoon, in a waterless valley speckled with thorn trees, we came upon goats, and then again upon the Tuareg nomads. They had moved their camp and were expecting us. The women slipped away. I recognized the old master of the desert, and some of the children. Abdullah had changed into his finest robes, and was in a proud and happy humor. Aissa tried to distract me with chatter about the Sahara, but ran out of things to say. At such close quarters there was no way to keep the transaction from me. From behind the seat in the extended cab, Abdullah unloaded boxes of ammunition. Then he went to the back, threw the firewood to the ground, peeled back the tarpaulins, and handed down the cargo—a dozen Kalashnikov assault rifles.

I don't know why there were so few rifles. The rebel Tuaregs say they are fighting to make an independent nation of the central Sahara—an idea so obviously impractical that a dozen rifles may actually be the measure of it. But the rifles may also have been a sample of a larger order to come. Either way, I saw that the acquisition was important to the Tuaregs. And Aissa saw that I saw.

I had served my purpose. We drove toward Djanet, only twenty miles to the north. We did not speak. The atmosphere in the pickup was deadly. Abdullah had sobered. Aissa seemed lost in thought. I sat forward on the backseat, and watched his hands, alert for any move toward his pistol. I calculated my chances of breaking his neck, which were small. But we came to the paved road between Djanet and its airport, and drove smoothly into town.

I took a room at the hotel, and in the morning bought a ride with livestock traders hauling goats to Tamanrasset. I recognized one of the goats as an animal that Aissa had brought to Djanet. The traders smiled about this, and we agreed that it is in the nature of business. We had a pleasant two-day trip across the Hoggar Mountains. We listened to tapes of the Koran. We stopped often to water the goats, all of whom survived.

In Tamanrasset I stayed with Salah Addoun, and never mentioned Aissa. We dined again with the merchant Moulay Lakhdar Abderhadim, who asked about the trip he had arranged. What did I think of the Tadart?

I answered that it was beautiful.

Abderhadim beamed, and offered to find a similar ride for my continuing trip south along the Trans-Saharan to Niger.

I thanked him and said that I had already made arrangements to travel by more public transport—two large trucks exporting dates to Agadez.

Addoun named the drivers.

Abderhadim looked satisfied. He predicted that the ride would be safe because of all the travelers who would accompany such a convoy. Trips to the south were unfortunately no longer frequent. He asked me if I knew of the Tuareg trouble, because he forgot that we had mentioned it before.

18

YAZID'S

DESERT

THE CHIEF JUDGE of Tamanrasset was a young and soft-spoken moralist who was widely feared. His name was Moulay Yazid. He shaved closely, and dressed in slacks and pressed shirts. Citizens cringed before him. They fawned over him. A lesser Saharan would have savored the power, and profited by it. But not Yazid, who resisted all temptation. He had read widely, and had traveled, and had learned to understand himself in a world larger than his surroundings. He was strong not because of his power but despite it.

He may have been the most educated man in Tamanrasset. He spoke Arabic, French, English, Spanish, and a bit of Tamachek. He woke up early every morning, and worked hard all day. He did not go home at midday, and did not take naps, and rarely relaxed. We became friends, and spent late nights talking about the larger world. In a desert confused by conspiracist simplicities about the functioning of power, he recognized the limits to it.

When he said, "There has never been a bad American president," he meant that the worst ones had been checked by the Constitution. He mentioned ruefully that the same had not been true for the nations of the Sahara.

I never met Yazid's wife, but knew his two young children, a boy and a girl, who reminded me of my own. They climbed on him joyfully. He spoiled them, and saw in them a reflection of himself. He said, "I would never want them to become judges. There is no peace for a judge. You see how hard it is for me."

The tension was inside him. We brewed tea alone in the desert, and even there he could not find peace. He could not shut off his thoughts. He said, "If someday you commit a crime, remember what I say. Do not run into the desert. Do not try to hide in the Sahara."

He would have been happier as a professor than a judge. He grew up in In Salah, and was a bright boy, and went off to the university in Algiers, and as a law student chose the judiciary track in a legal system that afterward offered him no change of mind. He requested a position in the Sahara, and was sent to Tamanrasset. He was required to join the ruling party, and for years he had to attend weekly party meetings, where he saw firsthand the venality of the government he was bound to defend. By the time I met him, he had long stopped attending the meetings. So great was his scorn that he could barely bring himself to speak in full sentences about the men in power. He had retreated to the bench, to which he felt bound by an abstract duty to society. He made no secret of his disdain for the military dictatorship, and yet no secret of his disdain for Islamic law, the sharia, proposed by the revolutionaries. He refused the political cases—few of which made it into the court system anyway. He worked alone or with a panel of junior judges, and accepted his responsibilities because he believed abstractly in law, more now than ever.

Citizens were accused. Yazid pondered their dossiers, listened to their arguments, released a few, and found the others guilty. Their crimes ranged from murder to theft, and were rarely interesting. He condemned some of the criminals to death, some to long imprisonment, and most to shorter terms. By the standards of a tough country, he sentenced them fairly. He knew about conditions in the Tamanrasset jail, where prisoners peered from dark openings in the walls, and even the street reeked of their excrement. He said he did not want to sentence people to such a place, but had no choice. It was his burden.

He said, "The desert looks big, but it is not. It's a village, small and up-close. You end up judging your neighbors. You end up judging your friends."

I asked him why he didn't leave.

He answered with a practical question. "Where would I go? What would I do?" He had a family to support.

One day he invited me on an official errand. We were driven by the chief of police in a government Land Cruiser with blue lights, a two-way radio, and a siren. The chief had a bushy mustache, a uniform, and a peaked cap. I called him Bronson because when we met he stuck his thumb up and said, "I should have been born an American. Char-les Bronson is number one."

Yazid gazed out the side window at the passing buttes and mountains. We drove south from Tamanrasset and came to a settlement of black African refugees, where Yazid had ordered the municipal government to drill a well; he wanted to see that the work had been done, and that water indeed was flowing.

Bronson disapproved, on principle. He hated these southern blacks. "They've brought AIDS to the Sahara. It's a very serious problem. Already we have had a dozen cases in Tamanrasset. Do you know how they got AIDS originally? AIDS is a monkey's disease. It's proof that Malians perform acts against nature."

Yazid waved him on impatiently.

Bronson refused to be denied. With a practiced burst of his siren, he pulled up beside a group of refugees sitting on an embankment. They stood nervously. Bronson walked over to them and demanded identity papers. Through the open windows, I heard him trying to intimidate them. He spoke in French, and said something about "*le juge,*" and something about "*l'Américain.*"

The refugees seemed afraid.

Yazid looked angry and embarrassed.

The refugees had papers with legitimate Algerian visas. Bronson was disappointed, and got back in the car. He would have liked to arrest the refugees, or have them deported, killed, or enslaved. But not in front of the judge Yazid, who would have found some way to make trouble for him.

We drove to a homestead far down an *oued,* where an old man named Moulay Tayeb had built a small vegetable farm. At age eighty-four, Tayeb no longer bothered even to come to the market in town and had made a life for himself away from the silliness of society. Yazid said he loved him as a student loves a teacher, and he visited him once a week to remind himself of the desert. He wanted me to understand: to be in Tayeb's presence was enough. He had Bronson wait by the car.

Tayeb lived in an unwalled compound of mud-brick houses, which he had built on a rise above the *oued.* His Tuareg wife, unveiled and handsome, was forty years his junior. She welcomed Yazid fondly and offered us a drink of cool water before directing us to the field where Tayeb was working.

The fields lay in a string down one side of the *oued,* in swatches of melons, potatoes, onions, eggplants. Lines of orange trees and date palms formed windbreaks. We found Tayeb cleaning an irrigation channel with a hoe. He was a tall, thin man in robes and a turban. He had a white beard, high cheekbones, and penetrating eyes. Yazid kissed his cheeks. I shook his hand. Because he was nearly deaf, we had to yell to make ourselves heard. His voice was strong and clear. He had fought in Libya for Mussolini, and spoke broken French and good Italian.

Standing in his field, looking me squarely in the face, he said, "I came here in 1967, when there was nothing. After nine wives, after seven sons, after ten daughters, after thirteen years at war, after sixteen years hiding in Niger, I came home with nothing. But for the man who considers himself dead in war, everything afterward is a gift. God intended this home for me. I dug the first well on seven October. I built the first house. I dug the first fields. I took a Tuareg wife, a good woman. You have met her, so you know already. She gave me a son, who is now twenty-six. I will introduce you. My son is a great gazelle hunter. He will take you hunting. He raises chickens not for the eggs but for the meat. He has four hundred chickens. Five chicks were born last night. Yazid has told me about you. You have a son, too. Did you bring a picture? Come, we will make tea." He shouldered the hoe and started walking.

I smiled at Yazid.

Yazid said, "He has a mind so sharp, he remembers suckling his mother's breast. He is the greatest man I know."

We spent the afternoon with him. He was virile, and vital, and undiminished by age. His son, the gazelle hunter, joined us. He was soft-spoken. We ate together, and made tea. I thought: these people are part of a Sahara we would all like to find, a place like a dream. I could see why Yazid escaped to them.

But Yazid did not see it as an escape. That evening during the drive to Tamanrasset, he said, "In his entire life Tayeb left the desert only once, for two weeks in Italy during the war. He won't live much longer. But I will think of him."

I had asked him why he didn't leave, and he had been chewing on the question ever since. Tayeb was again an answer. Yazid was not the type to boast about his desert bloodline, but he wanted me to know that his sense of kinship with such a man mattered to him. The desert offered him frustration, but richness as well. He meant to admonish me. Yazid and I were equals, men of the same age born into different circumstances, and he did not want my sympathy.

19

A DOOR

IN THE

DESERT

SALAH ADDOUN HAD arranged my passage south with
the two trucks hauling dates down the Trans-Saharan 600 miles
to Agadez, Niger, but now I had to wait. The trucks were battered Berliets with years of the desert on them. They stood
empty like abandoned wrecks near the Tamanrasset camel market. Day after day, I heard rumors that soon they would depart.
Then one hot afternoon word came that they had loaded and
started their engines.

Salah Addoun came to see me off. He introduced me to the
chief driver, a bearded man with a permanently amused expression, whose name was Ali. He wore stained trousers, a ragged
shirt, and no shoes. Addoun had told me that Ali was the best,
that he practically lived in the desert. He was a trader as well as
a driver; the trucks and their cargoes belonged to him. The
trucks were piled high with low-quality export dates in burlap
sacks.

Ali expected me to act like a reporter. From the way he stood and waited, I saw that he expected to be interviewed. Not to disappoint him, I asked what he would bring back from Agadez on the return trip.

Ali looked at Addoun. He looked at me. He answered, "Chickens."

I had a pad, and wrote it down. I asked him for his full name. He took the pad and printed it carefully in block letters.

I later learned that he wanted to be asked larger questions. The future of the Russian republic was his favorite subject. So he was disappointed with the interview, and assigned me to the other driver's truck. I never did catch the other driver's name. He was a gaunt Tuareg, who spoke no French and little Arabic. It didn't matter anyway, since I would ride in the back, crouched on top of the cargo with the other passengers.

The judge Yazid came to say good-bye and to tell Ali to treat me well. I was embarrassed by the attention. Addoun disappeared into the market. Yazid and I stood together, enduring the awkwardness of departure. Addoun returned with a *chèche* against the sun and dust, a blanket for the nights, and a sack of oranges to share with the passengers. On my truck there were ten: itinerant Tuaregs and black Africans—workers, traders, and refugees, men heading home. They peered down at me from atop the cargo. I threw my suitcase to them and climbed up after it. They made room. We did not talk.

There was drama to the departure. The engines rumbled. The drivers stood apart, smoking cigarettes. Their assistants made the final adjustments to the cargo ropes, then wandered into the crowd to chat. The drivers climbed into the cabs. The assistants ignored them. The drivers shifted into gear. The assistants pretended still not to notice. The trucks began to roll. The assistants feigned indifference, and at the last moment turned and swung easily into the cabs.

It was midafternoon; I was glad to be on the move. We drove to the edge of Tamanrasset, joined the pavement of the Trans-Saharan, and headed purposefully out of town. Ten minutes later, where soldiers had barricaded the road, we stopped. The soldiers ordered us to climb down with our papers and luggage. The drivers turned off their engines.

As roadblocks go, it was not a bad one. Ali told the officer in charge that I was a tourist. The officer stamped my passport and wished me good luck. He said he did not see many Americans. He asked if I had visited Foucauld's hermitage at Assekrem. He was glad to inform me that the border was officially open this week. He even complimented my French. He was less gracious with the other passengers. But we were delayed for only two hours, which in Saharan time is the merest moment.

Afterward, the pavement broke apart. I spotted the first of Addoun's concrete pylons, which had been run over and lay on its side. We ranged out across a desert of diminishing mountains. The ride atop the cargo was cushioned by the dates; the passengers swayed among the sacks, facing forward, their heads wrapped in indigo cotton. By sundown we had settled into a rhythm. The terrain was treacherous. The trucks wallowed and rolled, hesitated, backed, and shuddered. Their gears ground. On high-speed level ground, the engines bellowed, and the tires heaved dust, and we hit twenty miles an hour.

Darkness closed around us. The trucks competed for the lead. Now our truck rolled ahead and we looked back to watch our dust swirl through Ali's yellow beams; now our truck fell behind, and we tasted his dirt and followed his single red taillight. I don't know how the drivers navigated. High thin clouds dimmed the stars and blackened the horizons. We crossed a confusion of tracks that appeared in the short throw of our lights to run in all directions. When late at night we made camp, I counted twenty-three men. We drank water from fifty-gallon drums lashed to the chassis, and built two miserly cooking fires. We baked unleavened bread in the sand, and ate from communal bowls. The air turned cool. I walked away and rolled into a blanket.

Hours later the murmur of a truck's engine roused me. Lonely lights crept through the distance. The truck crested a rise maybe five miles away and disappeared to the south, pushing hard for the border, giving dimension to the night.

We left before dawn and spent the day passing through torn hills where sand lay in deep pockets. The heavily laden trucks bogged down often. You could sense the trouble coming on: the double-clutching of uncooperative gears, the desperate shifting down, the shuddering loss of momentum, the halt, the surrender. The drivers never spun their wheels. They stepped out to survey the sand. Calmly, they smoked their cigarettes.

The trucks did not sink into the ground, but pushed the sand into dikes that blocked their wheels. The passengers climbed down and excavated the dikes by hand and shovel. We became intimates of the tires, which were massive and heavily scarred. We inhaled the fumes of hot machinery, and embraced the dirt, oil, and leaking diesel fuel. I thought that if Mohammed had lived in a time of trucks, he would have praised them richly; if God is everywhere, then a truck must certainly be His expression. We kneeled by our Berliets. We submitted to them without question.

When the digging was done, we laid heavy sand ladders in front of the wheels. The sand ladders were ten-foot segments of military landing mat—perforated metal strips designed to link together to form a metal runway. Each truck carried a pair, like portable metal pavement, and so could roll forward ten feet at a time across even the softest sand. Then it would bog down again, and we would dig and reset the sand ladders. In places I had the feeling we were digging our way across the Sahara ten feet at a time.

When we found firm ground, and the trucks could keep rolling, and the passengers would run alongside to hang the sand ladders and climb aboard. There were various handholds and routes to the top. I preferred to do my climbing from the back, so that if I slipped I would not be crushed under the wheels. But most of the passengers were less careful. They assaulted the moving trucks enthusiastically from all angles, climbed breathlessly to the top, made jokes, and laughed. They were pleased by the smallest victories.

But other travelers had been defeated. We passed the half-buried hulks of their cars, abandoned to the Sahara, and later stripped of engines, wheels, and usable parts. These relics emerged from the ground like monuments to misfortune. The oldest models dated from the 1930s, the first era of regular desert driving. The newest ones dated from half a century later, during the last tourist traffic before revolution and civil war. Most occupants must have survived, continuing with a convoy, or more haphazardly with passersby. The wrecks did not rust, but they were soon blackened by the sun and wind. They became part of the desert geology. Some captured the dew, which allowed bushes to root in their shelter. Across one difficult mile I counted fifteen hulks—Volvos, Volkswagens, Peugeots, a Renault, a Fiat, and a Morris Mini.

I never saw another of Addoun's markers. When I mentioned this to Ali, he said, "It's better to find your own way." I did not doubt the essential, that we were southbound along the Trans-Saharan. For as far as I could see in any direction, the desert was dense with tire tracks.

Toward evening, nomadic Tuareg children materialized from the empty land. They ran toward us in a flock, waving empty plastic bottles. We stopped and gave them water. They begged for sugar, but we had none. We gave them flour and a sack of dates. They were the poorest of the poor, worse off than the refugees around Tamanrasset or the nomads who had taken delivery of Aissa's rifles. They looked spindly, gaunt, undernourished. Their skin was caked with dirt. They had ragged robes, and hair in wild dreadlocks. I spotted their camp at the base of a cliff—two tents, two goats, a woman watching. The men may have been hiding or hunting, or they may have been dead. Army reprisals in Niger and Mali had killed thousands, scattering their families into the wilderness.

We climbed back onto the trucks. The children watched us dully, shielding their eyes from the sun. As we rolled away, they trudged off, lugging the heavy water bottles. It was obvious that they could not keep living this way, off the diminished traffic of the Trans-Saharan. I thought, these are the circumstances under which parents will arm themselves and blur the distinction between robbery and revolt.

That night, Ali and I drank tea alone. I asked why we had stopped for the Tuaregs—was he not afraid of attack?

He answered, "And if they wanted to attack, do you imagine these Berliets could outrun them? They don't need to shoot. They can just wait for us in the sand. This is their desert."

"So why don't they rob us?"

He shrugged. "They rob others. This is my desert, too. For twenty years I've lived out here under the sky. I have no house, or wife, or children. I have these two old trucks. I drive round-trips every month, and always share my water and food. Sometimes I give them a sack of dates or a chicken or two." He stirred the coals. "I don't get involved in other people's affairs. You Russians are not so wise."

I smiled. "I'm an American."

He smiled. "Ah! What difference does it make?"

He had opinions about European union, North African union, and the Falklands War, but he preferred the old standard of the United States and Russia, because it still held the special appeal of an all-out nuclear exchange. Imagine every continent a Sahara.

I asked him when we would get to In Guezzam, the government outpost on the border with Niger.

The question amused him. "Maybe not tomorrow," he said.

Maybe not ever, I thought the following afternoon. The terrain had widened, and the drivers were ranging miles apart, finding their own ways through, bogging down or not, refusing to wait for one another. They were playing the averages, I realized, employing a method that, between equal drivers, produces the best speed across the desert. The old caravans had used the same method—they would have gotten nowhere had they kept the camels in line and waited every time one spilled its load. I tried now to ignore the other side of the method, which often amounted to the death of stragglers.

Abandonment in the desert had made me sensitive. From my perch atop the dates, I kept a careful watch on Ali's truck. It rumbled close, wandered off, rumbled close again, then became the merest glint to the west. Finally I lost sight of it altogether. The other passengers did not seem to care. We kept driving. After another hour I noticed that we had strayed into a part of the desert without tracks. I thought this was unusual. So apparently did our driver. He stopped, killed the engine, and without a word, climbed a nearby hill where he stood looking. I followed him. The land was empty. I returned to the truck, and sat, and waited. The desert was calm. I had hours to remember the worst. Somewhere out here the Belgians had been lost. Sit, wait, you will find your orientation.

Ali drove up after several hours. He had been stuck in sand over his wheels. We had not been lost at all. But afterward we stayed closer together. The roughest terrain lay behind us. The desert became a gravel plateau. Late at night, in blackness, we came to the border settlement called In Guezzam. We made camp deep in the desert in the middle of town.

HERE IS SOME practical advice: To find In Guezzam, go to the end of the earth and keep driving. Ignore the maps. Ignore the guidebooks. Arrive at night, because darkness will soften your impressions. Sleep soundly before morning, because the border crossing will require patience.

The dawn spread over a plain where nothing grew. A rooster crowed. In Guezzam was a sad settlement of concrete and adobe—a police station, a shuttered café, a government gas station, a dirt runway, a few houses, and at least one rooster. I guessed a thousand people still lived there.

More had lived there before. During the Sahelian droughts of the 1980s, the town had accommodated 25,000 Tuareg refugees from Niger who had lost their herds. The Tuaregs settled in tents and zeribas, required little, and clung to their remaining possessions. The odd part is that despite the trickle of international aid, In Guezzam could find no way to squeeze money from them. When Algeria finally expelled the refugees, In Guezzam was so poor that it hardly noticed the loss.

The international boundary line lay just over the southern horizon. We left In Guezzam and drove south to the crossing point, where the Algerian customs post stood alone in the desert, like a door without a wall. It was a whitewashed concrete building, stained orange with dust and ancient rain. It had a flag, a hand-painted warning sign in Arabic and French, and a patrol car. For a thousand miles in each direction, the border lay open, yet travelers leaving the country were expected to stop here, humbly to request permission. And permission was not gladly granted. Addoun had warned me that the commanding officer was as cruel as he was corrupt.

We were lucky. The commander was sleeping late that morning, and the inspectors on duty were merely sullen. The low quality of our dates did not put them in a better mood. Ali was insulted because one of them called it "monkey food" and refused the gift of a sack. Ali knew and hated these men. They told him he was lucky that the border was open again. He had to listen. They made a show of going through my notes. We spent the morning filling in forms and answering their questions. Around lunchtime they released us, and we drove off into the braided no-man's-land between the two countries. Somewhere out there we crossed the map into Niger. And life did change.

The customs post in Niger was called Asamakka, as if it were a village. It lay an hour south of the Algerian post, on the same infernal plain. A line of fifty-gallon drums stood in the dirt, like

a roadblock without a road. On the other side stood a collection
of tin and mud hovels, a single tree, and a barracks. The soldiers
were black-skinned southerners, strangers to the desert. They
emerged from the barracks wearing jungle camouflage, sandals,
and sunglasses. The captain among them packed twin pearl-
handled revolvers. The sergeant wore an Australian bush hat and
carried a bare-bladed knife under his belt. They were backed up
by an edgy private cradling an automatic rifle as if he expected
us to attack. I counted a dozen other soldiers, coming over
slowly, and I wondered what they had done to be banished here.
They seemed discouraged by fate, and resentful at waking from
their midday stupor. There was a war going on, but they had
been shackled to the Trans-Saharan.

The captain ordered us down from the trucks, and he made
us line up in the sun. He looked each of us over, while his
blank-faced soldiers stood behind him. Some of the passengers
grew anxious. Others seemed relieved, as if they found themselves on familiar ground. I took my cue from Ali, who looked
bored and unruffled.

The captain collected our papers and ordered Ali to have the
trucks unloaded, every sack, for inspection. He said the border
was closed, and would remain closed until later. He did not
specify the hour or day. He assigned two guards to us, and returned to the barracks. The other soldiers drifted away.

Asamakka had traditions. The squatters, who had watched
from their hovels, came over to offer assistance, and Ali hired
two crews to unload the trucks. Despite the heat, they set to
work immediately. I sat in the dirt beside Ali. He said that the
laborers worked for the soldiers, and would give them a cut of
their wages. The guards' real job was to keep track of business.

Ali said, "We could have unloaded the trucks ourselves, but the captain would have found other ways to make his money. These soldiers have not been paid in six months. So don't expect to go anywhere today. The captain will take everything he can before he lets us leave."

We sprawled under the trucks through most of the afternoon. We made tea. The offloaded sacks grew in mounds in the dirt. Children moved among us hawking cigarettes, soft drinks, and chickens.

Two Ethiopians approached me for help. They had been deported by Algeria, but refused entry by Niger. For weeks they had been stuck between the countries, living on donations from passing strangers. They were thin and hungry and sick. I gave them my blanket and oranges. Imagining that I might have the influence to pluck them from their misery, they handed me a crudely written letter to the United Nations Committee on Refugees. I promised to deliver it when I got to the capital, and I eventually did, although to an unimpressed official who had heard many such stories before.

The soldiers emerged again from the barracks late in the afternoon, and with help from the laborers began to probe the burlap sacks one at a time with sharpened steel rods, searching for weapons. Ali was amused. He said quietly, "And if we were smugglers why would we come through this checkpoint? It is a big desert."

Those soldiers not probing the sacks rummaged through our personal luggage. They did not steal. When they found something that pleased them, they had the manners to ask for it as a gift.

"Cadeau?"

"Bien sûr."

From me they took the small stuff—pens, batteries, rolls of film. They did not ask for money. We spent the night. The search continued the following day.

A bearded man in a police uniform approached me and said simply, "I am the constable." I gave him only a solar-powered calculator, which did not please him.

By the second afternoon, when the soldiers saw that Ali could outwait them, they allowed him to have the trucks loaded. The captain called me to his office—a room full of flies, with a cot in one corner, and a high open window through which the smell of stale urine drifted. The captain sat at a wooden desk. He had red eyes and beer breath. He stamped my passport, but said I could not continue with the date trucks, which would head directly for Agadez across the desert. I said that Agadez was my destination as well. He shook his head: I would have to go first to Arlit, Niger's northernmost town, and register there with the police. Arlit lay 150 miles to the southeast. I asked how I would get there. He said he didn't know; maybe I would find someone going that way. I thought he wanted a bribe, and asked what would be required to allow me to accompany the trucks. He insisted that nothing would change his mind. I asked why. He looked somber and said, "Because the direct route to Agadez is not safe. The Tuaregs are bandits, you know. There have been attacks."

Ali looked worried when I told him. He was carrying Tuareg passengers, and had a Tuareg driver, and in the minds of the southern soldiers was, as an Algerian and Saharan, probably a rebel conspirator. Now that the only Westerner had been removed from his convoy, he had to wonder if he was being set up for attack. The Tuareg war has been marked by just such misguided killing.

He left me bread and water. I told him I would find him in Agadez. He said, "God willing." We embraced without emotion, and I watched the trucks rumble slowly out of Asamakka. I trusted Ali's judgment. If he sensed danger, he would double back that night across the unmarked border. If the passengers gave him trouble, he would find some way to abandon them. I had my own worries.

FINDING THE RIDE to Arlit required no special talent. I simply waited. And I was lucky. The next day, a four-wheel-drive Toyota camper appeared across the no-man's-land, south from Algeria. It was driven by a tough old Frenchman and his leathery wife, who treated the soldiers like houseboys, and blustered through the entry formalities in less than an hour. Their names were Claude and Marie. They had retired from somewhere in southern France. I don't think they had quite gotten the word about the Islamic revolution or the Tuareg rebellion—or for that matter about the independence of Niger. When soldiers inspecting the camper tried filching their *pastis* and refrigerated cheese, Claude threw them out. He did this with an explosion of French vowels. Marie slammed the door. They were the last trans-Saharan tourists, operating on a hair-trigger of indignation. They liked me because of my race.

The rebels weren't ready for tourists who moved this fast. The way to Arlit was marked by black barrels filled with rock, one every kilometer. They led across a bare stone plain. The camper was nimble; Claude ran it full-out and did a lot of unnecessary swerving. He assaulted the sand pockets. He swore prodigiously. Sweat soaked his shirt. When he worked up his emotions, his neck swelled and his face turned red. Marie sat primly beside him with her seatbelt on. I sat in the back, braced against the sink. There was no time to talk.

That changed when we stopped for the night. Claude unrolled an awning, and set up three lawn chairs and a folding table. We had *pastis* mixed with bottled French water. Marie made a tidy dinner of *cornichon* and canned sausages. She regretted the lack of bread, but offered up a plate of cheese with crackers. Under her surveillance, I cut a thin slice for myself. She took the plate away. I did not begrudge her this stinginess. She and Claude were headed to Abidjan, and the beaches of the Ivory Coast, and had brought along just enough of France to last them. She mentioned that it was their final trip to Africa. I asked if they had made others. "*Oh oui,*" she said, and pushed back her hair in exasperation. Claude enjoyed these trips. They gave him an opportunity to indulge in dissatisfaction.

Claude was what the French call a *gueulard,* which is difficult to translate into English because it is a particularly Gallic type, a mixture of the loudmouth and the grumbler. I liked him. He was a social fellow. He sought confirmation with the French nasal "*Non? Heh? Non?*" and little pokes to the shoulder. He said he had been a sergeant in the army, and afterward had gone into the construction business. He wanted to talk politics. The conversation turned to Indochina. He deplored the French and American defeats there. He said, "Everyone is against torture, *non?* In principle torture is something bad. But you have to be realistic too, *non?* You have to admit that from time to time torture is necessary. Sometimes you ask questions and you need the answers."

The lawn chair was luxurious. Between the food and company, the evening felt like summer holiday on the coast of Brittany, only lacking beach tents and the toy shovels. The alcohol spun my head. I was glad to have escaped from Asamakka. Claude seemed admirably stupid. Rare is the man who does not grow cautious with age.

They slept in the camper. I slept on the ground wrapped in a jacket, because I had given away my blanket to the Ethiopians, and Marie did not want to lend me another. Claude would have lent me a blanket, but he did not want to quarrel with Marie. I got the impression she worried about skin lesions, parasites, and perhaps the transmission of venereal disease through polyester and wool. I had neither shaved nor bathed since leaving Tamanrasset, and I was dusty.

In the morning we drank Nescafé *au lait* from bowls, then rolled up the awning, folded up the lawn chairs and table, and got back to the furious driving. At noon we left the plain and sped across an undulating desert where scattered bushes grew in the depressions. The bushes were stunted, thorny, small-leafed plants, edible only to goats. Their speckled shade was hardly enough for snakes. But to me they looked as lush as tropical trees. I shouted this forward to Claude as he smashed over one.

"The tropics?" he called back. "These bushes are nothing! They're useless! They're getting the hell in our way!"

In the afternoon we came to Arlit, a new town built since independence around Niger's only national resource, a uranium mine. The town appeared abruptly out of the desert—a black African colony deep in Tuareg land. The main street was noisy and energetic, and so dense with pedestrians that even Claude had to slow. Despite the fierceness of the sun, the men wore no hats. They were sinewy southerners in tattered shorts and short-sleeved shirts. The women were more dignified with the print dresses and turbans and their perfect posture. Ragged children ran in bands.

The people besieged us. Claude kept advancing. The crowd grew to a hundred, young and old, trotting beside the camper, competing for our attention with laughter, shouts, and general good humor. They wanted to sell, buy, and provide, or simply to talk. Faces appeared and disappeared. Arms snaked through the open windows offering cigarettes, candy, matches, peanuts, and small thick-skinned oranges. By hooking both elbows through the window above the sink, one young man managed to get his upper body into the camper. The effect was unusual, as if he had suddenly dropped into the privacy of our kitchen. It seemed to surprise him as much as me. He hesitated for only a moment.

"*Bienvenu à Arlit,*" he said.

"*Merci.*"

He squirmed the rest of the way through the window, and picked himself off the floor. The crowd shouted its approval. "You've come from far?" he asked. He smiled.

I laughed in relief, feeling I had been too long in the desert. Arlit was an old and familiar delight. In its kindness and celebration, in its acceptance of life, Africa can feel like the most human place on earth.

Marie was worried again about disease. She rolled up her window, pulled in her elbows, and looked stiffly ahead. "*Do something!*" she said to Claude.

Claude didn't hear her. He had leaned his head outside, and was palavering with the crowd in pidgin French, what the French call "*petit nègre,*" a caricature of native grammar performed in a generalized African accent. No one in Arlit seemed to mind. Claude and the crowd got along famously. He drove with one hand and bargained with the other. During the short trip to the central police station, he bought a pack of unfiltered cigarettes, an unopened jar of Nescafé, and a cheap camel-skin wallet.

At the police station we pulled into a compound enclosed by high mud walls. The crowd stayed back, and the police shut the gates. Having squirmed through the window, our passenger stayed with us. He introduced himself as André. We got out of the camper. Claude had the sense to drop the pidgin talk. The guards at the gate were heavily armed. The men who searched the camper were unnaturally efficient. They stole nothing, and after their inspection led us into the station to see their commander. André started acting important. The commander ignored him. He was a hard-eyed man. He verified briskly that we were headed south for Agadez, and for our own safety, he forbade us to travel at night. He stamped our passports, and let us go. For this he demanded no payment.

Marie approved. "*Très correct,*" she said afterward. "He was a gentleman."

Claude agreed. "He has respect for France."

But there was a closer explanation. Arlit stands as insult to the Tuareg rebels. The commander guarded the mine. He did not have to extort money, because he was paid on time. He did not have to invent enemies and spies, because he was surrounded by real ones.

20

A

POLITICAL

PARABLE

THIS IS A story told among the sedentary people who
live to the Tuaregs' south in Niger, about a time when animals
could cultivate the earth. A certain mother goat had a magnificent garden in which she grew crops of onions, manioc,
potatoes, and all the other good vegetables necessary for her
children's meals. The garden was protected by a fence of spiny
branches. Nonetheless, one morning the goat discovered that
a gazelle had gotten into it, and was calmly eating up the
crops.

"You!" she said. "Gazelle! What are you doing in my garden?
Do you think it is just another place in the desert where wild
grasses grow? Don't you see that the garden is fenced?"

The gazelle answered scornfully, "We nomads, we desert creatures, we recognize no fences. Everything that is green we will
eat. The earth and everything that grows on it belongs to our
God, and he created it so that we could use it."

"Get out of my garden or I will fight you!"

"I'll get out only when I've had enough to eat. Nothing proves to me that you own this place!"

The goat charged the gazelle and the two animals began to fight. Just then a jackal passed. He stopped and said, "Why are you fighting like this? Stop, and tell me what the problem is."

The goat and the gazelle explained their disagreement, and decided to accept the jackal as a judge.

The jackal said, "Mother Goat, go home to your children and come back tomorrow morning. Tomorrow morning I will make my judgment, and not before."

The goat went home, but, fearing the duplicity of the jackal, she invited over her friend the dog for dinner. She prepared a tasty meal for him, and while he ate, she explained her predicament. The dog agreed to help her.

Meanwhile, the jackal conspired with the gazelle, and came up with a plan to cheat the goat of her garden.

In the morning the goat and the dog went early to the garden. The goat harvested the ripest vegetables, and placed them in a pile within which she hid the dog.

When the gazelle and the jackal arrived, the jackal began to distribute the harvested vegetables according to his scheme: nine handfuls for the gazelle, one handful for the goat. The goat protested, but the jackal ignored her, and continued his unequal distribution.

The pile grew smaller until suddenly the jackal spotted the ears of the hidden dog. He said nothing, but in a panic immediately reversed the scheme and began giving nine handfuls to the goat, and only one to the gazelle. When the gazelle complained, the jackal said, "I see the truth now in this pile of plenty."

But before he had time to correct the earlier injustice, the dog sprang out of the crops. He killed the jackal first, and then the gazelle. And that is how the goat retained her garden.

21

A

T U A R E G

T R A G E D Y

THE FRENCH CONQUERED the Sahara easily. Once they decided that they wanted this desert, it was theirs for the taking. Their only real problem was its size: for a while it was more than they could control. Tuareg resistance persisted not because the Tuaregs were great fighters or idealists, but because drought and distance protected them. We may cherish the image of desert-hardened warriors, but by European standards the Tuaregs were weak.

In the 1920s the French finally assumed control of the central Sahara with the most simple expedients. They beefed up their garrisons, declared the rule of law, established a postal service, and killed a few dissidents. But their most effective tactic was to replace the camel with the wheel. They did this in standard-production automobiles, which they drove into all the remote corners of the desert. The superiority of the automobile was immediately obvious. The French drove through the desert simply to leave tire tracks. The tracks endured. The Tuaregs submitted without further argument.

Then a strange thing happened. The French became the only protectors that the Tuaregs had ever known. The French were not entirely easy on them: they forced the nobles to abandon their raiding and to free their slaves; they made them pay a small tax as a symbol of their allegiance; they required at least one child in each family to attend "nomad school," to learn the French language and history. But beyond that, they also shielded the Tuaregs from their enemies to the north and south. By making a human preserve of the central Sahara, they provided the Tuaregs with what everyone agreed was a splendid sort of isolation.

It is said that by imposing the rule of a foreign law, and forbidding the old business of raiding, they strangled the Tuaregs. But the truth is that the world outside had changed anyway, and cargo ships, trains, and trucks had killed the caravan trade. In the central Sahara there was nothing left to raid—a dry desert had become even drier. The French could not keep these changes from happening, but they could protect the Tuaregs from facing the consequences. As colonial masters, the French were sincere and well intentioned. They thought they should help the Tuaregs to maintain their nomadic ways. They encouraged the Tuaregs to indulge in a way of life that became a fiction.

It was a fiction dreamed up in Europe. The French did not choose the desert by default, as is sometimes said. They were a densely civilized people, frustrated then as now by the competence and rigidity of their society. The Sahara was everything that France was not: big, clean, wild, dry, hot, hostile, and empty. It was uncivilized. It gave the French the escape they badly needed, a land that was empty and untouched and already so barren that it could not be spoiled, an especially pure sort of wilderness. There was no need even to go there; for ordinary French citizens, enclosed by all the refinements of their civilization, it was enough to have established this claim on the greatest open space on earth.

Never mind that during the years before Algerian independence, oil was finally discovered there. The French originally had higher intentions for their desert. They drew boundaries through the middle of it for the purpose of colonial administration, but allowed those boundaries to have little effect. The soldiers and civilians sent to rule the Sahara prided themselves not on what they did to the desert but on what it did to them. They were malcontents, ethnologists, and adventurers—not missionaries. The Sahara was their refuge. The Tuaregs who wandered through its heart were the noble savages of Rousseau's vision. The women were long-bodied beauties; the men wore swords and veils. They were aristocrats and brave warriors. They rode through the French imagination like characters in a romance novel. So much the better that these were the very people who had held out longest against French influence. Their resistance made the wilderness all the more authentic. It is hardly surprising that the French wanted the Tuaregs to remain proud, and encouraged them to remember a mythical past.

The Tuareg rebellion today would be uninteresting were it not for the complicity of this European wishfulness. It would be unimportant were it not for its kinship to wars elsewhere. Mano Dayak, a Tuareg rebel in Niger today, has written this best-selling account of his childhood under the French:

Before going off to school, I knew the happy childhood of the encampments. What memories! Those of children playing with the dry dung of camels. Memories of the first words of *tamachek* that my mother taught me to write in *tefinagh,* our script, on the sand of dunes. Memories also of all the late nights up around the fire.

With my father and Ebayghar, it was the school of the desert: the apprenticeship of trails, and of navigation by the wind and stars. A whole nomad science to acquire the knowledge of places, of the *oueds* of the Aïr, of the enormous dunes of the Ténéré. An intimate ancestral geography of the Sahara, our universe.

Every time I think again about the desert of my childhood, I feel sad and nostalgic. I see it like a sort of image, a very beautiful dream that I grieve for, that I would love to find again and to touch with my hands and my soul. I don't know how better to describe such a feeling. It is so difficult to explain and to share.

Born in the desert, one remains strongly attached to it, no matter what one does afterwards. He who leaves it, keeps a part of his *oued* with him, his paradise that awaits him. There is a Tuareg proverb that says, "No matter where he wanders, the nomad will always return to his first encampment." This is so true.

Mano Dayak is typical of the aristocratic Tuaregs who after generations under special French treatment learned to see themselves as the French saw them, with all the romance of outsiders. This is hardly an unusual syndrome—other people see themselves as the movies might portray them—but it can produce dangerous exaggerations. Dayak served up his memory of childhood in a 1993 book entitled *Touareg, La Tragédie,* which, significantly, he did not write alone, but rather produced with the collaboration of a professional French author. Published in Paris, the book is perhaps the most perfect Saharan artifact of our times. It has enjoyed success because it is still easy to convince the French that nomads are happier than city dwellers, and that they are more free.

This explains why there is no Tuareg emigration. Forced exile, yes, it exists. Our enemies make sure of it. But not voluntary emigration. Those Tuaregs who have been able to study in Europe—sadly, there aren't many—have all returned to the desert.

At this moment, hardly more than fifteen Tuaregs live more or less permanently in France. A number that must be compared with that of North African immigration, for example. It's true that the Moroccan and Algerians don't leave their countries for the pleasure of it. That is correct. We too are poor, but we can endure misery better than we can the absence of the desert.

When, as an adolescent, I left my home to discover the world of others, I soon began to burn with the desire to see the desert again. And I did return there, as have all our other travelers. Despite the droughts and the massacres, the Tuaregs remain so adapted to this Spartan existence, so in love with the desert. We cannot imagine living elsewhere. If I were told that I would have to stay permanently in Europe, I think I would die from it. And yet, I love Europe.

Touareg, La Tragédie is full of this. It reminds the French of old Saharan holidays when they wore *chèches* and squatted with nomads. It plays on life in northern France, and on current understandings of colonial history. The reader is hardly surprised, about halfway through the book, to discover that Mano Dayak once ran a tourist agency in Agadez.

He is probably an intelligent man. No doubt he is a brave and dedicated one. He writes from the front lines of a dangerous struggle. Despite the overwrought tone of his musings, elements of an obscure truth come through.

Under the French colonization, we still had the impression that we could move about without constraint, since the boundaries were not the sort of obstacle that they are today. Certainly, the [colonial] tax humiliated us, but to a certain extent our daily lives, away from the towns, continued peacefully. Some people now accuse us of nostalgia for the colonial times. What an aberration! No one fought the colonist as we did. Colonization hurt us enormously, but we have known worse since then. One must say things as they are.

The concept of pure ethnicity is as dangerous as that of pure race. All people are mongrels. "Indigenous" societies are subject to the same requirements for change as others. There is no such construct as an inauthentic culture. The worst thing the French did to the Tuaregs was not to defeat them in battle, but to treat them afterward like a privileged people. The worst thing the Tuaregs did was to deceive themselves. They were arrogant. They believed they were better than their neighbors and did not have to make peace with them. They let their desert fool them. They thought they could live in isolation from the world, though they never had before. They ignored what new technologies meant to the caravan trade. They ignored what changing ideologies meant to the practice of keeping slaves. And they were slow learners. Even today, generations later, there are many who cannot bring themselves to accept the obvious—that their camel culture is doomed, that their raiding days are over, that the central Sahara is too dry to sustain a purely pastoral form of nomadism, that they have to find some other way to survive. Were they Americans or Europeans, we would call them hopeless reactionaries. One must say things as they are.

The tragedy of the Tuaregs is that today they must pay for these delusions. By now the choices are indeed limited. The crisis started around 1960, when in a last-ditch attempt to retain Algeria, the French gave independence to their West African colonies, and abandoned the Tuaregs to the new national boundaries. The boundaries were invisible and largely unmarked, but they were real nonetheless. The Tuaregs could cross them undetected, but they could not escape their effects. Mano Dayak writes:

> We didn't really know what happened. During colonial times, the French divided us. They sat around a table to draw a map that denied our existence as a people. But because all of these territories, despite some internal French technicalities, were part of the same empire, the borders were not very important.
>
> With independence, all that changed brutally. Suddenly, the policemen and soldiers representing the new nations demanded to see passports, and even required visas when impoverished nomads from the Aïr wanted to visit their cousins in the Hoggar or in Adrar des Iforas.

He simplifies. The Tuaregs had never formed a cohesive nation; they operated within anarchic groupings that sometimes fought one another, and shared little beyond their Berber language and cultural identity. The effect of the borders was not to separate loving families, or to deny the Tuaregs' existence, but to force them into the modern world. They had lived artificially in a European dream, but this now was the real Sahara.

The Tuaregs who belonged to the Algerian side of the divide were the lucky ones: they joined a mostly Berber nation into which if they chose they could melt. Only a few miles away, the Tuaregs of Niger and Mali had an entirely different experience. In each of those two countries they accounted for less than 10 percent of the population. The remaining 90 percent were black Sahelians—Mandé, Fulani, Songhai, Djerma and others—who were the very people that the Tuaregs had traditionally preyed upon. The Tuaregs were from the start outgunned.

With these people from the south, hate came to the north. At night, in our desert encampments, travelers told us stories of what was happening to the Tuaregs of Agadez. During public gatherings, southern soldiers were stripping off the turbans of our chiefs, an act which represents the worst dishonor for a Tuareg. They were also taking away our swords, another grave insult.

The government of Niger set about terrorizing the nomads. It could not stand our pride, which the people of the south took for arrogance. Our dignity, even during colonial times, would not allow us to kneel to administrators. One did not bow before a man who, because he was armed, thought he had the power of life and death over civilians. The French at least respected our pride. But the Republic of Niger decided to make the Tuaregs pay dearly for their "insolence" and their past as "slave masters."

Their punishment was to be excluded from national development schemes—the new schools, hospitals, roads, and lucrative administrative positions. For proud and independent nomads, you might think this would not have posed a problem. But the symbolism grated on them. They thought that these things, which they did not want, were being denied to them by men who had no natural right to deny them anything. Arlit made the insult worse. Uranium was discovered there in 1968, and within two years the profits were being whisked 700 miles down the new "Route de L'Uranium" past Agadez to the capital city, Niamey. The Tuaregs who followed became street beggars. Those who went to Arlit found only menial jobs.

The situation was more difficult still in Mali, where as soon as the French pulled out, the government imposed heavy taxes on livestock and began strong-arming the northern population. In 1962, around Gao and Timbuktu, the Tuaregs rebelled and were crushed. The leaders crossed the border into Algeria, but were arrested and returned to Mali. Diplomacy between the uneasy neighbors required the gesture. Public executions followed, and have continued sporadically ever since.

In 1968 the summer rains faltered. In 1973 and 1974 they failed entirely. Across West Africa 50,000 people died, not of thirst but of starvation after their goats, cows, and camels had perished. Niger lost 60 percent of its herds. In itself this was not unusual—the southern Sahara has always been a treacherous place to live—but the difference now was political. In the past the Tuaregs would have shifted south with the drought, pushing their herds to the banks of the Niger River and beyond, shoving aside the black tribes of the Sahel. Those tribes, collectively, had a long memory of such apocalypses during which, just as the crops failed, masked swordsmen would appear out of the desert like the agents of hell. In modern Niger and Mali, in 1974, the southerners did not think that the Tuaregs could hurt them anymore, but they would not forgive them either.

The ancient pattern reversed: in the depths of the drought, traders from the Niger River moved north into the desert and bought up the emaciated Tuareg herds for the equivalent of a few cents. Towns like Agadez and Arlit swelled with destitute Tuareg refugees dying for the lack of charity. By 1975, when the rains returned, many Tuaregs were too poor to rebuild their herds. The old aristocrats had to slip secretly into Algeria to huddle by Tamanrasset or to work illegally in the northern oases.

Libya offered a more attractive alternative, because Muammar Qaddafi, a true Saharan, embraced the Tuareg refugees, employed them in his oil fields, and recruited them into his Islamic Legion. Qaddafi set up a radio transmitter and began beaming Tamachek broadcasts into Niger and Mali. This was unhelpful, since both countries were run by frightened Sahelian dictators already obsessed with conspiracy theories.

In 1980 Qaddafi called for an independent Tuareg republic, and promised to provide the guns and military training to make it happen. Indulging again in a massive act of self-deception, thousands of young Tuaregs took him up on the offer. Qaddafi sent them to fight against Morocco in the distant Western Sahara, and in 1987 gave them a taste of defeat in Chad. By then the price of oil had dropped, and with it the wages and conditions in Qaddafi's oil fields. The few squads sent into Niger had been wiped out. The Tuaregs in Libya felt betrayed. They continued to look outside for an enemy.

They were condemned already to their nihilistic war. Another great drought had hit the southern Sahara in 1983. It lasted three years, and was so severe that for the first time in recorded history the Niger River ran dry in Niamey. No one knows how many people died. Starvation spread across Africa at its widest, from the

Red Sea to the Atlantic. Saharans by the tens of thousands fled
north to tent camps in Mauritania and Algeria. I remember the
crowds in Tamanrasset, which included as many black tribesmen
as Tuaregs. In Algeria, the Tuareg refugees temporarily again had
the upper hand, and they used it. Twenty-five years after national
independence, they reverted to shoving around their fellow coun-
trymen, to treating the blacks like slaves. Had they forgotten what
a border could do to them? Did they think this refuge would last?

Qaddafi was not the only one leading them on. The colonial
empire had disappeared from the desert forever, and had indeed
become irrelevant, but its strongest tradition still flourished. If
the world now was growing smaller it meant this: more Westerners than before surrounded the Tuaregs with cameras and
mirrors, and extended their friendships and their sympathy, and
encouraged the Tuaregs to remain something they never had
been. These Westerners were jealous of their relationships with
the natives, and they outdid each other in their expressions of
understanding. This mattered because of who they were: like
Charles de Foucauld, many had come to the Sahara precisely
because they wanted to separate themselves from the national
powers that stood behind them. But every Westerner in such a
desert, no matter how full of Christian love, is an agent of the
West. And the West is seen as stronger and more clearly intentioned than in practice it is. The Tuaregs heard compassion
among visitors and in the European press, and they misread the
emotion as political commitment.

The drought ended, and the savanna turned green. Even in the
desert near Arlit, in the highlands of the Aïr, there was grass again.
In 1989 a new military leader in Niger made peace with Qaddafi
and agreed to the repatriation of the now-subdued Tuaregs from

Libya. The following year, faced with Islamic revolution in the north, the government of Algeria expelled the remaining refugees. Nearly 25,000 Tuaregs were held on the border at In Guezzam, while officials argued about which country they belonged to. The United Nations got involved. Promises were made for emergency food and supplies, and in January 1990 Niger finally agreed to accept 18,000 of the refugees. Men, women, and children climbed into trucks, and were driven to "transit camps" on the southern edge of the desert, southwest of Agadez, near a village called Tchin-Tabaradène.

The camps already held the returnees from Libya, and conditions there were difficult. The Tuaregs were kept under loose guard, and not allowed to leave. They had little food or shelter. The promised supplies were delivered to Niamey, then siphoned off by corrupt officials, and sold in the commercial markets of the capital—a standard destination for international aid to West Africa.

In May 1990 three young men from the camps stormed the police post in Tchin-Tabaradène. Mano Dayak says that they were unarmed, and wanted simply to protest against conditions in the camp. Maybe. They killed two policemen and a prisoner, ran away, and were never identified. Soldiers arrived within hours. The refugees in the camps panicked and fled. The soldiers went on a violent rampage, shooting Tuaregs on sight, stripping and torturing the elders, raping the women, slaughtering the children.

The campaign lasted several weeks. A few encampments were surrounded and machine-gunned, but the desert did most of the work: having occupied the wells, the soldiers sat back and let thirst drive their enemies into rifle range. No one knows how many people were killed. The army later admitted to seventy, but the real number was many times higher. Government spokesmen officially regretted the massacre, and tried to dismiss it as an "isolated event," though Tchin-Tabaradène lay like the final stepping stone on a straight path to war.

The Tuaregs rose up in a rage that spread across the Sahara. Many of the rebels were men who had been trained in Libya, and had kept their weapons. They dreamed still of an independent Tuareg nation, but died now more simply for their hatred. They attacked government forces in the Aïr, near Arlit. The army accused the rebels of collusion with Qaddafi, and of trying to sabotage the uranium mine. It did not distinguish between combatants and peaceful Tuaregs. In the towns, it rounded up suspects. In the desert, it simply hunted them down.

Something similar happened in Mali, where in June 1990, only a month after the massacre of Tchin-Tabaradène, a team of international aid workers was ambushed by Tuareg rebels. The rebels took the team's Toyotas and attacked Ménaka, the Malian town where fugitives from Tchin-Tabaradène had been detained. Fourteen Malian policemen died in the attack. The rebels escaped with weapons and ammunition. The Malian Army arrived and went on a rampage, killing, burning, raping. This time the Tuaregs shot back. In July 1990 fighting broke out on the streets of Gao. In September 1990 the rebels wiped out a force of 200 Malian soldiers on the hot plains of the Tanezrouft.

The rebellion spread slowly to Algeria where the national government was distracted by the Islamic revolution. At first the war in Algeria was fought by foreigners—rebels from Mali or Niger who refused to accept the borders, though in fact they hid behind them. Later, however, the cause was taken up by Algerian Tuaregs as well. The main effect was to make the desert dangerous.

The Algerian government brokered a tri-national truce in 1991, which lasted two months. It brokered another truce in 1992, which lasted three weeks. There were no further attempts. Plans for semiautonomous Tuareg regions in Niger and Mali disintegrate under the pressures of continued killing. Experiments with democracy fail because the democratic majorities refuse to share power. Defeat at the polls is seen by both sides as defeat in battle. The Tuaregs refuse to participate. Dreaming instead of their impractical nation, encouraged by the cheap sympathy of outsiders, they keep fighting. Along its entire southern edge, the Sahara spawns such wars of ambush and reprisal.

22

SOUTH

TO

THE

SAHEL

CLAUDE WAS NOT the type of Frenchman to sympathize with the Tuaregs. He could have settled happily in Arlit and worked his way into a new life as, say, an advisor to the government forces. But Marie was in a hurry. She wanted to get to Agadez before night, and Claude had the habit of obliging her. He checked the Toyota's tires, and climbed into the driver's seat. A policeman swung open the compound gate.

Unhappy with our sudden departure, André, the young man who had crawled through the window, said, "You must pay me now for my services."

Marie turned on him. "What?"

André said angrily, "One must never cheat one's friends."

Claude looked stonily ahead. Marie said, "I will call over the police!"

Wisely, André sulked off. Marie instructed us to close the camper's windows and lock its doors. By the edge of town only children chased in our wake.

We headed south down the Route de L'Uranium, an asphalt ribbon laid on an elevated gravel bed across the desert floor. Claude shared my enthusiasm for the engineering. The blue Aïr highlands rose to our left, but Claude saw only the road. "You'd almost believe this was France!" he said. He drove at ninety miles an hour, stopped for army roadblocks, and got us to Agadez in time for dinner.

Agadez was an ancient caravan center, a poor, hot, mud-walled town dominated by a sixteenth-century adobe mosque with a Sudanese-style minaret rising ninety feet above dusty streets. Dinner was on me. The hotel was a sultan's palace as old as the mosque. It was dark and dingy, and had thick adobe walls. The Tuareg Kaocen had lived there during his one-year occupation of the town, though this was nowhere written. For dinner we had a stew washed down with good African beer. I said good-bye to Claude and Marie, who went off to their camper for an early departure.

My room was a stifling, windowless cell with a concrete floor, stained green walls, and a bulb hanging from the ceiling. It had a cot with a foam-rubber pad and unwashed sheets. I checked for scorpions, then lay sweating, wishing for the open sky.

In the morning, I walked through town. Agadez once sat on the southern fringe of the Sahara, and prospered on the trade in slaves, gold, and salt. But by the time I got there the desert had moved farther south, and the town ran on a little commerce, charity, and international aid. It had wells and government offices. The population had swollen to 75,000 with refugees from drought and war. They lived in shelters of tin and straw tacked onto the sides of the mud-walled buildings in town, and in large squatters' camps on the outskirts. The atmosphere was uneasy. People did not approach strangers. I saw evidence of recent fighting in the tension of the soldiers, and in the obvious distrust between Tuaregs and southerners on the street. The two sides mingled at the market because they had to, but even the children's park had separate swings. The poorest children were too poor to play. They ran naked and stole their food at the market.

When I asked among truckers near the mosque about Ali and his cargo of dates, they grew suspicious, said they knew nothing. A drunken policeman demanded my passport. Wearily, I let him have it. He became friendly when he discovered my nationality, because he thought he should go to America to become rich. He took me to the station house so that I could register and share my wealth.

The station house was an adobe shack with open windows and a verandah swarming with flies. The three policemen there broke off a card game to write my name in a notebook, and to request a transit fee. I had to remind them to stamp my passport.

By the next morning, Ali had arrived. I found his trucks parked on the street near the market. The passengers had disappeared. Emaciated laborers were unloading the cargo of dates, and carrying the sacks into a warehouse. Ali was amused that I had beat him to Agadez.

Days later I took a bus 550 miles down the paved road to Niamey, and watched the desert disappear. It was a good, clean bus, with air-conditioning and a stereo. It left Agadez with a mound of luggage on the roof, and a full load of passengers. I found a place toward the back, next to a southerner with whom I shared no language. We smiled and left each other alone. The driver sat upright and wore lightly tinted sunglasses. There was drama in the way he drove, flashing through villages, overtaking the cars ahead. He had a multitone horn, and he could make it talk.

Thanking, scolding, proclaiming, the Niamey bus was coming through.

Music was the driver's pleasure. He carried a case of cassettes, among which he chose carefully. Over the sixteen hours of the trip, he repeated not a single tune. Most of his selection was West African pop, with its melodic guitar work. But he also liked American dance tunes with an emphasis on drumming and sex. The passengers listened impassively to this stew, swaying in unison to the lurching of the bus. But after the silence of the desert, the music pleased us all.

We stopped for God and government. At prayer time, the passengers knelt in groups in the dirt, and the driver obliged with recordings of the Koran. At the army roadblocks, illiterate soldiers peered at our identity papers and tried to record our names in ledgers. Some asked for my help. Near the camps of Tchin-Tabaradène, a sergeant made a show of holding up the bus while he questioned me about my purposes. But the other roadblocks were merely time-consuming. At the big town called Tahoua we had to pass through three of them—at the entrance, at the center, and again at the exit.

Nonetheless, we fled the Sahara fast, the changes passing as smoothly as the frames of a movie. The desert by Agadez was a barren land of cactus, gravel, and gully, but then acacias appeared and became more frequent, and the country turned to rolling, eroded grassland, inhabited in the valleys by isolated families. Where the grass grew thicker, the country began to resemble American rangeland, with goats and long-haired cattle. There were villages of round huts and granaries, and the conical thatched roofs, and cultivated fields of hand-planted corn. We came to a reservoir, the first open water I had seen since leaving the Mediterranean at Algiers. It was not a big reservoir, but the wind pushed up lovely little waves that lapped its sides. The land around it was irrigated and farmed. Someone had planted saplings in rock enclosures on the shore.

After dark we drove along the border with Nigeria, through villages with no electricity. The night was moonless and black. In the markets lining the road, vendors lighted their wares with kerosene lanterns, hundreds of them, casting orange light on the milling crowds. The huts were dark masses, some lit by cooking fires in the yards. I had a feeling that everyone was outside, enjoying the softness of the African night. Our driver had turned off the air-conditioning, and we had opened all the windows. Passengers hung their heads outside. We stopped for dinner in Dogondoutchi, and I wandered through the crowds, listening to the constant calling. Sitting at a bench with others, I ate a bowl of rice with a spicy sauce, impossible to see in the darkness.

At Dogondoutchi a crazy woman boarded the bus. She had a torn dress, hair in wild tufts, the slightness and exuberance of an adolescent, but an older face. She pranced to the back of the bus, sat across from me, and in French said "*Cigarette?*"

It was a request or an offer. I said I didn't smoke. The passengers watched solemnly. She giggled, then repeated herself because *cigarette* was the only French she knew. That and "*SIDA*." French for AIDS, which also made her giggle. She appreciated the driver's choice in African music. She started singing along, laughing, singing louder, dancing on the seat. When the driver put on American songs she picked up the melodies, and mimicked the words.

She refused to leave the bus at the town that was her destination. The driver came back to convince her—it wasn't for the money, he said, this was where she lived. She answered that she wanted to stay up with the music all night, wanted to dance, wanted never to sleep. Passengers in the front turned to smile. Those sitting closer tried persuasion. She debated them for half an hour before the police were called. I saw Africa in the stand-off: in this police state, this oppressive, ignorant, warring, disintegrating nation, the police when they finally arrived were gentle with her too. They tried their own arguments. She argued back as she had before. A few passengers grew impatient and said they didn't feel it was right that we should all be delayed. They wanted to throw her off. But other passengers had been taken in by the debate, which they followed eagerly back and forth with their eyes. There was no point, of course. Finally the police had to carry the woman off, and she fought them, and screamed and sobbed. But consider the horror of a more efficient Africa.

In Niamey I went to the national museum to find the remnants of a famous tree. It was an acacia, and it had grown in the Ténéré, the sand desert east of Agadez. For hundreds of miles in any direction it was the only tree. Maps showed it. Then, in 1973, a Libyan truck driver collided with it and knocked it down. The trunk was hauled to the museum. Out in the Ténéré a simple metal statue was erected. Someday I will go to see it, a peculiar monument to driving in the Sahara.

PART III

THE EDGE
IS A DESERT TOO

23

THE SAHEL IS a band of dry grassland, a savanna with no independent identity, the Sahara's southern shore. The Africans who inhabit it are a desert people. They do not contemplate the tropics to their south, but face instead toward the barren north from which every few years the Sahara surges across them. This has always been true. Instability is part of life in the Sahel—the good years give, and the bad ones take away. The difference now is not that the Sahara surges harder, though it may, or that the Sahel shifts southward, though it has, or that population growth magnifies these effects, though it must. Up close, it all amounts to the same old disorder of local drought. The Sahel has never allowed itself to become crowded. The difference now is mostly philosophical: Sahelians have enough contact with the outside world to know that a better life exists elsewhere, and they are less willing than in the past simply to submit to the weather and die. Some flee drought into the temporary refugee camps where international charity may provide for them. Others make the more permanent move to a city, preferably to a national capital, where by the magic of critical mass almost everyone can survive. That alone explains the new Niamey, now a half-million strong, which stands on the east bank of the Niger River where French colonial administrators happened in 1926 to plant a few buildings and trees.

Niamey is one of the poorest capitals in the world—a scattered, low-rise settlement spreading loosely from the river in an irregular pattern of dirt streets, broken pavement, and crumbling mud and cement buildings. Despite its size, it never quite becomes a city. Patches of savanna remain even at the center, crisscrossed by footpaths like the heavily traveled trails outside a village. The streets are uncrowded, and the few private cars move cautiously among overloaded minivans and buses spewing black smoke. Most people walk. Thin and poorly dressed pedestrians wander about looking for scraps of opportunity, or begging. Those with a little money do some shopping. There is an official marketplace, where established vendors sell their goods in rows, but prices are better on the street, where energetic hustlers offer as much as a person could need, and more than most can afford. The newest buildings, which house government ministries, are ultramodern monuments to national pride, never quite finished, slipping already into disrepair. Inspirational billboards proclaim the eagerness of the people to follow their leaders. One says FOR NIGER, ETERNAL VIGILANCE IS WORTH ANY PRICE. Democracy or dictatorship, it doesn't matter. You can turn on the television most nights and find some government official getting a medal.

The Niger River, which flows past the center of town, is a trick of nature. It draws its water from the wet tropical highlands of Sierra Leone and Guinea, but rather than flowing directly to the nearby Atlantic, it drains northward across the West African interior, then flows in a great arc through the southern Sahara, past the old caravan centers of Timbuktu and Gao, to emerge finally from the desert heading south for Niger, Nigeria, and the Bight of Benin. By the time it passes Niamey, about 2,000 miles from its headwaters, it has taken on some of the character of the desert, and is a wide, shallow, and volatile river. In Niamey it is spanned by a modest bridge named Kennedy that has allowed the city to spread along the west bank. Upriver on both sides, people have planted vegetable gardens like little jungles. Fishermen pole dugout pirogues close by the banks. Larger planked vessels known as *pinasse* carry passengers and a bit of cargo. On the floodplain below the bridge, hundreds of laundrymen scrub clothes in the brown river water. They lay the clothes on the rocks to dry, then fold them and carry the piles away on their heads. It is not a good life. The laundrymen have to lay claim to their tiny scraps of riverbank, then fight off competitors. They live nearby with their families, in miserable mud hovels. The slowly decaying Grand Hôtel stands above them by old shaded houses on a bluff overlooking the river. The bluff is cut by ravines dribbling sewage. Downstream, leatherworkers process animal hides in reeking pits of black slime. I mention this because of what it represents about life in Niamey. People who live away from the river in the less obvious misery of the shantytowns suffer equally to survive. But for all their troubles, they don't make revolutions. Opportunistic robberies don't count.

I liked Niamey for personal reasons: the police did not threaten me, and the whores left me alone when I asked them to, and I met a few educated Africans, and the trees shaded my eyes from the sun. Niamey gave me a rest from the desert. I enjoyed walking for days through its dusty streets, listening to the mixture of languages and to the music playing from a thousand tape decks. For tranquillity I walked north through the wealthy tree-lined district where diplomats and government ministers live in magnificent compounds behind mud walls with iron gates and Uzi-toting guards. When I grew thirsty, I would head back toward the center to gulp a cold Coke. I picked up a month-old copy of *Newsweek,* and read it hungrily. I made international phone calls by satellite. Airliners flew overhead directly to and from Europe. I whiled away hours at the museum, at the market, at a sidewalk café. Niamey is the only place in West Africa where strangers recognized me as an American: they walked up and said, "Hello." Startled, I answered them in French. But their judgment impressed me.

The Westerners I saw were Europeans, mostly French and German technicians of the class that keeps Africa running. Known locally as *"coopérants,"* they lived with their families by the remnants of colonial privilege, which amounted now mostly to having a few servants.

Sunday evenings they gathered on the terrace of the Grand Hôtel for cocktails and dinner. There was a small playground for the children. The adults talked quietly, laughed a little, and watched life on the river. Niamey ended out beyond the water, and the sun descended over the last views of the open Sahel. The terrace waiters wore soiled white jackets and got the orders wrong. They might have tried harder if their customers had been the African elite. But the *coopérants* had no real power.

I talked to the Belgian representative for a diesel engine manufacturer. He was a stocky, middle-aged engineer with a wife somewhere in the crowd and a daughter at the university back home. We sat side-by-side at the edge of the terrace and watched the sun go down. He had been three years in Niger and Mali, and before that in Togo, and before that in Chad. His work now took him the length of the Niger River. His attitude was at once wry and suspicious. He judged the world as a technician.

"It's impossible here," he said. "There is no solution. These people are like children who are always given new toys. They get tired of them, throw them away, and wait for new ones."

He seemed profoundly tired. Through half-closed eyes he watched an African in a ragged shirt who lay on his back on the riverbank below us. The African stretched his arms languidly and let them fall. "Impossible," the Belgian repeated. He looked away. He thought again about his work. "Everything falls apart here. The Africans care nothing about maintenance. They don't have the slightest concept. And then the spare parts! There is so much different equipment here that it would be impossible to keep all the parts in stock no matter how well organized you are. The inventory would have to be enormous."

I decided he had been hearing complaints from his customers. He mentioned seeing a shipment of Russian goods in Benin that included a snowplow. His enduring sense of order interested me.

The terrace waiters lit oil lanterns. After dinner a few couples danced. I found myself again with the Belgian. He said he regretted ever coming to Africa. "But once you enter into it you get stuck. That's where the new offers are, where the money is. It's practically impossible for me to find work that's *not* in Africa."

His wife came to take him home. She was the trim, tanned, tennis-playing, cuckolding type. I had noticed others like her in

Niamey. They drove company Land Cruisers with the ease of long experience, and shared the look of bored practicality that marked their withdrawal from Africa. A group came every morning to the walled-off hotel pool where they disrobed and rubbed lotion onto their brown breasts while the pool attendants looked studiously away. The women had fossilized. They talked incessantly, but had nothing to say. Restlessly, I headed by bus up the river road to Mali and the Sahara again.

24

A CITY BUILT OF MUD

Bᴜ AFRICAN STANDARDS, the bus trip upstream from Niamey to the ancient river port of Gao, in Mali, was neither slow nor difficult. We covered the 275 miles, including a border crossing, in a mere two days. The road stuck determinedly to the riverbank. It ran paved for the first morning, then turned into rutted track that slowed the overloaded old bus to a crawl. There was no music on this bus, just the unmuffled roar of an engine. The emergency windows flopped open and shut. Dirt danced on the floor.

We ground through fishing villages too sleepy to greet us, and through two larger market towns too busy to care. The country between seemed empty, motionless, nearly dead. It is said that these grasslands were once dangerous because of lions, and that more recently, during French colonial times, the telegraph line was cut regularly by galloping giraffes. The wildlife was exterminated not by drought, but by modern rifles. Nonetheless this may merely have been a matter of timing—of weapons getting to the animals before the dryness did.

We passed rapids in the river. The floodplain was in places shady and deep green. Crocodiles and hippopotami lurked in the water. The savanna undulated in yellow and gray to the horizons, and had a few trees, but dried as we drove north. In the afternoon we passed a few emaciated cows.

By the border with Mali, where we arrived at the end of the day, the trees were desert trees, and the soil was mostly bare gravel, a land good only for goats. The Malian border guards held the bus until dark, then prohibited it from driving on. They said they worried about a Tuareg attack, but the truth was they had found a prosperous market woman on the bus, and wanted to rob her. By the light of kerosene lanterns, they rifled through her stock of colorful cotton bolts and children's clothing, found nothing of interest, and announced that she had to pay a heavy customs tax.

The market woman was fat, smart, and brash—one of the many such West African businesswomen who manage somehow to succeed amidst so much failure. She came from a village up-river from Gao, and twice a year made the arduous trip to Niamey by boat and bus to purchase her goods. She wanted no sympathy and got none: the passengers on the bus seemed to resent her, and some now took the side of the border guards. But the woman would not be intimidated. She pretended that she had never heard of such outrageous demands. She folded her arms over her ample chest and refused to pay.

The guards locked her goods into a hut, and seized all passports and identity papers. To me they muttered ominously about a spy they had captured the week before, a Dutchman with a camera. I did not worry. From the start their threats had the familiar feel of an old opera. I knew that the guards intended no real harm, and that the market woman was less stubborn than she pretended, and that the passengers were in no hurry to get to Gao anyway. It was all quite comfortable.

A village of adobe and corrugated metal had grown up beside the border post. I walked through it in darkness, chased off a dog, and found a two-room hut where a family served meals to the public. The hut was hot and stuffy, and dimly lit, and had a single plastic-covered table. The proprietor was an uncommunicative old man with a fez and a goatee. He sold me rice with a fish sauce, and a Coke, and rented me a woven sleeping mat. I took the mat outside, spread it in the dirt beyond a pile of construction rubble, and listened to snatches of music floating across the village above the rushing of the river. Mosquitoes whined. The sky was a bright desert sky, but the air smelled of water.

GAO IS THE downstream port for the riverboat that plies the Niger's Saharan bend. It is an ancient trading center—like Timbuktu to its northwest, a place where the river highway meets a trans-Saharan track. At its height it was the capital of the Songhai empire, which during the fifteenth and sixteenth centuries included an area twice the size of modern France. But that is by now a disconnected heritage, and Malians don't bother to refer to it. One reason is that mud walls crumble and vanish, and if they are to endure, they require frequent rebuilding. As a result, they tend to reflect the immediate circumstances of people's lives. There are exceptions, of course—the Sahel's fantastic mud mosques were maintained for centuries even as religion weakened, and Gao still has a Songhai royal tomb made of adobe. Nonetheless, in ordinary residential and commercial neighborhoods, mud walls force a brutal honesty on architectural expression. Gao today is poor and forgotten, and it looks that way. Archeologists travel there to dig for its greatness, and to remind an astonished world of Africa's former competence. But the Songhai, who still live in Gao and along the Niger's bend, are overwhelmed by the present, and reminded of a more immediate decline by the crumbling of their childhood homes. It seems impossible that conditions could get worse, but they do. The Songhai blame Bambara bureaucrats sent from Mali's distant capital, Bamako, to rule over them. With greater justification they also blame the Tuaregs. The Tuaregs cannot win their uprising, but by closing the desert routes to Algeria and frightening tourists, they can strangle Gao. Their rebellion is still relatively new, but because Gao is built of dried mud, already Gao shows it.

Gao's streets are built of dried mud, too, and are rutted and dusty and full of trash. Raw sewage cuts channels the length of them. Houses fall into them. The sun beats pitilessly on the people driven to walk about in them by hunger and unemployment. The people are Songhai, Tuareg, Bambara, Bozo, Peul, Dogon, and others. They mix within the town uneasily, creating a harsh little culture that is predominantly Muslim, but suspicious and uncharitable, not the culture of modern Mali, or of any one group, but something unique to Gao, where even the marketplace is poor.

I waited in Gao for the riverboat, which was due to arrive whenever it arrived. I bought a ticket and reserved a berth. The ticket agent was an important fellow. He told me that the boat had left the river port of Mopti, 500 miles upstream, and later had passed by Timbuktu—that much was officially known. The problem with the downstream run was that when the boat ran aground, as inevitably it did, the river's current held it fast, and the crew had to kedge it off the shoals—a procedure that took hours or days. The Niger's water level depends not on the local weather but on the seasonal rains at its sources in the faraway tropical highlands. The dry season had come to the highlands, and the river's water level was dropping fast. The ticket agent told me I was lucky, because the next run upriver from Gao to Mopti might be the last for many months. He predicted that the trip would take five days or longer.

I walked while I waited, wandering throughout the town and out into the butte-studded desert beyond. At night I drank beer in a pleasant outdoor bar. One afternoon I took a *pinasse* across the Niger to the red dune that rises 300 feet above the river upstream from Gao. The boatman was a dignified gray-haired man with a beard. His *pinasse* was forty feet long, and was driven by an outboard motor. It carried about twenty people heading home from the market to a string of villages that lay inland from the river, across the dune. They eyed me with frank curiosity. I mentioned that I was waiting for the riverboat, which was not unusual, but which did not explain to them why a white man would travel here alone.

At the base of the dune they began unloading their bulky purchases of local rice and sorghum and American wheat. The boatman promised he would wait for me. I scrambled up the dune and walked along the crest to its summit, where I stood breathing heavily, looking down over the *pinasse,* the great muddy river, and in the distance the town of Gao, which was faint with dust and smoke and the color of the desert.

Carrying parcels on their heads, the villagers climbed the dune more slowly than I. They crossed the crest in a steady column, trudged down the far side, and made their way across a shimmering sand sheet toward their mud-walled houses beyond.

When I got back to the *pinasse,* the boatman said in French, "It's very *touristique* here."

He meant, at the dune. We pushed away from the riverbank as the sun was just going down. A breeze ruffled the river's surface, raising little brown waves across which the pirogue slapped. Birds flitted overhead. A hippopotamus swam languidly along the shore. A fish jumped. Our outboard motor purred.

The boatman spoke from the depths of his experience. "The Niger River is so beautiful. You will enjoy your long trip up the river."

How could I not agree?

He added, "We would be lucky, all of us, also to be leaving Gao."

When I drank from a bottle of purified water, then offered it to him, he refused and proudly said, "Here we drink the river water."

But the river at Gao is a sewer.

At the hotel, the Atlantide, water was brought to the washrooms by the bucket, for bathing. My room was an airless hole with torn mosquito netting over the bed. Every evening an employee with a flit gun helpfully sprayed the room with pesticide. It must have worked, since I never saw a mosquito. He also sprayed the hotel dining room while people ate, which helped to distract the customers from their food.

In the lobby I met a German anthropologist, a specialist on life in a certain river village, who acted surprised to find an American in Gao. He was taller than I, and had a beard, and stood close to me to talk. His English was laced with the exaggerated nasal intonations of a consciously Americanized accent. He was upset about a simulated African river trip he had taken at Disneyland. "The natives run like monkeys from wild animals! They attack the boat with spears! They are chased off by a single shot! It's incredible!"

I said, "I've never been there."

He was angry with me anyway. "Oh come on, everyone knows that the United States is a racist country."

I agreed, and indelicately brought up Germany's reputation. I might have brought up Mali's, too. One day the town grew excited because an army patrol had skirmished somewhere in the desert with a band of rebels. The mood in the streets turned festive and maybe dangerous, apparently in sympathy with one side or the other, but actually in grateful release from the tedium of slow decay. For a few hours after the fight, the police roared around looking for Tuaregs to arrest. I don't know if they found them, but I was pleased that during my stay in Gao they executed none publicly.

25

THE
DESERT
NATION

THESE FIGHTS WILL not end. A new Tuareg nation would be like an inversion of Mali, Niger, or Chad—one in which the light-skinned northerners would gain the upper hand and the blacks would rebel to save themselves. The evidence exists already in Mauritania, the nation of Moors that lies north of the Senegal River, and extends from the Sahara's Atlantic coast deep into the desert. The Moors are not Tuaregs, but they are Berber nomads, and the Tuaregs' closest cousins. Their nation is wretched and poor. It has few roads, schools, or hospitals. Malnutrition and disease are endemic, and in bad years there is famine. Politics are driven by fear and racial division. The military rules repressively. The towns are in disarray. For all this you can blame the deepening desert.

I once flew to Nouakchott, the capital city, which is hemmed in by enmities to Mauritania's north and south, and is accessible virtually only by air. The flight, from Casablanca, left me unprepared. I sat comfortably in the airplane watching the sun set against the ocean horizon, drinking strong black coffee. A fog bank lay offshore. To the east, the Sahara stretched in graceful plains. I sampled a pastry. I wiped my hands with perfumed towelettes. Then we were on final approach over a coastal desert of sand and gravel. Shacks passed under the wing. We landed, and disembarked by a ramshackle terminal. The dusk was thick with heat, dirt, and humidity. Within minutes my shirt was soaked through.

With some regret, I watched my airplane depart. The remaining daylight seemed gray, and I did not like the looks of the soldiers who loitered on the ramp, eyeing the passengers. I stood in the crowd, fighting mosquitoes and flies. Ahead, the police were carefully checking identities, and bodily searching the men. I wondered what they hoped to find.

The other passengers were fine-featured Moors, returning from the hadj pilgrimage to Mecca. They spoke the Arabic dialect known as Hassaniya. The men wore white Saharan robes; the women wore full dresses with colorful scarves, and like the Tuaregs did not veil their faces. Though many of the passengers undoubtedly spoke French, none would talk to me. They were reluctant to be seen with a foreigner.

Mauritania was given life by the French in 1960 as a desert nation to be ruled by desert nomads, and that is exactly what it became. Mauritanian society is among the most closed and hierarchical in the world. Below the ruling castes of Moors stands a Haratin class of slaves and ex-slaves, known as Black Moors. Slavery was officially banned in 1980, but in practice it continues today. The reason is that free people die of starvation in Mauritania, and for practical reasons slaves may prefer their servitude. And

Haratins in any case do not occupy the lowest level of Mauritanian society. That level is made up of cultivators and herders from the extreme south—black Africans with tribal ties to Senegal and Mali, who have never assimilated into the desert society. They inhabit a narrow strip of savanna and the farmland along the Senegal River, and constitute fully half the population. These people of the savanna are a problem for the ruling Moors, who despise and fear them, and worry that they will rebel. The Moors would like to reduce their numbers. They call their country an Islamic republic—a typical play on words, but one with relevance to the nation. The severe Islamic legal code called the sharia was instituted in 1980. In Mauritania, it now amounts to martial law.

In April 1989 riots broke out for three days, during which 400 of these "foreign" blacks were hunted down and slaughtered. Afterward, Mauritania expelled as many as 170,000 of them, calling them Senegalese. Senegal responded in kind, expelling Moorish shopkeepers. The two nations settled into the state of near-war that exists today. In Mauritania, the persecution continues. Along the Senegal River, the army keeps driving farmers from their land. There are rumors of killings. In the name of national security, the area is closed to outsiders.

This no doubt was what the airport policeman had in mind when he saw my visa. He scowled and ordered me to stand aside. He went to fetch his lieutenant. The other passengers stared at me as if they had not noticed my presence earlier. They now seemed equally upset.

The lieutenant was a shrewd pockmarked Moor with a sharp nose. He escorted me into a side room, held me there for an hour, and accused me of course of being a spy. I denied it. He said, "I do not believe you."

Having grown used to this elsewhere, I made no demands, volunteered nothing, and did not complain. I waited. Flies bathed in our sweat. Since the lieutenant did not pick up the phone, I suspected he was bluffing.

He asked, "What are you writing about?"

"The desert."

"What is there to say about the desert?"

"How dry it is."

"I do not believe you."

But he was softening. His underlings came in and searched my luggage. He impressed them with his command of the situation. "Monsieur says he is writing about the desert." They smiled at the idea. Later he impressed them with his generosity: he stamped my passport, and said I could go. He added, "But if you are caught taking photographs, you will be arrested."

"Understood," I answered.

"Here, we do not like spies."

"Understood."

Outside the terminal, the night was black. A crowd milled about. I caught a ride to the hotel through the unlit streets of Nouakchott. Our car lifted clouds of sand and dirt. At the hotel, French aid officials sat sullenly at the bar. Alcohol is prohibited in Mauritania. The Frenchmen drank Fanta.

IN MAURITANIA THE savanna has turned to sand. Erosion has cut the land. The river runs lower every year. There are places now where the desert extends right to its banks. And the drought has done more than damage the savanna; it has deepened the desert itself. Dunes have buried whole villages. Wells have gone dry.

In theory, there are solutions. You can drill deeper wells, irrigate crops, stabilize dunes, and plant trees. You can teach people to use the land more carefully, not to overgraze, overcut, or overpopulate. You can balance indigenous and imported technologies. You can preach hope that agriculture in the south might someday feed the country's two million people. In the meantime, you can ask them to stop killing each other.

In fact, there is little reason for optimism. Only rain can threaten the desert, and in recent years there has been mostly drought. The power of weather dwarfs human effort. In the past decades, the pluviometric limit of six inches of annual rainfall—the minimum for grazing—has moved south sixty miles. Nouakchott, once surrounded by grasslands, is now swept by blowing sand.

The Sahara is mercurial, and does not attack in regimental formation. It sprouts in barren patches here and there, perhaps a hundred miles ahead of the absolute desert, and bypasses the greenbelts planted to block its advance. Greenbelts are trees, Maginot lines in a losing war against the climate. If they survive, they protect only themselves. Farther on, around a well, near a village, for miles outside a city, the land goes bad. People steepen the decline once it has begun. There are more of them than ever before, wielding better tools. But it is hard to blame them. They cannot wish themselves away, and they must eat. The land cannot support them. The rains have stopped. This is the process now called desertification. It is an old story.

NOUAKCHOTT IS A political creation, planned in 1957 as the coastal capital of the soon-to-be nation. It is a dispersed, low-rise city of boulevards and block-house architecture—a place that speaks of the Mauritanian expanse. Goats wander the alleys. Donkeys haul loads of precious firewood to be sold in small bundles. The buildings are concrete, crumbling, dirty, and hot. There are few cars, and fewer trucks. Scant downtown traffic lights regulate the flow of Toyota vans packed to the limit with thirty or more passengers. There is a large African-style market, where women do most of the selling. Once there were two grocery stores, but during the riots of 1989 the largest was looted, and it has not reopened. Beggars, many diseased or physically deformed, cluster around the remaining store. Despite the penalties imposed by the sharia, theft is a problem. Many people are hungry. The better households employ guards. The wind blows constantly, carrying the desert with it. Sand is everywhere. Slowly it is turning even the busiest streets into tracks. Inside the buildings, workers sweep it, shovel it, and take it back outside.

The most surprising fact about Nouakchott is its size. Downtown, you might guess it at 100,000 inhabitants. The actual number is closer to 800,000—more than a third of the nation's entire population. Most of the people are Moors. They live in the squatters' camps that ring the city, and are discouraged from coming downtown by government policy and lack of transportation. Many are seminomadic: if the summer rains come, they leave with their goats for the open desert. When the season changes and the land can no longer support their herds, they return to the capital where there is electricity and water. The goats graze on refuse, at times on cardboard alone. The people have more elaborate needs. They suffer from sickness, but in Nouakchott, at least, they may stay alive. Nouakchott is the most efficient distribution center for the grain and medicine sent to

Mauritania by the United States and Europe, and managed on the ground by an array of international charities.

I drove out to the squatters' camps with a Moorish business-man who explained his work as "sometimes import-export." We went to the animal market, which stood in a sea of tents and flimsy shacks. Pencil-thin nomads crowded around us. My host said, "They are not as miserable as they seem. They think that by living like this they can force the government to give them housing and land. It is mostly fakery." And these were his fellow Moors. I did not ask what he thought of black Africans.

We bought a struggling lamb at the market, forced it into the trunk, and drove home. The businessman lived in a two-story concrete house with a large parlor. It was too hot inside, so we sat out back on a rug in the sand, and drank Coke and tradi-tional Saharan tea. Nearby, a slave slaughtered and skinned the lamb. I write slave without being sure. He was a Haratin, and had a peaceful face. He wore no chains. If I had asked, he would have been called a friend of the family. He was clearly more than a servant.

It was the week of the tree. On the television news we watched a government minister plant a sapling in the desert. There was no mention of world events. The businessman sneered. "They are confused and afraid, and don't know what to say. So they say nothing."

We went to his office, in a shabby building. He sat in grand style behind a large desk. On the wall hung the mandatory por-trait of the President Colonel—a handsome man with a mus-tache. I sat at a coffee table. We talked business about the economic potential of Mauritania, the iron deposits in the north, and the rich fishing grounds off the coast. We talked imports and exports. He argued that American magazines needed permanent representatives here. He discussed the strategic importance of the country. He was like a man on dry ground pretending to row a boat. The room had not been swept, and sand was accumulating in the corners.

INSHALLAH. GOD WILLING. You hear it again and again in conversation, a sort of cultural reflex, a constant reminder of faith. We will meet for tea, God willing. The weather will change, the rains will come, and our herds will survive, *inshallah*. And if none of it happens, that too is God's will.

Westerners accuse Islam of excessive fatalism, but fatalism is just the ingredient necessary to function in such a place. I talked to the director of the Peace Corps in Mauritania, who said the American way is to take action today for a better life tomorrow—which is equally a statement of faith. In Mauritania, the Peace Corps has proved largely impotent. The desert twitches, and sweeps aside good intentions. If nature has been subdued in the industrial West, in the Sahara it, or God, remains the primordial power. You live here as a guest. After a while you learn to think like others, and find yourself even in your most private thoughts saying, *inshallah*.

THE AMERICAN EMBASSY called a security meeting. New troubles had erupted in the Arab world, and there was fear of riots and reprisals in Mauritania. The Americans in Nouakchott formed an isolated, tight-knit community—members of the embassy, USAID, the Peace Corps, and Christian relief organizations. Perhaps fifty of them came to the meeting. They gathered at the American Center, a private club where alcohol is served. The mood was quiet and attentive. People greeted each other across the room with nods and quick smiles. There had been anti-Western riots before, during which cars had been burned and windows broken. No one had been hurt. But as unpopular guests in a radically Islamic land, the resident Americans did not dismiss the threat.

The chargé d'affaires was a strapping blond-haired man fresh in from an easier posting in Paris. He stood in front of the group and spoke in a measured, reassuring tone. He summarized the news, and repeated official policy. He said he had spoken to Mauritanian officials, and had demanded proper security. Nonetheless, he expected demonstrations. He mentioned as a worst case that everyone could be accommodated at the embassy, but that getting to it might be dangerous. He talked about an established "buddy" system for warnings and evacuation. He recommended that the Americans travel in pairs, and that they avoid the beach and the mosques. He urged calm. He smiled. His lovely wife smiled. It was a competent performance.

Several days later the rioting broke out, more as official policy than as an outpouring of genuine sentiment. The rioters were awkward and self-aware. Groups of chanting, flag-waving men circulated downtown. They carried unloaded guns. They chased one American, but he outran them. They hit a Frenchman in the head with an egg. They slaughtered a camel, stoned a window, and set fire to a few cars. I walked around town and watched. By evening Nouakchott had returned to normal.

The Westerners did not bother to feel offended. They had come to Mauritania to fight the desert, but had grown weary and realistic. At the American Center, a distinguished gray-haired man in a suit and tennis shoes introduced himself to me by saying, "I've been associated with every major foreign policy disaster of the past thirty years." His wife and children lived in Falls Church, Virginia. He was charged with reducing the American donations of wheat. I asked how he felt about such a duty. He said, "This office is pretty far removed from feeding people anyway. My problem is, I can't keep up with the acronyms." He may have worried about how he sounded. Later he came up to me and said, "But what are you going to do about a country like this?"

KIFFA IS THE capital of a region called the Assaba, 300 miles to the east of Nouakchott, on the paved road that crosses southern Mauritania. The road is interrupted by frequent security checkpoints. Immediately to the south, there is trouble on the river; immediately to the north, there is desert. The law is as capricious as the weather. The soldiers are uncertain. I went by air to Kiffa, and overflew their scrutiny.

Once a fertile savanna, the Assaba has come under full assault by the Sahara. The airport at Kiffa is a dirt runway scraped through the brown scrubland outside of town. I waited to disembark while an old woman tried to descend the airplane's stairs. She was a backcountry Moor, a nomad from the open desert. For minutes she hesitated in the doorway. She gripped the rails, and surveyed the angle. Her problem was not physical inability, but lack of understanding. These were her first stairs: she had climbed them to get on the airplane, and now she had to figure a way down. A crowd at the bottom shouted advice. She turned one way, then the other, and finally started down backward. Halfway down she ran out of ideas, and froze. She looked anguished. Men came from below and lifted her to the ground.

It was summer, the end of the rainy season. A single cumulus cloud towered in the haze and humidity. No one dared hope for a storm; for months the sky had been full of false promise. The land was sparse. The people at the airport looked idle and unhealthy. I was carrying messages from Nouakchott, and caught a ride with an aid worker into town.

Kiffa looked like a town of 10,000, and probably held three times more. Still, it seemed dispersed and uncrowded. Stone houses lined empty dirt streets. Groups of young Moorish men in white and pale blue robes walked abreast. They were haughty and unwelcoming. Relations between the races were difficult. The few European aid workers had naturally taken sides with the blacks. A weary Englishman, a nurse, said to me, "We are the new slaves here. We even pay our own way." There was a market run by black African women where the heat was magnified by the confines of airless alleys. There were a few small groceries with butane refrigerators to keep bottled drinks cool. There was no electricity. There were no telephones. There were few cars. During my visit there was no gasoline. People dug individual wells and drink tainted water. There was no sewage system. There was no hospital. There was a medical clinic with no medicine. Cholera, polio, measles, tuberculosis, malaria, typhoid, hepatitis, parasites, and probably AIDS thrived. One death was hardly distinguished from another.

I stayed in Kiffa with a Peace Corps worker named John Stingely. At age forty, he was a wizened, balding man with a full beard and a cautious expression—hardly the poster image of an enthusiastic volunteer. Stingely was a sometime rock musician and forester from coastal Oregon. His last job there had been as a low-paid technician, trudging the rainy slopes and counting

saplings. He told me he joined the Peace Corps out of frustration. He said he wanted to dry out his boots.

But he was idealistic, too. With three years of forestry school
behind him, and a lot of practical experience, he thought he
could do the world some good. The Peace Corps sent him here
to fight the Sahara and plant trees. He was a better soldier than
most; near the completion of the two-year tour only fifteen of
his original group of forty-one volunteers remained. The others
had quit because of sickness and discouragement. Stingley himself had lost thirty pounds, and gained back only fifteen. He lived
in Kiffa utterly alone, with little backup from the Peace Corps
headquarters in distant Nouakchott. His relations with the local
authorities were poisoned by corruption, mistrust, and racial
politics. Stingley stayed on, but he no longer believed he could
help. He had grown his trees and watched them die. He blamed
Mauritanian neglect and the weather. Now he was only counting the days until the end. It is not easy to fight a hopeless war.

The Peace Corps rented his house from the biggest landlord
in town. It was a two-room bungalow at the center of walled
dirt yard. With the exception of a scraggly tree by the porch, the
yard was bare. This embarrassed Stingley, who said he would
have planted shade trees and vegetables except for the herds of
neighborhood goats. They were the bane of his existence. They
bounded over the walls and wandered the yard at will. Goats are
the worst culprits in desertification. They eat even spined plants,
and destroy young trees by cropping them down to their roots.
Stingley hated them with professional vigor, but would have
missed them if they were gone. Together he and the animals
danced a mad ballet. When he spotted them in his yard, he
stepped threateningly off the porch and waved his arms. They

watched, and pretended not to care. He started after them, and they thundered around the house in mock fright. He was nimble and sly, and doubled back to catch them by surprise. They thundered the other way, just out of reach. He threw stones; they pranced. If he cornered them, they escaped over the wall and returned later to test his vigilance.

We drew water from a deep well at the front of the yard. It was a laborious job of hauling up buckets hand over hand, and filling plastic jerricans. Stingley did not mind. Preparing the water was the kind of ritual that had kept him sane. He filtered and sterilized it with the patience of a castaway. His housekeeping was immaculate. He cooked on a campstove and ate simply. He weighted himself daily. He kept himself clean. He kept an evening journal in tight handwriting. He was proud that he had not been sick for months.

At night we sat outside to escape the heat of the rooms, and we drank his homemade bush wine—a grapeless concoction that smelled like an experiment in fermentation. We mixed it with Fanta, and listened to the BBC through the static of a shortwave radio. We talked about rain. Stingley had a gauge in the yard, and had measured only two inches for the year. We talked about the Sahara—an enemy he fought yet had never clearly seen. We slept on straw mats in the dirt, thankful for the slightest breeze.

In brilliant morning sunlight we went to the nursery, where a crew of Africans cared for seedlings under Stingley's direction. The laborers were employees of the Mauritanian forestry department, to which Stingley was attached as a sort of extension agent. They had not been paid in months, and were growing weak from malnourishment. Stingley said that the bosses were stealing their wages. He could not bear the suffering of his men, and had loaned them money from his own meager salary. In return, they treated him as their friend and protector. He had protested on their behalf, to no avail. He was frustrated by his inability to help.

Still, he brightened up among his seedlings. There were some 40,000 of them in the nursery, grown in sacks for transplantation. He led me through the nursery, bending over the young plants, cupping their fragile leaves in his hands, discussing the attributes of the different species. Mostly he raised mesquite, which roots well in difficult soils, finds water, grows fast, and can be cropped to the ground and survive. The other seedlings were acacias and desert bushes, a local tree called tikifeet, and another called the neem, which was his favorite because of its resistance to goats.

Within the confines of the nursery, the project was successful: after several reseedings, Stingley had achieved a 90 percent germination rate. I asked about the longer term prospects of survival. He shook his head. In the United States the survival rate is roughly 80 percent; he guessed survival in Mauritania to be at the most 8 percent, depending on the project. He described walking through old projects in which every sapling had died. He described watching his own saplings die.

We discussed the current crop. Most of the trees were intended for planting along the roads leading out of town. The idea was to fight drifting sand. But there were no trucks or crews available, and already the planting season was ending. Stingley had heard rumors that in reality many of the trees were destined for the yards of the governor and the chief of police. He shrugged. "At least they might get watered."

Other trees were being given away on the street. One afternoon as we watched, the nursery crew handed 15,000 seedlings over the fence to crowds of women. The women seemed delighted. Stingley was skeptical. He had wanted to sell the seedlings for a token fee, and include instructions on how to plant them. I asked him if he thought any would survive. He smiled quizzically and answered, "*Inshallah.*"

We went to see recent plantings at the northern edge of town. They were mesquite bushes, regularly spaced across the upwind slope of a long, powdery dune. A group of children from nearby houses followed us across a fence, and along the crest. The land to the northeast was a vast eroded plain, the desert shadow of an earlier savanna. A few sturdy trees remained, but the grass was gone, turned to dirt and sand. The land was harsh, but not lifeless. Spiny bushes had taken root along an *oued* and in the shelter of rocks. A car track led across the plain, and disappeared into the distance, where the main mass of the Sahara stretched in eternal buttes and sand seas.

Here on the dune the mesquite plantation had failed. The sand had kept moving, exposing the roots of the bushes, slowly killing them. The fence sagged where we and others had climbed over it. Soon it would let in the goats. I asked the children which way the dune was drifting. They pointed here and there. But I could see for myself that it threatened their houses. The sand was slipping into town. The sun pounded the earth.

2 6

T H E

R I V E R

THE RIVERBOAT GOT to Gao at night, and while it refueled it loaded. The town woke up for the event. I left the Atlantide and joined the throng heading through the dark streets to the port, where a noisy market had sprung up around the boat's lowered gangplanks. After forcing my way onto the crowded lower deck, I found a staircase by the light of a caged bulb, climbed to the crowded middle deck, found another staircase, emerged onto open-air portion of the bridge deck, and secured a place by the railing that faced the town.

Steel cables held the boat against the river's sluggish current. The fuel hose snaked like an umbilical cord into the hold. Heavily loaded *pinasses* floated in the strip of water by the muddy bank. Thousands of people moved about on the shore by the light of kerosene lanterns. Piles of cargo materialized and vanished as porters streamed through the town. The gangplank sagged under the weight the mob. People lost their balance and fell into the water. Men and women, the young and the old, they all went in. The crowd noticed, laughed, and pulled them out. Sodden cargo was retrieved just as willingly. Only the police seemed to be in a bad mood. One of them waved a riot-control stick and shouted because no one would listen. A *pinasse* capsized, and filled with water. From the boat's bridge, the silhouette of a man watched quietly, pulling on a cigarette. I assumed he was a river pilot.

Minutes after the fuelers withdrew their hose, the deckhands raised the gangplanks and cast off from the shore. The engines rumbled, belching black exhaust, and the boat shuddered out into the current. Thieves dashed to the railings and dove away. Gao soon disappeared into its black haze. By dawn we had pushed two hours upriver.

The boat was built in the old East Germany, and had a plaque that called it a gift, in solidarity, from those people to these. It was 150 feet long, thick hulled, and of shallow draft. Its three twelve-cylinder diesels were capable in theory of driving it at fifteen miles per hour, in practice at less. But the Niger here is a sluggish river, rarely flowing faster than three miles per hour, and more important than speed was the boat's ability to carry passengers: designed for a maximum of 350, it regularly carried three times that. I won't guess the number aboard now, so dense was the humanity. We moved up the river, stopping at settlements along the way. More people boarded. The boat teemed.

It functioned like a concentration of Africa. The lower deck, which lay only inches above the river and had open sides and communal cabins, was where the poorest passengers were expected to remain. In its misery and squalor it was like a Brueghel painting come to life—the tangled mob of people and goats living among their bundles; the accumulation of the blackest filth; the smoke drifting from cooking fires built directly on the deck; the sharp stench of diesel fuel, sweat, and human feces; the sounds of argument and laughter; the bawling of children, the splash of water, the constant drumming of the engines. I heard that Europeans sometimes traveled this way, participating in lower-deck life as an expression of their love for Africa. But this was hardly the native life to admire. It was not loving or picturesque. A woman and a small boy died during the trip upriver.

The middle deck was smaller, and contained second- and first-class cabins along outside passageways. The cabins were little cells with just enough room for bunks, but they had lockable doors. I was unlucky, because mine was by the communal toilets, which had quit working. The passageway was crowded by refugees from the lower deck, who soon created similar conditions here, too. The police were supposed to control that sort of thing, but accepted small bribes instead. And they were right—within the confines of a single boat, the attempt to enforce the rules would have been absurd, even dangerous. I felt no solidarity with these neighbors who crowded my corridor, who would not make room for me to pass, who cursed me when I jostled them, who kept me awake at night with their shrill voices and the shuffling of their rubber sandals. But I also recognized the element of chance in their births and in mine. As an act of self-discipline, I would not allow myself to resent their encroachment. When I could no longer stand the smell of the toilets, I climbed to the bridge deck, which grew equally crowded, but was swept by the clean Saharan wind.

One night when the crew invited me forward to the bridge itself, I discovered there the same sense of competence and sober duty I once knew in the cockpits of airplanes. The bridge was dark except for a small charcoal fire kept alight for tea. Three Songhai river pilots in robes and desert turbans stood by the helm, peering steadily into the night. We shared no language beyond nods and a glass of tea. The boat trembled beneath us. The steering mechanism clicked softly. The bow wake splashed. There was no moon. Beyond the faint green glow of the engine controls and the occasional flaring of a cigarette, the river ahead lay in blackness. The thinnest trace of a shoreline slid by, blotting the stars. Only from the work of the pilots could I tell that the water was shallow, that it braided through shifting channels, that it required many small turns. The boat ran at full speed. The pilots navigated without map or depthfinder, by confident feats of memory.

They made mistakes, of course. Anyone would. Late that same night they ran us aground in midriver, and the boat came to a jarring stop. I got up from my bunk and went to the bow, where deckhands had opened a cargo hatch and were shining lights down into the hold, listening to the echo of water. One of them spoke English to me, explaining that an existing leak had grown stronger, but that the pumps and perhaps the occasional bailing brigade would keep up. His English was thick and strangely ornate. "One grows accustomed to decrepitude," he said. He was more worried about the depth of the river. "If their excellencies on the bridge cannot find the channel, we shall be obliged to return to Gao." He was a university student in Bamako, and had taken a leave of absence to support his old mother. He himself did not look like a young man. I asked how long his leave had been. He said, so far about twelve years.

It took only minutes to back off the shoals. The boat shuddered in reverse, stirring sand and mud, then smoothly slipped free. Leaning from the bridge above us, the pilots allowed it to drift backward with the current before starting upstream again, closer to the shore. With crew members positioned at the bow to pole for depth, we felt our way slowly, nudged a shoal, drifted back, tried again, and after an hour found a way through. The pilots called again for maximum speed.

In the morning I visited the engine room, which occupied the aft section of the lower deck. It was a deafening place, choked with exhaust and hot fumes, filthy with black oil. The engines churned under metal grates, on top of which slept the engineer's wife and two children. You could not imagine a more poisonous home. I admired the furnishings, then went back to the bridge, where I discovered that the pilots had brought their families as well: Children and chickens scurried about; women lit cooking fires, talking shrilly; blue smoke drifted into the helmsman's bloodshot eyes; there was hardly room on the bridge to stand. One of the pilots hauled up a tethered pot of river water and did not quite boil it before he made tea. I drank the tea reluctantly, and later fell violently ill. But even then I knew it was the suffering of those others who could not leave that mattered.

Day after day I watched the banks go by. The river changed constantly, narrowing between barren bluffs, widening to a mile across open land. We moved up one side or the other, working the turns and channels. The desert was sandy and pale, and rolled in low hills to the water's edge. Here and there, a tree or bush had taken root and survived. We passed Tuareg encampments with goats and camels and animal-skin tents, and small Songhai settlements of one or two mud houses. People bathed in the river, and washed their clothes in it. Children swam, and fisherman fished. But aside from the occasional vegetable patch, there was no attempt at irrigation or farming. The Niger should be the Sahara's greatest oasis, but because of Mali's poverty, it is not.

A passenger in a business suit had a different theory. He said, "It's because these northerners are lazy. They are nomads. They would rather starve than work."

He himself was a southerner, an unhappy traveler, a hard worker, a big eater. He bottled soft drinks in the capital, and was rich. He spent the trip in the deckhouse behind the bridge, sitting with his wife, who was thin and elegant and had beads in her hair. They had taken the boat on a mission which he described only as his wife's family affair. I asked her if she came from the Niger, and he answered for her, yes, from Timbuktu. She looked as if she would feel at home in Paris. She spoke to no one but her husband, and even to him barely murmured. He complained to me that for lack of customers the Malian national airline had stopped flying Timbuktu. He and his wife had driven all the way from Bamako to Gao, and had taken the boat from there because the overland route to Timbuktu was arduous and was threatened by the Tuaregs. Getting out of Timbuktu would be difficult now if this boat was, as he too had heard, the last of the season. "But the wife . . ." he lamented. I could not get him to finish that sentence.

He was determined at least to suffer in comfort, and had brought along a servant to prepare his meals. Twice a day he took his wife below to their cabin to eat in private. The rest of the time he sat in the deckhouse with her, expressed his disgust with the desert, and allowed himself to be fawned over by the boat's official jester—a barrel-chested man crippled by childhood polio, who was known as the *"animateur."*

The *animateur* was a Bambara with family connections in the capital. He had been hired by the Malian boat company in a mimicry of national development, as if this river trip might be made into an inland pleasure cruise. His job was to keep the upper deck amused—a difficult mission which he undertook with insistence and desperation, as if his family connections might fail him. If they did, and he lost this job, he would end up like other African polio victims, condemned to the streets, forced finally to sell his crutches to buy food. His immediate problem was that so many passengers faced similar worries. It was like this on every trip. The people who took this boat were usually not in the mood to be entertained.

I sympathized with the *animateur,* and insisted that I enjoyed watching the desert, and even promised to write a nice letter to his employer. But he could not be reassured. He thought I needed stimulation. One night to my embarrassment he organized a dance in my honor. A hundred people crammed into the deckhouse. I don't know who they were, or how they were invited. They were not the poor of the lower deck. The *animateur* had put on a polyester party shirt that made him sweat. He introduced me to a fat woman who clearly expected to be my partner for the night. She wore a full-length print dress and a matching turban. We had to take the first dance, while the others watched. The *animateur* played the stereo at high volume. My date danced fluidly. I did not. I was grateful when, with the second song, other dancers joined in. Eventually I managed to stop dancing by offering my date a beer. We discovered we had nothing to say to each other. When I did not ask her to dance again, she grew offended and walked away.

The *animateur* came up to me looking worried. Over the music, he shouted, "You've made her upset. She was yours for the night. Look at her body—she's made for the bed. She has meat on her. I thought you'd be pleased."

"I have a wife at home," I answered apologetically. "I have a family."

He stood beside me watching the dancers, thinking through my case, then frowned and said, "You're worried about AIDS. A man can't tell about Africans."

The dance was not his only disappointment. In the days following, as the bridge deck filled with illegal passengers from below, he abandoned any hope of providing a cruise ship atmosphere, and retreated into the deckhouse, where he sat beside the soft-drink bottler and his wife, and cursed the insolence of the poor. He blocked the door to the deckhouse with the stereo's cabinet speakers, and blasted the passengers outside with the songs of a man and woman known as "the blind couple from Mali." The song he hurled again and again was an accusation springing from the bitterness of his own experience. It had a French refrain that observed, "Il'y a toujours des menteurs, des trompeurs, et des traîtres." The song was backed by a melodic guitar. "There are always liars, cheaters, and traitors." That is the real desert now. Through a deepening Sahara, the refrain propelled us upriver.

TRUTH

AND

FALSEHOOD

T RUTH AND FALSEHOOD were both traveling, though for different reasons, when by chance they found themselves on the same path. Falsehood saw Truth ahead, and hurried to catch up with him.

"Hello, traveler," said Falsehood.

"Hello to you too," answered Truth. "How was your night?"

"It was peaceful. May I ask who you are and where you are going?"

"My name is Truth, and I am on my way to collect a few debts from those who owe money to me."

"My name is Falsehood, and I am on my way to give hope to people, and to tell them whatever will please them. Shall we travel together?"

"Yes, of course," said Truth.

"Since you were ahead of me already," said Falsehood, "I will ask you to be my guide."

Truth accepted, and the two companions continued on their way. At every village they came to, Truth approached the people honestly, to collect his debts. The people answered by chasing him away. This went on for days. Truth and Falsehood grew steadily hungrier, until finally Falsehood could stand it no longer.

"Truth, you are not a good guide," he said. "Everywhere we go we are turned out. If we keep going this way, we will both die of hunger, and thirst, and fatigue. Let me be the guide now, and you will see, at the first village we will have plenty to eat."

With a light heart, Truth agreed to let Falsehood become the guide. When they came to the next village, Falsehood spotted a hut from which old women were emerging. The women were bent over, somber, and very quiet. Falsehood understood immediately that something had happened. Bringing Truth with him, he found a place to sit by the hut, not far from a freshly dug grave. Truth sat there quietly, and with dignity, but Falsehood began to cry loudly. The mistress of the hut, a peasant woman, came outside and asked, "Stranger, why are you crying so?"

Falsehood answered, "We are on our way, my friend and I, to resurrect a dead child, but we have not eaten for days, and our genie has stopped us here because he is hungry. He says if he doesn't get his food, others will die too."

The peasant woman was astounded. "I have just lost my only son, who was just twelve years old. Maybe you could resurrect him?"

"Resurrecting the dead is our job," said Falsehood. "But we work with a genie who eats all the time."

The woman finally understood. She prepared a large meal for the travelers. After they had eaten, Falsehood asked her to build a small hut over her son's grave. She set about doing this, and while she was working she mentioned that the king's father had died only two days before. Falsehood asked her to send word to the king of their presence.

The king was overjoyed, and promised a hundred horses, a hundred cows, a hundred slaves, clothes, silver, and many other things to anyone who could bring his beloved father back to life.

After the Friday prayer, at two in the afternoon, Falsehood entered the hut over the boy's grave. He dug open the grave and climbed in, and after a long and muffled conversation emerged covered in sweat.

To the mother of the dead boy he said, "Your son wants to return to life, but the father of the king is holding him by the hand. Go tell the king that his father will only return if he can return with the child."

The peasant woman went to tell the king, who in turn now consulted his mother. The king's mother was categorical. "And if your father returns, who will occupy the throne? Is there enough room in a pond for two male crocodiles? Leave the old king in peace. Pay the magicians what you owe them, and be done with this."

The peasant woman returned to her hut in tears. Falsehood was paid his fortune. He mocked Truth, who as yet had received none of the debts owed to him.

After a long silence, Truth sighed and said, "He who purchases with lies must someday pay with the truth. Today you may laugh, exalt, and beat your chest. But when people realize that you have tricked them, they will make you suffer dearly."

But when Truth and Falsehood separated, each took the path to his own destiny, and the disagreement between them was never resolved.

28

SKIPPING
TIMBUKTU

T HE BOAT STOPPED along the way at the villages where deep water allowed it to nestle against the shore. The scenes played like small repetitions of Gao, but without the thieves. The boat blew its whistle upon arrival. People emerged from adobe houses and came to the river down wide dirt streets. Food markets sprang up by the lowered gangplanks, selling smoked fish, a few vegetables, batteries, and rice. Villagers and passengers streamed through the boat. Pirogues circled around. I took every chance to leave the boat and walk through the villages. Away from the river, they were somnolent places of ruined walls, where women ducked out of sight and children chased after me asking for presents. I gave the children pens. They responded by showing me the local attractions—a well, a garden, a litter of day-old puppies, a ruined French fort.

At most of the villages I was accompanied by a man I had met on the boat, a quick young Fulani named Amadou, who came from the capital Bamako and was wandering through the back-country eager for any opportunity. Amadou was twenty. He had a flat-top haircut, a strong chin, and wore neatly pressed trousers and a short-sleeved shirt with the short sleeves rolled up. He smoked. He spoke seven African languages and French. He had seven brothers and five sisters. Sitting in the shade of a tree one day, I asked him why he had left Bamako, and what he was doing here. He grinned and showed me a shoebox of music cassettes from the capital that he had thought he could sell along the river.

"How is business?"

He shook his head. "Bad, very bad. These people here don't have any money. If I had known I would not have come, but once you are on the river you stay on the river, *n'est-ce pas?*" He had spent the last of his own money on the fare. But he smiled because he remained strong, and he was accustomed to adversity.

He befriended me because he thought I might prove useful. I befriended him because he shared my interest in the world. He was energetic. We climbed the slopes above the villages and stood looking over the wide brown river sweeping from the horizons. Amadou seemed to enjoy observing his country through the eyes of a foreigner. He loved Mali and he worried about it.

He said, "It's good of you to give gifts to the children, but they should not be such beggars."

A straight answer would have been awkward. I said, "Amadou, I promise you, children everywhere are natural beggars."

But of course I pitied those children. This desert, no fault of their own, would take away their lives.

Amadou lived in it too, and despite his energy was unlikely ever to find opportunity there. The Sahara is not cruel, but it is indifferent. An American can pass through, thankful that the boat's whistle blows before every departure. Because a Malian cannot, I could never quite talk honestly with Amadou.

In the larger villages, traders stacked sacks of American and Canadian wheat on the muddy banks. The sacks were marked with the symbols of international aid. The wheat was not originally intended to be sold, but nevertheless had slipped past corrupt officials and into the market. I mentioned my annoyance to Amadou: it was precisely such siphoning that had sparked the Tuareg rebellion in Niger. Amadou acted mystified. He wanted to be my friend, so he agreed with me. But given the chance he would have bought and sold the wheat as well.

The bottler from Bamako said, "Do you think your American farmers don't make money on these supplies? Why shouldn't we Africans make money too?" He pinched his fat forearm. "Is it because of our black skin?"

"It's because of your famines."

The bottler chuckled and spread his hands. "But look around you, there is no famine this year."

I did look, and had before, and knew this much: famine in the Sahel never quite resembles the images of it that appear on television and in the newspapers. Even during the worst years of drought, whether in refugee camps or villages, the sort of living skeletons who have come to symbolize African famine are, in fact, quite rare. This is because among the poor, they are the resilient ones. Ordinary Africans get sick and die before losing so much weight. They also murder each other. And a large number of them continue to prosper by robbing the weak. If at its origin famine is a natural phenomenon, it inevitably also becomes a political one. Even in the hardest hit areas, the rich and the well armed never lack for food.

The bottler from Bamako was right that the rains this year had been ample, that the rice harvest was good, that international donors had continued to send wheat, that there was plenty of food to go around. What he did not say was that the Tuaregs who chose neither to fight nor to flee, who tried to live peacefully within the new democracy of Mali, continued nonetheless to go hungry. And they were not the only ones. Nearing Timbuktu late one afternoon, the boat stopped at a village that was no longer just desperately poor, a place where people were actively going about the dying of starvation. The residents were not Tuaregs or rebels, but were black Africans on the Malian government's side of the war, and would have farmed or fished if they could have. The bottler from Bamako kept calling them nomads because he did not care.

Gone were the sacks of grain. No cargo came off the boat. At the gangplank market, vendors offered only peanuts and soap bars. I walked away from the riverbank through the silence of the dead. There were adults here who did not hide from me, but simply turned to watch listlessly. Dressed in rags, they had arrived at the pre-skeletal stage of open sores and predominant mouths. I'm sure there were others who were stronger. But the children who followed me did not smile or offer to show me around. They had contracted a respiratory infection, which choked them, and caused mucus to run from their noses. They coughed constantly, and could not bother to keep the flies from their eyes. A young boy stood in front of me and silently extended his hand. I gave him a coin. The others crowded around.

Hopelessly, I distributed the last of my cash—a few dollars' worth of French and West African francs. When my pockets were empty, the children continued to watch me numbly. Amadou came wandering up looking somber. The whistle blew dully for Timbuktu. Twilight flattened the sky.

TIMBUKTU, LONG FAMOUS for being far away, has again become difficult to reach. It is a town of about 20,000 people, of sandy streets and mud-walled houses, six miles inland from the river. Founded by wandering Tuaregs, inhabited first by their vassals and later by black merchants of the Niger, it became a caravan center during the twelfth century—one of the string including Gao and Agadez that dotted the Sahara's southern edge. The Tuaregs did not live within the town, but they claimed the right to it, and they extracted tributes. Only when they were chased off could Timbuktu prosper. This happened under the empires of Mali and Songhai, from the fourteenth through the sixteenth centuries. A mud mosque and a university were built. Word filtered back to Europe of a mysterious and powerful city of native palaces, where the ruling classes ate on plates of gold. The city was thought to lie somewhere in the West African unknown, below the hostile Sahara, in a land of warrior kings, near a great river that might someday be discovered. Geography left plenty of room for embellishment. The myth of a glorious Timbuktu endured because of the real city's nearly perfect isolation.

Time was hard on Timbuktu. The Songhai Empire collapsed in the early seventeenth century, and the new Moroccan masters lost interest in the city. Although money was still made in the caravan trade, the Tuaregs returned, and Timbuktu reverted to its natural condition of chaos, suspicion, and civil war. Then as now, the anarchy choked off commerce and kept visitors away. The situation was made worse by the growth of the European trading and slaving posts on the African coasts, which undercut most trans-Saharan trade. By the end of the eighteenth century, even the myth of Timbuktu had suffered: for lack of news, astute Europeans surmised that the famed city had declined. Their interests in it were now largely scientific. But they still had Timbuktu on their minds.

In 1824, the Paris-based Société de Géographie offered a 10,000 franc award to the first European to reach Timbuktu and return alive. The following year a British army officer, a rigid Scotsman named Gordon Laing, set out by camel from the Mediterranean at Tripoli. In the company of a paid guide, two African boatbuilders, a Jewish interpreter, a West Indian servant, and eleven camels, he angled southeast across the Sahara toward the famed city. Laing was an immodest and jealous man, convinced that he was destined for greatness, and worried that someone might beat him to it. He dressed in robes and a *chèche,* in reluctant acceptance of the climate, but at the start of the trip he declared his intention to don English attire every Sunday, and to read aloud from the Bible. From the string of letters he sent back to his father-in-law, the British consul in Tripoli, it is not clear that he managed to accomplish this. It was high summer. The way across the desert was hard and hot, with temperatures rising to 120 degrees. Banditry forced the men to take an indirect route. The Saharans they met cheated them. The boatbuilders, the guide, and the interpreter all misbehaved. The camels suffered, as camels do.

The unhappy little expedition went to Ghadames, rested, then passed below the Great Eastern Sand Sea, and came after five months to In Salah, where Laing was the first European the residents had seen. There Laing and his companions joined a southbound caravan of 150 merchants who had been waiting nearly a year, out of fear of the Tuaregs. It is said that Laing shamed the merchants into proceeding southward.

In January 1826 the caravan passed west of the Hoggar Mountains, not far from Tamanrasset, and headed out across the terrible flat Tanezrouft, making twenty miles a day. The emptiness of the Tanezrouft spooked the merchants, who were armed, but disorganized and frightened. Laing wrote disdainfully that "every acacia tree in the distance became magnified . . . into troops of armed foes." He should have paid attention.

Two weeks south of In Salah, twenty Tuaregs attacked—not by galloping over the horizon, but in the standard manner, by riding up quietly and joining the caravan. The merchants reacted with typical timidity, each distancing himself from the others in the hope of avoiding trouble. Laing, on the other hand, was fooled. He wrote that the Tuaregs were friendly, and had offered protection to the caravan. None of the merchants bothered to set him straight.

The Tuaregs realized that Laing was vulnerable. Late one night they made their move: they fired into his tent, then cut the ropes, and in the confusion of falling canvas, rushed in with swinging swords. Several of Laing's companions were killed. Laing survived, but suffered two dozen wounds, including deep cuts and broken bones from his skull to his legs and two nasty slashes that nearly severed his ear and his right hand. The Tuaregs left him for dead, and looted the ruins of his camp. The caravan reacted by packing up and leaving. Laing's remaining companions strapped him to a camel, and took him 400 miles across the Tanezrouft to recuperate in the camp of a friendly

Berber. There they all died of fever—except for Laing, who got sick but recovered.

On August 13, 1826, after more than a year in the desert, Laing reached Timbuktu. To Tripoli he sent back a message: "I have no time to give you my account of Timbuktu, but shall briefly state that in every respect except size . . . it has completely met my expectations."

But the real Timbuktu was a sleepy, sandy, inglorious place, with only the faint traces of history to recommend it. Then as now, war swirled around it—the Fulanis had recently seized the town from the Tuaregs, who nonetheless controlled the desert. Laing stayed in a mud house, which stands today. He sneaked one night to the river port at Kabara and sneaked back. He wrote furiously in his journal—what, we do not know. He was well treated, but after five weeks the local sheik received a letter from the distant Fulani sultan ordering his exile or execution.

Laing left town on September 22, 1826, heading northwest in the company of a guide from Timbuktu. The guide was a Fulani agent or a religious zealot, or both. On the second night, only thirty miles from Timbuktu, he demanded that Laing renounce his Christianity and accept Islam. When the stubborn explorer refused, the guide killed him with a sword. He cut off Laing's head, burned his writings, and left his remains to be eaten by vultures. An ex-slave escaped to tell the story. A passing Tuareg later discovered Laing's body and buried it. Eighty-four years later, in 1910, the French colonial army dug up Laing's bones at the base of a tree, and reburied them in Timbuktu.

The greatest tragedy about Laing's life was not his death, but his public devotion to the Timbuktu myth even after it should have been obvious that the myth was false. He may never have admitted even to himself his only important discovery: that

Timbuktu was not worth the visit. Such an admission would have seemed to him like a failure.

The man who finally brought the truth home, and who won the 10,000 franc prize, had an important advantage over Laing: he came from the lowest level of European society, and in his modesty he was willing to accept Africa as he saw it, and to report on it simply. His name was René Caillé—an uneducated French peasant, frail-looking, gaunt, uncommunicative, the orphan of a prison convict from La Rochelle. His family wanted him to become a cobbler. He became instead one of history's most supple travelers, a model for the thousands of young Frenchmen who drift through the world today, living close to the earth, managing usually to survive.

Caillé was an antihero, the opposite of a military man. He read *Robinson Crusoe* as a child, became obsessed with the idea of the tropics, and managed at the age of sixteen, in 1816, to sail for the west coast of Africa. He joined a disastrous British expedition, during which he learned firsthand the difficulties faced in Africa by large and overequipped European forces. Weighed down by weapons and trading goods, slowed by the sick, the expedition plowed ponderously through a land where native people practiced the lightest forms of life and travel. It was no wonder that the expeditionaries were seen as foreigners and fools, to be resisted and plundered.

Caillé left Africa, and returned in 1824 determined not only to reach Timbuktu, but to reach it alone. The trick would be to pass quietly, drawing as little attention to himself as possible. This meant that he would have to pose as a Muslim. In preparation, he went to live among the Moors of Mauritania, seeking religious instruction, and learning Arabic, the Koran, and Islamic ritual. Afterward he worked for the British at an indigo factory in Freetown, Sierra Leone. After saving up 2,000 francs, he decided the time had come.

Caillé was the freest of men. He lived unrestrained by a proper upbringing, unrestricted by family or friendship, unconcerned with his dignity or comfort, and unafraid of dying. His plan was simple. Carrying an umbrella and a few pounds of trading goods, he would approach his goal from the west, secretly taking notes in the Koran that he carried, explaining his "strangeness" by presenting himself as an Egyptian captured as a boy by the cruel French, freed finally in West Africa, wishing only now to go home, via the great Islamic city of Timbuktu.

In March 1827 he walked out of Freetown, and headed inland, unfinanced, unknown, and utterly alone. Laing was already dead, though no one knew. Caillé made his way slowly across the West African landscape, through forests, over mountains, across the savanna, following the narrow trails with slaves and native traders. He told and retold his story, and was accused of being an impostor. He suffered extreme hunger, thirst, fever, scurvy, and lay near death for weeks. He floated down the Niger in a slave boat, among chained slaves. He escaped Tuareg pirates. And thirteen months and 1,500 miles after leaving the coast, on April 20, 1828, he arrived in Timbuktu. The city was of course a disappointment. Having spent his entire life getting there, Caillé, the realist, stayed only two weeks. Posing still as an Egyptian, among hostile and increasingly skeptical Saharans, he joined a caravan northbound across the desert, and during three hellish months to Morocco managed to survive. After his return to France he wrote, "The idea I had formed of the city's greatness and wealth hardly corresponded to what I saw . . . It presented at first view nothing but a mass of ill-looking houses, built of earth. Nothing was to be seen in any direction but immense plains of sand of a yellow-white color. The sky was a pale red as far as the horizon: all nature wore a dreary aspect, and the most profound silence prevailed; not even the warbling of a bird was to be heard." Food and water were scarce and expensive; the streets were too quiet; the market was moribund. "In one word, everything was suffused with the greatest sadness . . . I was surprised by the lack of activity, and I would say even by the inertia that dominated the town."

After Caillé admitted it, there was little to add. The next European to visit Timbuktu, in 1853, was a German named Heinrich Barth who confirmed Caillé's judgment, laying to rest lingering doubts about the Frenchman's honesty. Since then Timbuktu has known few important dates.

In 1883, the Berlin Conference awarded Timbuktu to France, and nothing changed.

In 1893, the French arrived to take possession of it, and they were welcomed.

In 1960 Mali became independent, after which the French were missed.

In 1983, the Sofitel corporation built a forty-two-room hotel in Timbuktu, not to make money from it, but to find glory in a famous name. The name explains why, despite the onset of war, Sofitel kept the hotel open. In theory you could make a reservation there from the United States by dialing 1-800-763-4835. This was supposed to be amazing, more evidence of a shrinking world, because even to people who do not know where it is, Timbuktu still means "distant and far away."

In fact, even before the war, when the airline still flew to Timbuktu, the hotel drew few tourists. Blame good information, starting with Caillé. The consensus is now nearly universal: guidebooks, travelogues, and letters home all agree that there are better places to visit. I was tired. I was sick.

When the last boat of the season stopped there, at the port called Kabara, it was late in the night. I wandered through the darkness among the crowds on the riverbank, and on hands and knees vomited behind the ruins of a pirogue. I caught a ride to Timbuktu proper, and by the skewed yellow lights of a Peugeot saw crumbling mud walls and the closed expressions of soldiers at an army roadblock. There are three mud mosques in Timbuktu, as there have been for centuries. I returned to the river, where the boat was scheduled to leave before dawn. I preferred to miss Timbuktu. It has an attractive name, but is now known mostly for what it is not.

OVER THE DAYS that followed the boat often ran aground. We worked upstream around the curve of the Niger's bend, and south through the grassy swamps of an inland delta where the river broke into streams so narrow that at times we brushed against the grass. We passed close to hippopotami. I sought the shady sides of the upper deck, and watched the plains beyond the water's reach as they turned gradually from Sahara to Sahel. Now a bush, now a tree, now a lone shepherd, waving. The shepherd held a sheet of cardboard over his head for shade. His land was bright, thin, and yellow. His goats were sinewy.

Amadou came to sit beside me in companionable silence. I noticed that he had torn his shirt, and repaired it, and that he had lost weight. When I told him he looked hungry, he refused to admit it. Afterward I simply gave him food.

I do not know by what measure we finally left the desert. We passed herds of cattle standing on French-built dikes, and beyond them, a few irrigated rice fields. But away from the fields, the land stretched in parched plains. We neared Mopti, the boat's final port, after eight days on the river. We passed villages built around classic mud mosques with fanciful spires and protruding beams. After the sun set, the villages, which had no generators, were lit at night by orange fires, and by the yellow beams of mopeds piercing the smoke and dust.

Mopti was different. It had electric lights and a riverfront too busy to submit entirely to our boat's arrival. Built at the confluence of the Niger and the river Bani, it stood on three islands of solid ground, surrounded by swamp and water, connected to the mainland by a causeway. It was a poor place, with dirt streets and mud-walled houses, but also an important trading center. I walked through the town, luxuriating in its commotion, checked into a cheap hotel, and bathed from a bucket in the yard. The next day was market day, when women from the bush streamed in to trade, carrying bulky sacks of grain on their heads to exchange for fish and vegetables, and manufactured goods from Asia. People here suffered, but did not starve. Life's hardest edges had been softened by the river. The few Tuaregs walked about unmasked, and there was no sign of war. I stood in the shade of a tree by the river port, satisfied that in Mopti I had left the desert.

The following day I went by shared taxi through the brushy savanna south of town. The driver did not handle himself with the discipline of a desert man. He drove his old Peugeot too fast down donkey tracks, and spun the wheels ineffectually in pockets of loose sand. In the afternoon, on a stretch of dirt road, he accelerated aggressively toward goats that were crossing ahead, and ran directly into one of them without so much as a swerve. The goat flew over the hood, landed, and hobbled off bleating. Coolant poured out of the car's smashed radiator. The driver kept driving until the engine seized, then he broke into tears. I felt sorry for him, and for the goat, but secretly delighted in the freedom he felt to wreck his car. I took it as further evidence of the land's abundance.

That night back in Mopti, Amadou invited me to dinner at his aunt's house, which stood by the mosque in the old part of town. It was a poor, mud-walled house with a large and smoky room lit only by a cooking fire, too dim to make out the faces of the people there. We ate rice and sauce from communal bowls. Amadou's aunt turned out to be the cousin of his grand-mother. She was an old woman who had lived always in Mopti, and spoke little French. Amadou translated for us. She did not make conversation, but hearing that I had crossed the Sahara, said sternly, "The north is not good. The north is death."

I thought her fear was old-fashioned. But while we ate din-ner, the harmattan came. It is the hot wind that blows from the north, carrying the desert's soil. I walked alone through Mopti's dark streets in air thick with dust, and went to the river port, where the market had been shuttered and abandoned. The street lamps cast futile halos. The harmattan is not a bad wind, but it is a reminder. I stood facing it, tasting the Sahara. In the morning I left with Amadou by bush taxi for the capital, Bamako. The trip took all day. The driver drove carefully and complained about the damage caused to his car by the sand. He said it had gotten worse in recent years. That night, the harmattan blew through Bamako.

29

THE

DESERT IS

DOWNTOWN

Amadou lived in a desert that looked like a city. You can imagine that in ancient times his Fulani ancestors had inhabited the Sahara's central highlands, and had painted the rocks there, and had fought the first Tuaregs in the period before camels, and had moved south with their cattle. In the nineteenth century his ancestors were perhaps the savages who thrilled and frightened European explorers. And then only yesterday they were the type of tradition-bound tribespeople studied by classic ethnologists. They had elaborate ceremonies, surprising beliefs, and a rich vocabulary to describe cows.

Amadou was remotely aware of all this. He said, "I have cousins who live still as cattle herders. Somewhere in Mali, or in Burkina, I'm not sure where."

"Do you regret losing contact with them?"

He looked at me with surprise. "Regret? Why?"

He was right, of course. He could have saved his money and bought a cow, but where would he have grazed it? The pastures were already taken. In good years the savanna could support some wandering families, but in bad years it could support fewer. Population pressures and the new national boundaries to the south held the herdsmen hard against the droughts.

I asked Amadou about the family's move to Bamako. He shrugged and said he didn't know the details. All that was before his time. "Already when my parents were children the *brousse* had nothing for us."

This may explain why Amadou told me he did not worry about desertificaiton, the famous coming of the Sahara. Those were the concerns of his old aunt in Mopti. But for him, whether the grasslands endured or turned to sand, the savanna was already a desert. He was a Fulani, but a modern one, at home only in Bamako.

He said, "Country people are afraid of Bamako, but Bamako offers everything a modern man could want. It has cinemas that show the latest movies. It has the best discotheques in West Africa. It has the most beautiful girls, and the easiest. It is so well lit at night that you can find a dropped needle in the street. It is like your San Francisco. It is one of the world's greatest cities."

But Bamako is just an overblown African village—a dusty, smoky sprawl of cinder-block and mud-walled slums extending loosely from both sides of the Niger River below sparsely wooded hills. It has grown up around a gray stone train station, which stands at one end of the 800-mile track laid by the French to link the Niger to the Atlantic port of Dakar, Senegal. When the first train ran, in 1904, Bamako was a fishing village with a population of about a thousand. The French made it an administrative capital from which they could go forth and civilize the African hinterland. In the end the opposite occurred, and the hinterland arrived to civilize Bamako.

Today the fishing village has a population of nearly a million. It has a bridge that crawls with mopeds and communal taxis. It has a new mosque built by the Saudis, and a People's Palace built by the North Koreans. In its small and undeveloped center, the shaded colonial buildings have gently decayed, the pavements have crumbled, and the streets have filled with far more people than they were intended to hold. The crowding brings with it the commotion of markets and people, the richness of the African crowd. Bamako is not as great a city as San Francisco, but it is more vibrant. At night the air turns soft, and music mixes through the voices of the people. You can wander the streets, or sit in the outdoor cafés and watch all Mali go by. The bustle is surprising. By night or day, the capital rarely rests. But after a while you may notice something wrong: the commotion begins to feel frantic and seems to provide few results; when you look into the crowd and sort out the individuals, you find that they are malnourished, destitute, and even desperate. If Bamako is enterprising, it is also poor. Divorced from the unproductive land, connected to the sea by a thin thread of an old railroad, the poor sell to the poor in a cycle of slowly diminishing returns. Richer nations do not compete for Mali's love, and now even France is pulling back. There is no magic to the economy, no critical threshold to cross. Traders grab the famine aid not only in selfishness, but in despair. Country people are right to fear such a city. If Bamako could truly provide men with what they need, their children would not go dressed in rags, there would be peace in the north, and Amadou would not have tried to sell cassettes to Timbuktu. The Sahara takes many forms. Even a marketplace requires rain.

I stayed at the Hôtel de la Gare, built into the train station. One morning I climbed a hill above the city and followed a trail to an overlook. For hours I sat there, contemplating the expanse below. Seen from a distance, Bamako hardly moved. Smoke floated from piles of burning refuse. Traffic inched across the bridge that spanned the river. A pirogue floated by. Uniformed players sauntered down a soccer field. Dust hung in the air. I sweated and grew thirsty. A truck rattled down a bad road. An airliner climbed through the haze for Paris. The sky was pale, the earth was dry and hot. The view I had was a desert view.

I also saw it up close. One evening Amadou took me to his mother's house, where he still lived. We rode a communal taxi, a Toyota minivan which at one point carried thirty-two people, including the driver and his toll collector. Those who could not cram into the inside stood on the bumpers and running boards, and hung from the roof. The driver managed to steer. We endured the bridge crossing, and proceeded slowly along the convulsed dirt streets into the slums.

Amadou's family had claimed a plot thirty years before, and now had a nice cinder-block house with four rooms, cement floors, electricity, and a latrine and vegetable plot protected by garden walls. We sat in a brightly lit kitchen by a wood stove and a radio.

Amadou's mother was a wrinkled old woman who thought I was French, and treated me with deference. She mentioned that her husband had worked for the French on the railroad, that he had died, that the family had always been the friends of France.

She said, *"Vive la France."*

Times were harder now, but she had thirteen children, and they took good care of her, as she had known they would. Amadou was her youngest and her favorite. She kept attesting to his qualities, as if I might offer him a job.

"He is a good boy. He is smart, and a hard worker. He does not steal. I swear he will never give you trouble."

We drank powdered coffee. The house slowly filled with family: Amadou's older brothers and sisters, their spouses and children, and their children's children. All told, twenty-seven people lived in the house, sleeping on mats and mattresses. I asked Amadou how they earned their livings. He said two were mechanics, one was a watchman, and the others just tried to get by. He said the children sometimes did not eat well.

I later discovered that Amadou had offspring of his own, at least three of them, by different women. He was proud of this, and showed me wallet photographs.

"Nice children," I said, surprised that he had not mentioned them before. "Do you see them often?"

"Not too often," he said. "Birthdays, you know."

"You don't get along with the mothers?"

He grinned. "There are plenty of women here. Why should I marry?"

I thought at least one reason was AIDS.

Amadou took me to meet his friends, young men about his age. We sat outside a tin-roofed shack, drank beer, and listened to some of the cassettes that Amadou had been unable to sell along the river. The men laughed about Amadou's business venture, but had equally desperate schemes of their own. The best plan, they all agreed, would be to leave Africa entirely. This I now found was what Amadou wanted as well. The day I left Bamako for Dakar, he insisted on seeing me to the train. I gave him my address because he gave me his. But when he asked whether I wouldn't write to the American embassy on his behalf, I told him honestly that it would do no good, that I could not get him to America. He looked disappointed. He was young, and kept having to turn and face the drought.

THE CLOCK IN the Bamako station ran precisely five minutes fast. The clock in Dakar may have, too. The schedule that linked them was a small wonder of symmetry. Two trains worked the line—one Malian, and one Senegalese. Each made two trips every week—one out, and one back. This meant there were two trains weekly from Bamako, and two from Dakar. The timing called for simultaneous departures from both cities at 9:00 A.M., on Wednesdays and Saturdays, and simultaneous arrivals exactly thirty hours and thirty minutes later. The trains were meant to pass each other at the international border, which happens to lie halfway between the cities. The simultaneous border formalities were expected to take exactly one hour, through the midpoint of the night. All this came as a shock to me, and I was strangely relieved that none of it worked out.

The train left Bamako two hours late, with the whistle blowing. Traffic stopped as it rolled across the boulevards, westbound into the open Sahel. I sat in an open doorway in a hot wind of dust and diesel smoke, and let Mali go by. We passed through low rolling hills of red earth and tan grass, with scrub trees and baobabs, small rivers, footpaths. The villages had round mud huts with conical thatched roofs. Children ran beside the tracks. By abandoned plantations, the ruins of colonial stations still had signs proclaiming DAKAR—NIGER. We stopped in the larger towns—places with names like Sebekoro, Badinko, and Boulouli—where girls balanced buckets on their heads, and sold water by the ladle. We entered a burning valley where flames licked the tracks and ash swirled through the doorway. At night the moon lit pale grass.

We passed the border and by dawn had left Tambacounda, the principal town of eastern Senegal. The savanna was colored softly at first by the morning light. The day passed in growing heat. Families of monkeys now perched in the trees. A paved road ran beside the tracks. Among the huts in the villages stood French-style square buildings, power poles, and microwave transmission towers. In the town of Thiès we passed yellow commuter trains. The last huts were replaced by long wooden shacks like those once built for migrant workers in the American south. When the Atlantic came into view off our left, I was startled by the deepness of its blue.

We rolled west through shantytowns, which grew together and became Dakar. Passengers threw fruit to the crowds of children who ran alongside the train. Adults watched sullenly from a distance. The pools of green sewage that flooded their yards dried into dust beside the tracks and swirled into the train. The city grew denser, and rose into the central district of banks and luxury apartments. A billboard advertised direct flights to New York. A neon sign advertised a supermarket. Container ships nestled by cranes in the harbor. From the station a taxi whisked me to a hotel shower.

Dakar has a modern European downtown, but a porous one, through which seeps the Sahel. Beggars, cripples, and thieves inhabit the sidewalks. Senegal is another flawed jewel of the old French colonial empire. It keeps growing poorer. Crops fail. The Sahara lies close to the north in Mauritania. The Moors move south and set up small groceries to sell to the Senegalese, whom they have always detested. During droughts, the Senegalese riot for food, kill a few Moors, and loot their shops. This happens now even downtown. Dakar occupies the westernmost peninsula of continental Africa, as if it had been caught by the desert.

28 X DAYS